101 8

D0420621

Cathy H.C. Hsu, PhD
Editor

ONE Casino Industry
in Asia Pacific
Development, Operation,
and Impact

Pre-publication
REVIEWS,
COMMENTARIES,
EVALUATIONS . . .

"*Casino Industry in Asia Pacific* is a very informative book for those interested in the casino and gaming industry in the Asia Pacific region. This book has addressed both the positive and negative impacts of the casino industry quite well."

Manat Chaisawat, MBA
Associate Professor
and Director of the MBA
International Program
in Hospitality and Tourism,
Prince of Songkla University,
Phuket, Thailand

"This book will become the definitive work on Asia Pacific gaming. The editor has compiled a book blending cutting-edge academic researchers with world-renowned industry practitioners and experts who are working in the Asia Pacific casino industry. They provide an accurate account of the current and future state of the Asia Pacific gaming industry. This is an excellent resource book. It covers all of the countries that are players, wannabe players, and soon-to-be players in the casino industry."

James Wortman, ABD
Director of Gaming
Education & Research,
Conrad Hilton College,
University of Houston

More pre-publication
REVIEWS, COMMENTARIES, EVALUATIONS . . .

"This book provides valuable insights into the current status of legal gaming in key Asian and Pacific countries, and points out social, cultural, legal, and economic nuances that distinguish gambling in Asia from the West. The chapters provide a fascinating glimpse of Asian gaming — what currently exists and what might soon emerge in the world's most populous continent. Regulatory and other technical dimensions of modern casino industries are examined and applied in an Asian context. Insights into the relatively mature — and far more Westernized—Australian gaming market are also provided.

This book is a must-read for anyone interested in the opportunities and challenges that the proliferation of casino gaming will bring to Asia in the early twenty-first century. The economic and social consequences of casino gaming in Asia may ultimately prove to be far more significant than those encountered in the West, and this book opens the door as to what those consequences might be."

William R. Eadington, PhD
*Professor of Economics
and Director, Institute
for the Study of Gambling
and Commercial Gaming,
University of Nevada, Reno*

THHP

The Haworth Hospitality Press®
An Imprint of The Haworth Press, Inc.
New York • London • Oxford

Casino Industry in Asia Pacific

Development, Operation, and Impact

Casino Industry in Asia Pacific
Development, Operation, and Impact

Cathy H. C. Hsu, PhD
Editor

THHP

The Haworth Hospitality Press®
An Imprint of The Haworth Press, Inc.
New York • London • Oxford

For more information on this book or to order, visit
http://www.haworthpress.com/store/product.asp?sku=5541

or call 1-800-HAWORTH (800-429-6784) in the United States and Canada
or (607) 722-5857 outside the United States and Canada

or contact orders@HaworthPress.com

Published by

The Haworth Hospitality Press®, an imprint of The Haworth Press, Inc., 10 Alice Street, Binghamton,
NY 13904-1580.

PUBLISHER'S NOTE
The development, preparation, and publication of this work has been undertaken with great care.
However, the Publisher, employees, editors, and agents of The Haworth Press are not responsible
for any errors contained herein or for consequences that may ensue from use of materials or information contained in this work. The Haworth Press is committed to the dissemination of ideas and information according to the highest standards of intellectual freedom and the free exchange of ideas.
Statements made and opinions expressed in this publication do not necessarily reflect the views of
the Publisher, Directors, management, or staff of The Haworth Press, Inc., or an endorsement by
them.

Cover design by Lora Wiggins.

Library of Congress Cataloging-in-Publication Data

Casino industry in Asia Pacific : development, operation, and impact / [edited by] Cathy H.C. Hsu.
    p. cm.
  Includes bibliographical references and index.
  ISBN-13: 978-0-7890-2345-2 (hc. : alk. paper)
  ISBN-10: 0-7890-2345-8 (hc. : alk. paper)
  ISBN-13: 978-0-7890-2346-9 (pbk. : alk. paper)
  ISBN-10: 0-7890-2346-6 (pbk. : alk. paper)
  1. Casinos—Asia. 2. Casinos—Pacific Area. 3. Gambling—Asia. 4. Gambling—Pacific Area.
I. Hsu, Cathy H. C.

HV6722.A78C37 2005
338.4'7795'095—dc22
                                            2005009651

CONTENTS

SECTION I: HISTORY, DEVELOPMENT, AND LEGISLATION

SECTION II: OPERATION

SECTION III: GAMING AND SOCIETY

ABOUT THE EDITOR

Cathy H. C. Hsu, PhD, is Professor, Associate Head, and Graduate Programs Director in the School of Hotel and Tourism Management at The Hong Kong Polytechnic University. She is the editor and chapter author of the book *Legalized Casino Gaming in the United States: The Economic and Social Impact* (The Haworth Press), as well as co-author of the textbook *Marketing Hospitality and Quantity Food Quality Control.* She has served as a consultant to various tourism organizations and is the past Chairman of the Board and President of the International Society of Travel and Tourism Educators. She is Editor in Chief of the *Journal of Teaching in Travel & Tourism,* as well as serving on seven journal editorial boards. Dr. Hsu's research has focused on the economic and social impacts of casino gaming, tourism destination marketing, tourist behaviors, and hospitality education.

CONTRIBUTORS

Ki-Joon Back is Assistant Professor of Hotel, Restaurant, Institution Management and Dietetics at Kansas State University. His research and teaching interests focus on casino development and management, consumer behaviors, and research methodology. He has published in several academic journals, such as *Annals of Tourism Research* and *Journal of Hospitality and Tourism Research.* Also, he has professional experience as a casino marketing manager and casino executive in Las Vegas.

Helen Breen is Academic Coordinator for the Centre for Professional Development in Club Management and Lecturer at Southern Cross University. Her research interests include the development of adult education programs, tourism and hospitality management competencies, impacts of gaming, and the evaluation of responsible gambling strategies. Helen has been involved in many joint research projects, is co-author of Australia's first textbook designed for gaming management students, and has published extensively in national and international journals and conference proceedings.

Paul D. Bromberg is Director of Spectrum Oso Asia, Ltd. He has extensive investigative experience throughout Asia and speaks fluent Mandarin and Thai. He is also a recognized expert on mainland China and Southeast Asian business practices. He has conducted multifaceted casino-related investigations throughout Asia. Bromberg formerly was Director of Research for Kroll Associates (Asia) Ltd. He graduated with honors from the University of Leeds, England, and spent a number of years conducting research at Fudan University in Shanghai and at Xiamen University in Fujian Province, China.

Jeremy Buultjens is Senior Lecturer at the School of Tourism and Hospitality Management, Southern Cross University. He teaches economics and tourism planning. His research interests include employment relations in the hospitality industry, responsible gambling, and indigenous tourism. He has published in employment relations and hospitality journals. He is the joint editor of the *Journal of Economic and Social Policy* and is a member of the Centre for Gambling Education and Research, Southern Cross University.

Grace C. L. Chien is a full-time PhD student at the School of Hotel and Tourism Management, The Hong Kong Polytechnic University. She was a full-time college lecturer in Taiwan before she began her PhD study. She holds BS and MSc degrees in Hotel, Restaurant, and Institution Management from Iowa State University, Ames, Iowa. She received the 2002 Best Teacher of the Year award from the Taiwan government. Her recent research focus has been on knowledge management and market orientation in the hotel sector.

Fredric E. Gushin founded Spectrum Gaming Group, LLC, in 1993 and serves as Managing Director of the company. Spectrum is an international gaming consultancy specializing in services to casino developers and operators, Internet gaming companies, gaming vendors, and regulatory agencies. Since 1999, Gushin has been Intermittent Advisor to the U.S. Department of the Treasury, Office of Technical Assistance. He is also a member of the editorial board of the *Gaming Law Review* and a member of the International Association of Gaming Attorneys. From 1978 to 1991, Gushin served with New Jersey's Division of Gaming Enforcement, where he rose to the position of Assistant Attorney General and Assistant Director. He was responsible for overseeing compliance and enforcement activities that occurred in Atlantic City's casino industry. Gushin litigated over fifty cases before the Casino Control Commission and argued some of the most important cases that helped shape New Jersey's casino industry.

Nerilee Hing is Senior Lecturer in the School of Tourism and Hospitality Management at Southern Cross University in Lismore, Australia, and head of its Centre for Gambling Education and Research. Nerilee teaches in the areas of gaming, club management, strategic management, entrepreneurship, and food and beverage management. Nerilee's key research focus is the management of commercial gambling, particularly social responsibility in gambling and the management of problem gambling. She has conducted gambling-related research projects for numerous government and industry bodies and has published widely in gaming, tourism, hospitality, and management journals.

William R. Kisby is Executive Vice President of Gaming and E-Commerce for NFC Global, Inc. His responsibilities include supervising all gaming investigations for NFC worldwide and developing foreign due diligence clients in both government and e-commerce. In addition, Kisby was recently appointed to the board of directors for the Law Enforcement Intelligence Unit (LEIU) Foundation. Prior to joining NFC in 1996, Kisby served twenty-seven years with the New Jersey State Police, fifteen years of which were with the New Jersey Division of Gaming Enforcement Casino Intelligence Unit. He later became Unit Supervisor of the Casino Intelligence Unit, which is responsible for monitoring and investigating organized crime activity in all Atlantic City casinos. In 1985, Kisby testified on behalf of the New Jersey State Police before the President's Commission on Organized Crime regarding organized crime infiltration into the New Jersey casino industry. He also formulated and supervised the first money laundering "sting" investigation in New Jersey.

Choong-Ki Lee is Associate Professor in the College of Hotel and Tourism at Kyunghee University. His research interests include casino policy and forecasting tourism demand. He has published in numerous academic journals, such as *Annals of Tourism Research, Journal of Travel Research,* and *Tourism Management.* In addition, he has published a book titled *Understanding the Casino Industry.*

Andrew MacDonald is a highly respected Australian expert on casino operations and gaming statistics. Several of his works are utilized by the University of Nevada, Reno, in its Executive Development Program, of which he is a comoderator. He is currently employed by Australia's largest casino operator, Publishing and Broadcasting Limited, owner of the Crown Casino in Melbourne, as Director, Global Gaming Developments.

Glenn McCartney is an MPhil/PhD candidate at the University of Surrey, and a full-time lecturer and project manager at the Institute for Tourism Studies, Macao SAR, China. His research focuses on casino tourism development, particularly as it relates to Macao. Previously, he was Director of Sales and Marketing for the second largest casino hotel in Macao.

Sean Monaghan is Director and Head of Gaming and Wagering Research for East Asia and Australasia at ABN AMRO and is currently based in Sydney, Australia. He has covered gaming and wagering companies for the past decade and has previously worked at other investment banks, including Deutsche Bank and Burdett Buckeridge Young. He has also worked with companies in the gaming industry including Aristocrat Leisure Limited and Metroplex Bhd with their casinos in Subic Bay, Philippines. He has addressed conferences in many parts of the world, including Australia, Asia, and North America and sits on various advisory panels for major events such as Global Gaming Expo and the Asian Gaming Expo. Monaghan writes regularly for major publications such as *Global Gaming Business Magazine* and has a strong interest in the development of the global industry.

William O'Reilly serves as Managing Director of Spectrum Oso Asia, Ltd. (SOA). SOA is an investigative and research firm with offices in Bangkok, Thailand, Hong Kong, and Guam. He is an expert in white-collar criminal matters, Asian organized crime, and gaming matters. O'Reilly is an eighteen-year veteran of the Federal Bureau of Investigation, having served much of that time in Asia. O'Reilly formerly served as Associate Managing Director of Kroll Associates (Asia) Ltd. and Managing Director of Armor Group Asia Pacific. He is also the author of three books relating to his law enforcement and corporate experiences.

Kevin O'Toole has been Executive Director of the Oneida Indian Nation Gaming Commission since 1997. In this position, he oversees the regulation of casino gaming activities at the highly successful Turning Stone Casino Resort near Syracuse, New York. O'Toole formerly served as Deputy Attorney General with the New Jersey Division of Gaming Enforcement. He was Supervising Attorney for the Audit Section and had direct responsibility for reviewing internal control submissions of Atlantic City casinos.

William N. Thompson is Professor of Public Administration at the University of Nevada, Las Vegas. He received graduate degrees from

Michigan State University and the University of Missouri–Columbia. His research interests have focused upon public policy and the gambling industry since moving to Las Vegas in 1980. He wrote *Gambling in America: An Encyclopedia,* as well as *Legalized Gambling: A Reference Handbook.* He co-authored *The Last Resort: Success and Failure in Campaigns for Casinos, International Casino Law,* and *Casino Customer Service.*

Preface

Gaming has existed in Asia for millennia; in many Asian cultures, playing games is part of daily life. Even though Western-type casinos were only introduced in the past century or so, many Asia Pacific countries and regions, such as Australia and Macao, have an active casino industry. Many other Asian governments are also turning to gaming to bolster their economies and to capture taxes lost to illegal betting. Figure A illustrates the countries and regions discussed in this book.

India and South Korea have opened their first casinos for their own nationals. The Philippines is vowing to shake up its casino monopoly to facilitate expansion. Border casinos are flourishing in Cambodia and Myanmar, and longtime holdouts Japan, Thailand, and Taiwan are debating the legalization of casinos. The Tokyo metropolitan and four other local governments have urged the central Japanese government to draw up legislation that would allow them to build casinos, which the local political leaders view as a key to boosting tourism. The discussion on legalization of casinos on an outlying island in Taiwan has been raging for more than five years. A poll released by Taiwan's Ministry of the Interior indicated that 65 percent of polled respondents agreed with the legalization of gambling in the Penghu archipelago, while 22 percent opposed the idea. Even though most gaming activities are illegal in China, Hong Kong, and Taiwan, these three areas account for half of the region's casino spending, all outside of the borders.

The growth and future prospects of Asia Pacific casinos have not gone unnoticed by Las Vegas gaming corporations. In fact, many of them have been aggressively expanding and looking for opportunities to further develop in this part of the world. Wynn Resorts and the Venetian have been granted licenses to operate in Macao; Park Place Entertainment Corp. and MGM Mirage have each had discussions with representatives of the metropolitan Tokyo government to develop the industry in Japan; and a few Las Vegas giants have been reported to

FIGURE A. Asia Pacific countries and regions discussed. *Source:* mapresources. com.

work with local developers and Penghu county government in planning casinos in Taiwan.

Yet most gaming studies published to date in the English-language press were conducted in a Western context. Few publications with an Asia Pacific emphasis on the industry's development, operation, or impact are available. A handful of studies have been conducted on gaming in Asia Pacific countries or regions; however, most of them had a local focus, and rightly so. Thus there is a need to have a comprehensive source of information for all gaming research projects completed across the Asia Pacific region in the recent past.

The intent of this book is to incorporate casino gaming research studies, documented and undocumented development of the industry in this region, and industry professionals' accumulated experience to serve as a reference of the industry's development, operation, and impact. To provide a review of the gaming industry from various perspectives, authors of the chapters remain neutral on the gaming issue and simply report facts and experiences related to casinos in the Asia Pacific region.

Upper-level undergraduate students and graduate students will find this book useful as an introduction to the modern casino industry in the Asia Pacific region. Gaming researchers will find this book helpful as a review of current literature. Researchers can also gain insights from industry professionals' experience to help develop research agendas with practical significance. Important information is given and issues are discussed for policymakers and casino developers to consider in their long-range planning. All readers will gain an in-depth understanding of the scope of gaming development in the Asia Pacific region. Important and unique operational issues are addressed to raise readers' awareness. This book comprises not only academic assessment of the gaming industry's development and impact but also experience shared by veteran industry professionals.

This book is organized into three sections: development, operation, and impact. In the first section, each chapter includes a comprehensive history and development of gaming for a particular location, which includes Australia, Japan, South Korea, Macao, and Southeast Asia. Laws and regulations are also reviewed for each location to report changes and document current status. In Section II, each chapter examines an important casino operational issue, which includes effective regulations, licensing and due diligence, internal control and auditing, and rolling commissions. Examples are provided to illustrate the importance of proper operational control. Section III reviews economic and social impacts of gaming in Australia and South Korea; gaming and Chinese culture are also discussed to illustrate the intertwining relationship between gaming and people's daily lives.

Chapter 1 reviews the historical development of Australian gaming, starting from 1778. The four major historical periods in the transformation and redefining of Australian government policy in gaming are discussed. The three waves of casino development, starting in 1973, are also detailed. The chapter ends with a description of the characteristics, current status, governance, and opportunities and challenges of Australian casinos.

Chapter 2 starts with the historical development of Korean casino gaming and moves to current casino industry characteristics, including operations, customers, and receipts. Major casino events and casino receipts from foreign players are reported in a table format. The Korean gaming regulatory system is well explained in terms of licensing, regulations, operating policy, and opening up to the domestic market.

Chapter 3 documents Macao's history of gaming, in both legal and illegal forms, which dates back to the seventeenth century and continues in modern times. Macao gaming's colorful past is well illustrated. The recent liberalization of casinos, begun in 2001, is also reviewed. The chapter ends with a discussion on the incorporation of casinos into the bigger tourism development plan and on committed future casino investments by both a local company and two Las Vegas operators.

Chapter 4 begins with a personal discovery of gaming activities in Japan, a country where gambling is illegal. An introduction to pachinko machines leads to an inquiry into what gambling is. The addictive quality of pachinko machines and the history of pachinko further add to the ambiguity of whether pachinko is gambling. The author also looks at the lottery and various forms of racing, including horse, motorboat, motorcycle, and bicycle.

Chapter 5 provides an overview of legal gaming in Southeast Asia. Countries discussed include Cambodia, Indonesia, Laos, Malaysia, Myanmar, Singapore, Thailand, and Vietnam. The status of legal or illegal gaming in each country, prospects for legalization, existing gaming establishments, regulatory control, gaming control agencies, and enforcement programs are reviewed.

Chapter 6 begins Section II with suggestions for Asian gaming jurisdictions and standards that should be adopted in regulating and controlling casinos. The author urges jurisdictions to clearly articulate the reasons why casino gaming is being legalized and to incorporate public policy goals in gaming legislation. Recommended licensing standards and casino operational control elements are also explained in detail.

Chapter 7 discusses the need for government to have a process in place that provides a meaningful way to determine the suitability of casino applicants. The authors take readers through the investigation process of an applicant, starting from completing the application form, signing the release authorization, and being investigated through various checks. Detailed requirements for casino entity licensing, vendor licensing, and employee licensing are then explained. The chapter closes with a real-life case study of investigation that found the applicant unsuitable for a casino license.

Chapter 8 addresses the importance of accounting and internal controls as well as auditing. After reviewing the general principles of an effective accounting and internal control system, standards in protecting the casino cage, table games, and slot machines are elaborated. Casino auditing requirements, for both internal and external auditing, are then stated.

Chapter 9 illustrates the use of nonnegotiable chips as an instrument in calculating commissions paid to VIP or international premium players at casinos. The chapter starts with an explanation of what nonnegotiable chips are and how they are used, followed by a mathematical consideration of the practice. The use of nonnegotiable chips for the games of baccarat, blackjack, and roulette is compared, considering the wager, house edge, theoretical turnover, casino tax, theoretical win, and commission. An appendix of terminologies and definitions is provided at the end of the chapter.

Chapter 10 opens with a list of impacts of gaming. The remainder focuses on problem gambling and its impacts, which have captured a tremendous amount of attention in Australia. The author identifies the reasons for the rise of treating problem gambling as a social issue in Australia and explains the redefinition of problem gambling as a public health issue. The chapter continues with a thorough discussion on the government and industry responses to problem gambling and concludes with an evaluation of the effectiveness of responsible gambling measures.

Chapter 11 starts with a brief history of the casino industry in Australia, a review of the market structure and ownership regime, and factors that should be considered when assessing the impacts of gaming. Economic benefits of casinos discussed include consumer benefits, economic growth, and revenues to the public sector. Economic costs of casino development examined include the nature of employment, reduced business opportunities in other sectors, increased government reliance on gambling revenues, problem gambling, and community perceptions and impacts. The chapter finishes with a discussion of the future of the gaming industry in Australia.

Chapter 12 assesses the positive economic and negative social impacts of casino development in Korea. Economic impacts from foreign players are measured based on multipliers derived from an input-output analysis. Creation of employment opportunities by the casino industry is also compared with other export trades. Economic impacts from the casino opened to domestic players are measured by number of visitors to the community, tax revenues, and employment figures. Social impacts are reviewed from the societal level and the individual level, with references to previous research studies.

Chapter 13 traces Chinese gaming history back to almost 300 BC. Chinese games of cards and mah-jongg are introduced. The importance of Chinese players in modern casinos is documented and Chinese culture traits related to gaming are discussed, with suggestions for casino operators. The chapter also reviews the status of gaming legalization in Chinese societies focusing on mainland China, Hong Kong, and Taiwan.

Through illustration of the speed and spread of casino development in Asia Pacific, the importance of proper regulation and management becomes clear. However, a major challenge faced by several Asian countries in regard to casino legalization is the important issue of regulation and management. In many of the developing or newly developed countries, their political and regulatory systems are not adequately structured to monitor such cash-intensive operations as casinos. Information provided in Section II should provide some food for thought to policymakers and regulators.

The impacts of casinos on a society and economy are difficult phenomena to measure. With the great diversity in political, social, economic, culture, geographic, and demographic characteristics in the Asia Pacific region, the appropriate measurement of impacts for each country is unique. Many Asian countries are also small in size, in close proximity to each other, and closely intertwined in terms of economic and tourism activities. These factors further complicate the measurement issue. Even though chapter authors of this book have made an attempt to summarize research findings in terms of gaming's economic and social impacts, as readers complete their review of the chapters, they will realize that currently available research has only touched the tip of an iceberg. More research is desperately needed to help estimate the impacts of casino gaming in the Asia Pacific region.

One particular economic issue that ought to be investigated is the leakage factor. Many Asian countries have realized the importance of proper casino management; however, due to their lack of experience in operating large-scale casinos or lack of funds for the initial investment, foreign management companies or developers are brought in. Research is needed to investigate the net economic impact resulting from such arrangements, as foreign managers and developers would logically transfer their earnings back to their home country.

Literature has documented the benefits of residents' involvement in tourism development planning. However, little research has been published in English on local residents' opinions of or attitudes toward casino development in Asia Pacific communities. Economic benefits touted by government officials and lobbyists representing special interest groups, either through increased numbers of inbound tourists and tourism receipts, thus increased foreign currency earnings, or through decreased numbers of outbound players to foreign casinos, have been the primary reason for casino development in many countries and regions. However, unlike many American jurisdictions where, to legalize casino operations, an area-wide referendum needs to be voted on and passed, most Asian casinos have been approved either by their respective legislative council or by the prime minister. Residents' opinions and attitudes have not been sought nor taken into consideration. Even though they do not have a say in the decision-making process, their lives are impacted by the casinos. Thus, researchers have responsibility for unearthing their perceptions and opinions.

Since many North American and European casinos currently attract a significant percentage of their players, especially premium players, from China and other Asian countries and regions, more casino development in the Asia Pacific region could present a threat to Western casino industries. Thus, even though the focus of this book is on the Asia Pacific casino industry, development and operation in this part of the world will have implications for casinos worldwide. Such implications could be a worthy focus for research, and results could provide recommendations for strategic directions of casinos in different countries and regions. Thus, future research and discussion about Asia Pacific casinos would be of great interest and value to the global casino community.

The very task of compiling currently available information on Asia Pacific gaming is a contribution to the gaming literature by itself. However, great demands and numerous opportunities exist for further research and investigation as well as sharing the experience of industry executives. I call upon fellow academicians to further contribute to the documentation of Asia Pacific gaming activities by publishing more journal articles, monographs, conference proceedings papers, and books, which will no doubt facilitate the healthy development of the industry in this part of the world.

SECTION I:
HISTORY, DEVELOPMENT, AND LEGISLATION

Chapter 1

Casino History, Development, and Legislation in Australia

Helen Breen
Nerilee Hing

Casino history, development, and legislation in Australia can be best understood within the wider context of the development of gambling in Australia. Casinos are a relatively recent addition to the Australian gambling sector, with the first legal casino, Wrest Point, being established in the state of Tasmania in 1973. There are thirteen casinos in Australia, at least one in every state and territory, and each state and territory maintains its own legislation and policies regarding casinos. However, Australian casino history and development needs to be seen against a background of evolving social and economic conditions that affected government policies from the earliest days of European settlement in Australia. Four major historical periods have been identified by the Australian Institute for Gambling Research (1999) in the transformation and redefining of Australian government policy on gambling:

1. The period of early colonization from 1778 to 1900, characterized by selective prohibition of gambling
2. A period of selective legalization from 1900 to the 1940s
3. A period of government endorsement and market growth from World War II (1939-1945) to the 1970s
4. A period of commercialization, competition, and market expansion from the 1970s to the present (Australian Institute for Gambling Research, 1999, p. i)

Using these four major periods, this chapter explains how changing historical, social, and economic conditions created a legislative environment that allowed for the establishment and continuing development of casinos in Australia. However, a few definitions here will help clarify some of the terms used in this chapter. *Gambling* is defined as the "(lawful) placement of a wager or bet on the outcome of a future uncertain event" (Tasmanian Gaming Commission, 2002, p. 5). In Australia this includes gaming, racing, wagering, and sports betting. *Gaming* is "all legal forms of gambling other than racing and sports betting" (Tasmanian Gaming Commission, 2002, p. 5). This includes casino gaming, poker and gaming machines, lotteries, football pools, interactive gaming, and minor gaming. *Racing, wagering,* and *sports betting* are forms of legal betting on horses, greyhounds, and specified sports events though totalisators and bookmakers (Tasmanian Gaming Commission, 2002, p. 5).

EARLY COLONIZATION: 1778-1900

Government policy on gambling during the early period reflected class-based distinctions. Early Australian colonists brought British gambling practices with them to Australia (O'Hara, 1988). Although a prohibitionist approach to gambling prevailed for the lower classes, gambling among members in private clubs and betting on horse racing were tolerated for their contribution to recreational and social purposes. The wealthy classes saw card playing, billiards, and betting as matters of reputation, civilization, and honor rather than gambling "for mere money" (O'Hara, 1988, p. 246).

In this context, early clubs established themselves as not-for-profit organizations with social objectives. The Australian Club was established in 1838 in Sydney to provide accommodation and leisure facilities for its country and city members. It was a prestigious club with high fees and members were leading political, military, administrative, legal, and church figures (Williams, 1938). In contrast, the poorer classes saw gambling as one of the limited recreational pastimes available to them (O'Hara, 1988). At the far end of the social scale were convicts. Some convicts were transported to Australia for gambling crimes, and many used food and clothing as their gambling stakes (Cumes, 1979). Popular gambling among the lower classes included dog, cock, and rat fights, cards, dice, two-up, and coin games.

Horses were important for transport and communication in the colony. The popularity of horses gave horse racing a certain degree of respectability (O'Hara, 1988). In the state of New South Wales (NSW), organized horse racing was established by 1810; by the mid-1800s, racecourses, club facilities, and numerous sweepstakes based on horse racing were well established (McMillen, 1996). The first Melbourne Cup, Australia's premier horse race, was run in 1861.

The growth of gambling was not without opposition. The growing urban middle classes and rising evangelical Protestantism (Inglis, 1985; O'Hara, 1988) opposed the growth of gambling. The values of emphasizing the industrial work ethic and distrusting idleness saw gambling, especially by the working classes, as "a vice which distracted people away from the virtues of industry" (O'Hara, 1988, p. 104). Although the moral reform movement was successful in influencing antigambling legislation (Inglis, 1985), it had less success in reducing participation in gambling, both legal and illegal. All colonies passed laws between 1876 and 1897 to prohibit gambling in streets, shops, and private houses, but prosecutions were few and far between (O'Hara, 1988). Government objectives were aimed at trying to prevent gambling among the lower classes while turning a blind eye to gambling by the upper classes. As such, they reflected class privilege and the conservative moral principles of the time (Australian Institute for Gambling Research, 1999).

SELECTIVE LEGALIZATION: 1900-1940s

During the first half of the 1900s, government policy on gambling shifted from a class-based prohibitionist approach to selective liberalization that clearly linked gambling to social benefit. The Gaming and Betting Act 1906 NSW and similar legislation in other Australian states placed restrictions on lower-class entertainment (e.g., closing betting shops, restricting betting to racecourses, and licensing racecourses) (O'Hara, 1988). Despite this, horse racing and trotting continued to grow with betting made more efficient with the mechanical tote after 1911 (Watts, 1985). Elite gentlemen's clubs still operated.

Illegal betting shops and private bookmakers continued, although more cautiously (O'Hara, 1988).

The introduction of the state-run Golden Casket lottery in Queensland demonstrated that the state could be an effective gambling operator, with revenue used in a morally defensible way to relieve pressure on state funds and provide social benefits (O'Hara, 1988). It was so successful that in 1920 the Queensland government took over its operation from local charities and directed all profits to the Motherhood, Child Welfare and Hospital Fund (Selby, 1996). State lotteries were later introduced in all states and territories.

By the 1940s, bingo also had gained popularity. Clubs, hospitals, ambulance organizations, and the Catholic church operated bingo for charitable causes. Regulations on hours of play, number of games, and prize money were introduced to contain its growth (O'Hara, 1988). The first half of the 1900s saw state, church, and charitable involvement as gambling operators strengthened the legitimacy of gambling. Gambling gained new respectability through association with welfare purposes, attracting middle-class participation, particularly by women (McMillen, 1996a). Lotteries and bingo increased public access to gambling (Selby, 1996).

It was within this context of increased legitimation and public exposure to gambling that NSW clubs became established as major leisure institutions and gained the first foothold on machine gaming in Australia. Poor facilities in hotels and improved economic standards fueled public demand for better leisure facilities. The nonprofit status, membership requirements, and social aims of clubs were instrumental in gaining preferential treatment compared to hotels by officials and legislators. Police and public officials allowed NSW clubs to serve liquor outside hotel trading hours and operate illegal poker machines (Caldwell, 1972). Resulting profits improved club facilities and services, increasing their social benefit and popular appeal. The link between gambling and social benefit was being firmly established in government policy. Gambling for social purposes was seen as acceptable to a population who viewed gambling as an integral part of Australian popular culture (Australian Institute for Gambling Research, 1999).

GOVERNMENT ENDORSEMENT AND MARKET GROWTH: WORLD WAR II TO THE 1970s

Between the 1940s and 1970s, government policies on gambling continued to emphasize social benefit, although attention turned toward controlling illegal gambling operations, primarily in bookmaking and gaming machine operations. State-run totalisators provided the solution. Betting on horse races was officially restricted to on-course bets with licensed bookmakers. However, Painter (1996) argued that a thriving illegal off-course betting industry has always accompanied organized racing in Australia. By the 1960s, all Australian states had established government-operated off-course betting shops and totalisators called the Totalisator Agency Board (TAB).

Government moves to stamp out illegal gambling justified the spread of legalized commercial gambling in Australia during the 1950s and 1960s. The 1960s saw legalized gambling operations restricted mainly to state governments and not-for-profit organizations. Crime control and efforts to remove corruption added further legitimacy to legalized gambling. This was accompanied by the morally defensible purposes of raising revenue for churches, charities, governments, and not-for-profit organizations. Among the latter were NSW clubs, which gained the legal right to operate poker machines in 1956 (Hing, Breen, & Weeks, 2002).

In 1956, NSW clubs were successful in gaining exclusive legal rights to machine gaming operations, with the stated official justification focusing on characteristics that differentiated clubs from profit-focused, openly accessible hotels. These characteristics, including the social benefits provided to members and the community, restricted access to clubs and their poker machines, and the fact that poker machine profits did not accrue to individual business owners, were used as factors justifying exclusive gaming machine concessions. The importance of the clubs' not-for-profit status, membership requirements, and social role was clear when the Gambling and Betting (Poker Machines) Act 1956 NSW was passed. The community benefit rationale for clubs was very important (Hing et al., 2002).

From 1956 to the 1970s, the evolution of the NSW club industry was characterized by exponential growth in the number of clubs and club members, and increasing appeal to working-class people. Mackay

(1988) identified privileges underpinning the appeal of clubs, including more liberal trading hours than hotels, exclusive rights to operate machine gaming, and the introduction of a superior form of social drinking (Mackay, 1988). Thus, Australian gambling policies by the beginning of the 1970s were characterized by government ownership of the lotteries and TAB, tight regulation or restriction of private operators such as clubs and bookmakers, and prohibition of machine gaming in all jurisdictions except NSW clubs (McMillen, 1996b).

COMMERCIALIZATION, COMPETITION, AND MARKET EXPANSION: 1970S TO THE PRESENT

Economic pressures and social instability in the 1970s forced governments to rethink existing policies and find new stimulants for economic growth. Social, technological, and economic factors encouraged this transition (McMillen, 1996b). Social changes, such as increased leisure time and community affluence, along with economic trends such as the growth of tourism, made gambling more attractive to private investors. New technology enhanced management and control of gambling infrastructure and provided stable profits and taxes through predictable returns. The economic pressures of a series of recessions, cutbacks in federal funding, and an ideological move toward economic rationalization forced impoverished state governments to review policies and find new ways to stimulate growth. Although state government reactions to these developments varied, they all legalized new forms of gambling during the last decades of the twentieth century (McMillen, 1996b).

Competition for gambling dollars saw a fall in the popularity of lottery tickets but a rise in the number of new lottery products such as Lotto, soccer pools, Powerball, and instant lottery. Both government and commercial providers operate lotteries. Australia accounts for slightly less than 2 percent of world lottery sales, yet Australian lottery gamblers have a high frequency of gambling. Over half of lottery gamblers buy lottery products once a week or more (Productivity Commission, 1999).

The monopoly on gaming machines enjoyed by NSW clubs for twenty years ended in 1976. Other states and territories were deterred by pressure from existing gambling operators opposed to increased competition and by alleged corruption associated with the machines (O'Hara, 1988). Nevertheless, all Australian state and territory governments, except Western Australia, have legalized gaming machines in clubs and hotels—Queensland in 1991, Victoria in 1992, South Australia in 1994, the Northern Territory in 1995, and Tasmania in 1996. The leading type of gambling activity in Australia is now playing on gaming machines. Australia's share of the world gaming machine market can be interpreted in two ways. The market share can be estimated as high as 20 percent for regular high-intensity gaming machines or as low as 2.6 percent if pachislo, pachinko, and other amusement-with-prize machines are included (Productivity Commission, 1999). Australia has about 185,000 gaming machines, about half of which are operated in NSW. Gaming machines account for half the total business and tax revenue collected from all types of gaming (Productivity Commission, 1999).

In terms of venues with gaming machines, there are approximately 5,600 clubs in Australia with about 9 million members (Productivity Commission, 1999). The majority of these clubs have gaming machines. In contrast, the introduction of gaming machines into hotels has been much more recent, occurring mostly during the 1990s. In the state of NSW, hotels were permitted to have up to thirty gaming machines in 1997. There are 1,834 hotels operating 25,452 gaming machines in NSW, with a turnover estimated to be A$1.8 billion (NSW Department of Gaming and Racing, 2001).

Over the past three decades, market share and expenditure on racing have been declining in Australia, but off-course betting at the TAB has become very popular. Racing expenditure in 2000-2002 was A$1.7 billion compared to gaming expenditure of A$1.6 billion (Tasmanian Gaming Commission, 2002). The Australian Institute for Gambling Research (1999) identified four trends as being important for the future of racing and wagering:

- Privatization of the main TAB networks and their listing on the stock exchange. Privatization removes the TABs from the traditional public sector bureaucracy and perceived inflexibility, resulting in greater emphasis on commercial objectives and managerial autonomy.

- The rationalization of racing. This has taken the form of "growing the business" through providing more opportunities for punters to bet on racing, and removing those race meetings that add little to the business. This has included introducing Sunday, Monday, and Friday race meetings as well as night racing, and reducing the number of country race meetings.
- The promotion of special events in racing as part of a drive for increased tourism. This has occurred through promotion of the main racing carnivals and of particular racing stars, fashion, and gala events. These promotions have led to marked increases in both on-course attendance and betting turnover at the main carnivals.
- Interactive electronic wagering. Online betting on racing and sports is permitted in Australia and has introduced new people to racing as well as providing increased opportunity for current participants.

In 1992, the first sports bookmaking license in Australia was granted to Centrebet, then a private company operating in the Northern Territory. Sports betting in Australia is "the wagering on all types of local, national or international sporting activities (other than the established forms of horse and greyhound racing), whether on- or off-course, in person, by telephone, or via the internet" (Tasmanian Gaming Commission, 2002, p. 2). Each state and territory has different policy and legislation regulating sports betting. Prize money and the odds on sports betting at the TAB (such as footy-bet) are dependent on the total amount wagered, but bookmakers' sports betting is based on fixed odds (Productivity Commission, 1999). Expenditure on sports betting is rising and has grown from nil in 1991 to A$41.5 million in 2000-2001 (Tasmanian Gaming Commission, 2002).

Internet gambling began operating in Australia during 1996 in the Northern Territory (Independent Pricing and Regulatory Tribunal of NSW, 1998). However, in 2000, the Australian federal government placed a moratorium on Internet gambling. Initially, all forms of Internet gambling were banned, including gaming, wagering, and sports betting. In 2001, the focus shifted. The federal government introduced legislation, with the Interactive Gambling Act 2001 legalizing Internet betting on racing, sports betting, and lotteries. In contrast, gambling on computerized casino games and gaming machines was banned. The use of the Internet to play games of chance, or games of mixed skill and chance, such as roulette, poker, craps, on-line gaming machines, and blackjack, is an offense to customers physically located in Australia. Australian Internet gambling companies provide these particular games for overseas customers only (Independent Pricing and Regulatory Tribunal of NSW, 2004). Australian Internet gambling companies operate for overseas customers. No Australian nationals are allowed to gamble on these sites. In the Northern Territory, Lasseters, which operates Australia's largest on-line sites as well as a casino in Alice Springs, went online in 1999. In its first financial year, Lasseters online gambling operations recorded over A$100 million in revenue. Its online operation relies on 85,000 overseas customers for revenue (Schneider, 2001). Expenditure on Internet gambling in Australia was A$18.54 million in 2002-2003, of which A$18.51 million was spent with agencies in the Northern Territory (Tasmanian Gaming Commission, 2004). A further response by state and territory governments in countering some of the difficult social, economic, and political conditions in the 1970s was the introduction and establishment of casinos in the expanding Australian gambling arena.

CASINOS IN AUSTRALIA

Development

The development of the casino industry in Australia has been categorized by McMillen (1995) as having three waves. The first wave of Australian casinos was established in Tasmania and the Northern Territory, the two jurisdictions most vulnerable to the 1970s economic slump (McMillen, 1995). These were small, low-key developments, located in remote destinations, modeled on British club-style casinos and designed to draw tourist dollars to help with regional economic development.

The second wave of casino developments in Perth, Gold Coast, Adelaide, Canberra, Townsville, and Christmas Island in the mid-1980s and early 1990s aimed to stimulate tourism but was also intended to boost economic development. The states of Queensland, Western Australia, and South Australia sought to expand tourism to diversify their economies away from primary production and manufacturing. These casino developments differed markedly from their predecessors. With the exception of Christmas Island Casino (now closed), these casinos were located in large urban centers, drew much of their patronage from local residents as well as tourists, and were "fashioned on the glitter, luxury and showmanship of the American prototype" (McMillen, 1995, p. 14). There was a move away from the small, elegant, British-style casinos reflected in earlier developments in Tasmania and the Northern Territory.

The mid-1990s saw the third wave of Australian casino development, with megacasinos being built in major urban centers of Melbourne, Sydney, Brisbane, and the popular tourist destination of Cairns. These were established as a response to the economic consequences of the 1990s recession by the previously industrialized states. Victoria, in particular, suffered major declines in its manufacturing sector and was encouraging development to boost tourism to the state through sporting events such as the Grand Prix, and developments such as the Crown Casino. These casinos have been modeled on Las Vegas prototypes with the assumption that bigger is better (McMillen, 1995). Thus, all state and territory governments sanctioned casino developments, opting for private ownership with strict government controls and substantial, although diminishing, taxation rates. Each casino has at least a regional monopoly, with most having a state monopoly. Exhibit 1.1 illustrates the historical development of the industry in Australia based on McMillen's (1995) three waves.

At least three different casino models are recognizable at the international level, as McMillen (1996a) argued, based on British-, European-, and U.S.-style casinos. First is the British approach of tolerance but nonstimulation, in recognition of the inevitability of gambling in the community but a reluctance to encourage further growth. Governments have restricted market expansion and limited public access to casinos. Second is a European approach, which is more accepting of the integration of casinos and economic development, but which has strengthened the power of governments to deliver benefits to the local community. Third is the American model, which is driven by a mixture of regional development moral concern by restricting casino

EXHIBIT 1.1. Historical development of casinos in Australia.

1st wave: 1970s to early 1980s

1973	Wrest Point Casino, Hobart, Tasmania
1979	Diamond Beach Casino, now MGM Grand, Darwin, Northern Territory
1982	Launceston Country Club and Casino, Tasmania
1982	Lasseters Casino, Alice Springs, Northern Territory

2nd wave: 1980s to early 1990s

1985	Jupiters Casino, Gold Coast, Queensland
1985	Burswood Casino, Perth, West Australia
1986	Adelaide Casino, South Australia
1986	Breakwater Resort, Townsville, Queensland
1992	Casino Canberra, Australian Capital Territory
1994	Christmas Island Casino (now closed)

3rd wave: mid-1990s

1994	Crown Casino, Melbourne, Victoria
1995	Star City Casino, Sydney, New South Wales
1995	Conrad Treasury Casino, Brisbane, Queensland
1996	Reef Casino, Cairns, Queensland

Source: Based on McMillen, 1995, 1996a.

development to remote regions devoted to "fantasy" tourism. This model also recognizes principles of economic liberalism that include profit maximization and market expansion. Australia has increasingly tended to follow the American approach in its rapid expansion and style of development (McMillen, 1996a). However, it differs in that this third wave of development has seen new Australian casinos located in major urban centers drawing their patronage from local residents, not tourists (Hing et al., 2002).

Characteristics

The pattern of casino development in Australia has been quite distinctive, according to McMillen (1996b). She pointed to a number of characteristics of Australian casinos that differentiate them from international casinos, including access, location, and government policies:

- Australian casinos are very accessible. The European approach has been to allow many smaller casinos to operate throughout the country and generally require membership and a "cooling-off" period upon joining. In the United States, casinos were first allowed only in selected areas, such as Las Vegas and Atlantic City, in an attempt to export some of the potential problems. In some countries, locals are not allowed into casinos, and thus casinos do not rely on the local population base for customers. Thus, unlike casinos with restricted local access and unlike casinos located in isolated resort destinations, Australian casinos provide open access to the local population and aim to stimulate mass consumption and mass spending.
- Australian casinos are located mainly in major urban centers with a stable population base. Although tourism has always been a stated policy objective when a new casino development has been proposed, in fact in most Australian casinos, local residents are the dominant market. This is known as the "grind" market, made up of a large number of regular local players placing small bets, in contrast to the big-spending but smaller high-roller market.
- Australian casinos have not been established due to public demand, but due to the various state governments' desires for economic benefits. Australian governments have sanctioned casino development in their jurisdiction and enjoy the resulting taxation benefits. They have intervened in casino policy more than governments in many nations, to increase the capacity for effective regulation and theoretically to minimize any adverse social impacts by limiting the number of casinos (McMillen, 1995).

Current Status

Thirteen casinos are now legally operating in Australia. Since 1973, Australian casinos have expanded their market share from nil to 20 percent of total gambling expenditure in Australia (Productivity Commission, 1999). Yearly gambling expenditure in Australian casinos is A$2.54 billion, with the largest share (A$0.95 billion), being spent in the state of Victoria (Tasmanian Gaming Commission, 2002). Casinos pay state and territory taxes of about A$500 million per annum (Productivity Commission, 1999). The average annual profit margin for casinos is 3.4 percent or A$93 million (Australian Bureau of Statistics, 2000). Typical casino gamblers in Australia are males, aged eighteen to twenty-four years, and from Asian communities (Productivity Commission, 1999). The average annual per capita spending in casinos is about A$174 (Tasmanian Gaming Commission, 2002). Of the A$174 spent, approximately 80 percent is spent on gambling while 20 percent is spent on meals, alcohol, and accommodations (Australian Bureau of Statistics, 2000).

Governance

Each Australian state and territory has an act of parliament to allow the granting of a casino license and subsequent operation. The Casino Control Act 1992 NSW, for example, is the relevant legislation for casino operation in NSW. In addition, each state and territory has a gaming authority. In Victoria, this is known as the Victorian Casino and Gaming Authority, while in NSW it is called the NSW Casino Control Authority. Ultimately, responsibility for control of casinos lies with the relevant state or territory authority which, with a few minor exceptions, is not subject to the direction or control of the minister. Members of the authority are selected from recommendations made by the minister and should generally include persons with experience and qualifications in (a) business management, (b) gaming, (c) law, (d) finance, and (e) information technology (*Casino Control Act 1992* NSW, Section 135). In addition, membership should include a person with at least seven years' judicial or legal experience. The authority, headed by a chief executive officer, has the power and authority to investigate any areas of the casino that it considers may be in breach of the act and apply the relevant penalties. In addition to its reactive powers, the authority is also the body that the casino must apply to for any licenses. The casino must also pay any casino duty to the authority (Section 114) as set out by the state treasurer. As houses of gaming, most casinos must also pay a community benefit levy, which in NSW is paid into the Casino Community Benefit Fund administered by the Casino Community Benefit Fund Trustees.

Opportunities and Challenges

Many opportunities and challenges face casinos in Australia. Some of these, McMillen (1995) maintained, include a growing global market, increasing multinational investments, international competition, standardization of markets and casino games, regional differences, and offshore Internet gambling.

- Australia is well positioned geographically to take advantage of the growing global market for casino gambling. Burswood and MGM Grand casinos attract some of the highest per capita gambling expenditures, given their geographic proximity to high-roller markets in Asia. In 2000-2001, net gambling takings in Australia from international tourists were A$611 million, an increase of 13 percent from the previous year. Of this, premium players (high rollers) contributed A$500 million, an increase of 8 percent from the previous year (Australian Bureau of Statistics, 2001).
- Through branding, packaging, and sheer economic strength, multinational corporations with investments around the globe have established a high degree of market control, which small, localized gambling operators cannot match (McMillen, 1995). For example, the Darwin Casino has been refurbished by MGM Grand to attract a larger share of the Asian market. Multinational corporations also have a high capacity for pressuring governments for favorable operating conditions, such as lower taxes and less regulation.
- Australian casinos face increasing international competition. Not only has casino development escalated in many countries, but casinos themselves have become progressively internationalized. They are being forced to keep up with world—rather than national, state, or regional—standards. Thus, there has been a migration of casino management practices and a standardization of casino developments toward the large-scale U.S. model (McMillen, 1995).

- Homogenization of markets and casino games is reflected in the evolution and promotion of standard North American–style casinos and machine gaming. Many international games have been standardized, devoid of any local, cultural meaning. Traditional class boundaries in the types of gambling people participate in are also disappearing (McMillen, 1995).
- In each Australian state, government and casino operators have joined forces in a parochial effort to penetrate new markets and promote their own regional casino operations. State governments are coming under increasing pressure to make concessions to their local casinos to improve their competitiveness. This could threaten the regulatory effectiveness of state governments and reduce the economic benefits of casinos to the local economy. A collaborative approach between casino operators and governments in the various states is required to work cooperatively to overcome regional competition within Australia (McMillen, 1995).
- Offshore Internet gambling operations are thriving. They potentially threaten the competitiveness of traditional forms of gambling and effective government regulation and taxation in Australia. All forms of gambling are available on the Internet, including those provided at casinos (gaming machines, keno, table games, and sportsbook), clubs (gaming machines, raffles, keno), church and community halls (bingo), hotels (gaming machines, raffles), newsagents (lotto, pools, instant lottery), and the TAB (horses, greyhounds) (Toneguzzo, 1996).

CONCLUSION

This chapter has focused on the historical development, legislation, and current status of casinos and their governance in Australia. This explanation and analysis was based first on significant periods in the history of Australian gambling and second on the history of Australian casino growth. Distinctive features of Australian casino growth were explained using McMillen's (1995) concept of three waves. There are thirteen casinos in Australia, the first of which has been in operation only since 1973. Although changing historical conditions have created an environment that allowed for the establishment and development of casinos in Australia, they face considerable opportunities and challenges in sustaining and growing their market share.

REFERENCES

Australian Bureau of Statistics. (2000). *Gambling industries Australia 2000* (Catalogue 8684.0). Canberra: Australian Government Printing Service.

Australian Bureau of Statistics. (2001). *Casinos Australia* (Catalogue No. 8683.0). Canberra: Australian Government Printing Service.

Australian Institute for Gambling Research. (1999). *Australian gambling comparative history and analysis.* Melbourne: Victorian Casino and Gaming Authority.

Caldwell, G. T. (1972). *Leisure co-operatives: The institutionalization of gambling and the growth of large leisure organizations in New South Wales.* Unpublished doctoral dissertation. Canberra: Australian National University.

Casino Control Act 1992. New South Wales Casino Control Authority. Sydney, Australia. Available at http://www.casinocontrol.nsw.gov.au/resource/authority/cas act151992.PDF.

Cumes, J. W. C. (1979). *Leisure times in early Australia.* Cheshire/Reed: Longman.

Hing, N., Breen, H., & Weeks, P. (2002). *Club management in Australia: Administration, operations and gaming.* Sydney: Pearson Education Australia.

Independent Pricing and Regulatory Tribunal of NSW. (1998). *Report to government: Inquiry into gaming in NSW.* Sydney: Author.

Independent Pricing and Regulatory Tribunal. (2004). *Gambling: Promoting a culture of responsibility.* Sydney: Author.

Inglis, K. (1985). Gambling and culture in Australia. In G. Caldwell, B. Haig, M. Dickerson, & L. Sylvan (Eds.), *Gambling in Australia* (pp. 5-17). Sydney: Southwood Press.

Mackay, P. (1988). A profit is what it's all about. In Club Managers' Association Gosford conference (Ed.), *Proceedings of the marketing effectively conference trade exhibition* (pp. 13-21). Sydney: Club Managers' Association of Australia.

McMillen, J. (1995). The globalisation of gambling: Implications for Australia. *National Association for Gambling Studies Journal, 8*(1), 9-19.

McMillen, J. (1996a). *Perspectives on Australian gambling policy: Changes and challenges.* Paper presented at the National Conference on Gambling, Darling Harbour, Sydney.

McMillen, J. (1996b). The state of play: Policy issues in Australian gambling. In B. Tolchard (Ed.), *Proceedings of the seventh national conference of the National Association for Gambling Studies* (pp. 1-9). Adelaide: National Association for Gambling Studies.

NSW Department of Gaming and Racing. (2001). *Gaming analysis 1999-00.* Sydney: Author.

O'Hara, J. (1988). *A mug's game: A history of gaming and betting in Australia.* Sydney: NSW University Press.

Painter, M. (1996). A history of the regulation and provision of off-course betting in Australia. In J. McMillen, M. Walker, & S. Sturevska (Eds.), *Lady luck in Australia* (pp. 37-46). Sydney: National Association for Gambling Studies.

Productivity Commission. (1999). *Australia's gambling industries* (Report No. 10). Canberra: AusInfo.

Schneider, S. (2001). Australia. *International Gaming and Wagering Business, 22*(2), 9, 17.

Selby, W. (1996). Social evil or social good? Lotteries and state regulation in Australia and the United States. In J. McMillen (Ed.), *Gambling cultures: Studies in history and interpretation* (pp. 65-81). London: Routledge.

Tasmanian Gaming Commission. (2002). *Australian gambling statistics 1975-76 to 2000-01*. Hobart: Author.

Tasmanian Gaming Commission. (2004). *Australian gambling statistics 1977-78 to 2002-03*. Hobart: Author.

Toneguzzo, S. J. (1996). The Internet: Entrepreneur's dream or regulator's nightmare? In J. O'Connor (Ed.), *High stakes in the nineties: Proceedings of the sixth national conference of the National Association for Gambling Studies* (pp. 53-66). Perth: National Association for Gambling Studies.

Watts, J. H. C. (1985). Australia's best bet: The history of the totalisator. In G. Caldwell, B. Haig, M. Dickerson, & L. Sylvan (Eds.), *Gambling in Australia* (pp. 109-119). Sydney: Southwood Press.

Williams, J. L. (1938). *Australian club centenary*. Sydney: John Andrew.

Chapter 2

History, Development, and Legalization of Korean Casino Gaming

Choong-Ki Lee
Ki-Joon Back

HISTORICAL DEVELOPMENT

The history of gambling legislation in South Korea began with the passing by the Korean government of the first legislative action to prohibit any type of gambling activities. This legislation went into effect in November 1961. However, the Korean government amended it to legalize gambling only for foreigners in order to generate foreign tourist receipts in 1962. The Korean government did not have a clear definition of gambling activities, and gaming regulations were too strict to attract foreign travelers. Thus, an amendment was developed that allowed foreigners to gamble at casinos, which were exclusive tourism facilities for foreigners, to maximize tourism receipts.

According to the new amendment, the Olympos Hotel and Casino in Inchon was to become the first casino in 1967. The Walker-Hill Hotel and Casino opened in 1968 to accommodate alien and foreign travelers. Ironically, during the period between 1962 and 1968, the amendment was too liberal; therefore, it failed to prohibit domestic gambling at the casino. The Korean government decided to re-strengthen the regulation and revised the law to keep residents from gambling in casinos. The new law established in 1969 stated that casinos that allowed domestic customers into the casino areas would have their operations terminated and their casino license canceled.

In the 1970s, six casinos were built in several existing tourist destinations, including mountain and beach resort areas. In the 1980s and

1990s, a number of casinos opened on Jeju Island, the most famous tourist destination in Korea, known as the Asian Hawaii. Casinos on Jeju Island increased tourism revenues dramatically. In addition, the first casino in Kangwon Province, the Sorak Park Hotel and Casino, was given a license in 1980. In proximity to the beautiful scenery of the Sorak Mountains, foreign travelers enjoyed spending their vacation time gambling. Furthermore, the government loosened the casino license application procedure, which resulted in six additional casinos opening on Jeju Island. By 1995, the Jeju Ragonda Hotel and Casino opened as the eighth casino on Jeju Island. Table 2.1 summarizes the historical development of the Korean casino industry.

The Korean government has observed positive economic impacts from the casino industry as a result of increases in inbound tourism receipts. In August 1994, the Tourism Development Law (TDL) was designed to encourage the tourism industry by including the casino sector (Lee, Kwon, Kim, & Park, 2003). In the TDL, casino-related regulatory items were further improved. Prior to the TDL's initiation, the chief of police, the secretary of the interior, the governor, or the mayor were responsible for licensing, monitoring, and regulating casino operations.

According to the TDL, the Department of Culture and Tourism now has full responsibility for monitoring a licensee's compliance with all regulations, performing audits, and conducting investigations of possible violations of regulations. In December 1995, the Korean government legalized gaming in the run-down former coal mining areas of Kangwon Province for domestic customers (Lee, Kim, & Kang, 2003). These towns experienced a gold rush at a time when coal was used as a major source of energy for industries and households. As coal was replaced by new energy sources, such as oil and gas, the economy of these communities rapidly declined. The Korean government pursued various economic revitalization policies, but to no avail. After the four communities repeatedly urged the government to legalize gaming for domestic customers to revitalize the dilapidated mining towns, the government finally legalized a casino in one of the four communities (Chongsun). The Kangwon Land Casino opened to domestic customers in October 2000 and expanded in March 2003. This property is described later in this chapter.

TABLE 2.1. Historical development of the Korean casino industry.

Year	Event
1961	Korean government prohibited any type of gambling activities.
1962	Legalized gaming for foreign travelers.
1967	First casino, Inchon Olympos Hotel and Casino, opened.
1968	Seoul Walker-Hill Hotel and Casino opened.
1969	Restrengthened casino regulation by prohibiting domestic customers in casinos.
1971	Sokri Mountain Casino opened.
1972	Jeju KAL Hotel and Casino opened.
1978	Pusan Paradise Hotel and Casino opened.
1979	Kyungjoo Kolon Hotel and Casino opened.
1980	Sorak Park Hotel and Casino in Kangwon Province opened.
1985	Jeju Hyatt Hotel and Casino opened.
1990	Jeju Grand, Jeju Namseoul, Seoguipo KAL, Jeju Oriental Casino opened after government loosened the casino license application procedure.
1991	Jeju Shila Hotel and Casino opened.
1994	Department of Culture and Tourism gains full responsibility for monitoring a licensee's compliance with all regulations, performing audits, and conducting investigations of possible violations of regulations.
1995	Jeju Lagonda Casino opened.
	Legalized domestic casino in Kangwon Province.
1997	Slot machines were allowed in casinos.
1999	Foreign investments allowed.
2000	First domestic casino, Kangwon Land Resort, opened.
2003	Main casino of the Kangwon Land Resort opened.

Source: Adapted from Lee, Kwon, et al. (2003).

In 1997, the Korean government mandated a computerized data system that would enable every casino to report all transactions. In addition, the government allowed casino operations to offer up to nineteen different games on their properties, including slot machines, bingo games, and mah-jongg (Lee, Kim, et al., 2003). Slot machines had garnered much interest as a result of their simple game rules.

THE KOREAN CASINO INDUSTRY TODAY

Casino Operations

Fourteen casinos are registered to operate in Korea (Lee, Kim, et al., 2003). Thirteen of them exclusively accommodate foreign travelers and aliens, and only one casino is open to domestic customers. A majority of the casinos, eight properties, are located on Jeju Island. There are two casinos in Kangwon Province and one each in the cities of Seoul, Pusan, Inchon, and Kyungjoo. Ten casinos are operated by independent casino companies and lease their space from the hotels. Most of the casinos are housed in five-star hotel properties. In 2004, three additional casinos were legalized in Seoul and Pusan, and they are run by a subsidiary of Korea National Tourism Organization.

Casino Customers

The casino industry has had positive economic impacts as revealed by the number of foreign casino customers, increasing from 344,000 in 1988 to 680,000 in 1992, mainly from Japan, Taiwan, and China (Lee & Kwon, 1997). During the economic recession between 1993 and 1996, the number of foreign customers decreased (see Table 2.2). There are several reasons for the low demand among foreign casino customers. First, the Korean government prohibited Koreans who lived abroad from entering casinos between August 1993 and February 1994. Second, the Japanese economy seriously suffered as a result of inflation in its currency, and the majority of foreign customers were from Japan. In addition, casino bars (different from pachinko machines) were legalized in Japan, thereby discouraging Japanese people from going abroad to gamble. Third, the severance of the diplomatic relationship with Taiwan in 1992 had a big overall impact on

TABLE 2.2. Foreign casino customers and their receipts (except Kangwon Land Casino).

Year	Casino visitors	Growth rate (%)	Receipts (US$1,000)	Growth rate (%)
1988	343,843	—	58,015	—
1989	438,707	27.6	83,568	44.0
1990	499,362	13.8	93,164	11.5
1991	595,115	19.2	116,544	25.1
1992	680,397	14.3	136,351	17.0
1993	650,420	−4.4	173,176	27.0
1994	626,865	−3.6	255,507	47.5
1995	632,007	0.8	282,419	10.5
1996	517,672	−18.1	261,828	−7.3
1997	518,178	0.1	243,013	−7.2
1998	689,254	33.0	203,877	−16.1
1999	694,899	0.8	251,787	23.5
2000	636,005	−8.5	298,778	18.7
2001	626,851	−1.4	296,355	−0.8
2002	647,722	3.3	—	—

Source: Adapted from Korean Casino Association (2003).

the inbound tourism industry in Korea. Last, the completion of a new international airport in Macao in 1995 took away Southeast Asian casino customers from the Korean casino market.

However, the Korean casino industry increased in demand between 1997 and 1998, temporarily. Almost 690,000 foreign travelers visited casinos in 1998 because Korean currency was devalued by 50 percent as a result of a tough domestic economic situation. In 2000, the number of casino customers dropped again to about 640,000 (−8.5 percent from the previous year) when Korean currency regained its exchange rate against other currencies. Further, the negative growth rate in the number of casino travelers was due to a continuing terrible economic situation in Japan. Thus, numerous casino operators and marketers began developing new marketing strategies to attract casino customers from mainland China. In 2002, about 648,000 foreign tourists visited casinos, representing a slight increase of 3.3 percent over the previous year.

Table 2.2 presents interesting data showing that receipts in some years decreased while visitor numbers increased. This phenomenon was due to the devaluation of Korean currency in 1998. Receipts were reduced even though the number of visitors increased compared to previous years.

In the Seoul Walker-Hill Hotel and Casino (see Photo 2.1) received about 411,000 casino customers, which was equivalent to 65.5 percent of all casino customers (Korean Casino Association, 2003). In the same year, the Pusan Paradise Hotel and Casino recorded about 105,000 casino customer visits (16.8 percent), becoming the second most attractive place to gamble. The Inchon Olympos Hotel and Casino received 23,000 (3.6 percent), Kyungjoo Chosun Hotel and Casino (the former Kolon Hotel Casino) received 15,000 (2.4 percent), and Kwangwon Sorak Park Hotel and Casino recorded about 6,000 (0.9 percent) casino customer visits in 2001. Surprisingly, the total number of casino customer visits to the eight casinos on Jeju Is-

PHOTO 2.1. Seoul Walker-Hill Hotel and Casino. *Source:* Courtesy of Seoul Para- dise Walker-Hill Casino.

land was only 67,000 in 2001, accounting for 10.7 percent of the total casino visitors.

Kangwon Land Casino, the only casino for domestic customers, recorded about 208,000 visits during the first three months after its opening on October 28, 2000—the equivalent of 3,200 casino customer visits on a daily basis. In 2002, 915,000 casino customers visited Kangwon Land Casino (2,500 visitors on a daily basis), of which the majority of the visitors were domestic residents (Kangwon Land Casino, 2003). More than 1.5 million visitors and revenues of US$564 million were recorded when the main casino opened in 2003 (Kangwon Land Casino, 2004).

Casino Receipts

In the last ten years, the Korean casino industry has been successful in terms of generating casino revenues from foreign customers. As Table 2.2 shows, total casino revenues went from US$58 million in 1988 to over $116 million in 1991. In 1997, casino receipts of $243 million were recorded, equivalent to 4.7 percent of total tourism receipts ($5.2 billion). This positive economic trend continued, resulting in almost $300 million in receipts by the end of fiscal year 2000. During the period between 1996 and 1998, casino receipts declined slightly due to the economic recession in Japan. As mentioned earlier, casino receipts increased again at the beginning of 1999 because of the previous devaluation of the Korean currency during the Asian economic crisis. The average daily amount spent by each casino customer was $473, equivalent to 38.7 percent of the total daily spending by foreign travelers in 2001 (Lee, 2003).

THE KOREAN GAMING REGULATORY SYSTEM

The Department of Culture and Tourism has the authority to approve licenses, regulate policies, and control and supervise casino operations. In May 1996, the government mandated that all casino operations install a computerized casino data system to monitor each transaction (Ministry of Culture and Tourism Republic of Korea, 2003a).

Casino License

According to the TDL (Ministry of Culture and Tourism Republic of Korea, 2003b), casino operators must obtain approval from the minister of the Department of Culture and Tourism. This approval procedure follows a very strict set of guidelines, including building codes, business hours, number of employees, description of facilities, and the variety of amenities. There are four specific procedures for legally operating casino businesses, namely, registration, authorization, declaration, and approval. Unlike other types of tourism business, which have easy access to business initiation by either registration or authorization procedures alone, casino operations must follow all four procedures. Of these procedures, obtaining approval is the toughest process. It has been designed to minimize the potential negative social impacts on public interests.

There are three types of approval in the casino industry: new, modified, and conditional approvals. The new approval procedure occurs when a casino operator starts business for the first time. This specific procedure requires a representative person, name and location of the property, and full description of the facilities. The modified approval procedure applies to any changes made to the current approval. The conditional approval procedure is for provisional casinos that must meet all the guidelines set by the minister of the Department of Culture and Tourism within a specific time frame. Generally, the time frame is not over one year and is set by the president of South Korea.

Article 20 of the TDL states requirements for the casino approval process. A preliminary requirement for a casino license within a hotel or a convention center is that the applicant property be located in a tourist destination city with an international airport or harbor. In addition, there are several critical conditions that each applicant property should meet:

- Meet or exceed the predetermined minimum number of foreign travelers visiting in the previous financial period. These minimum required numbers are determined by the minister of the Department of Culture and Tourism.
- Provide a detailed business plan including feasibility studies and marketing strategies for attracting foreign casino customers.

- Provide proof of financial resources to support the planned activities.
- Develop financial transaction and internal control procedures.
- Meet other miscellaneous requirements determined by the minister of the Department of Culture and Tourism to promote the industry in the public interest.

An international cruise line must meet one more specific requirement: the vessel should weigh over 10,000 tons. All other requirements are the same as for hotel or conference center casinos, as mentioned previously.

The following documents should be submitted to the minister of the Department of Culture and Tourism as part of the casino license application process:

- Names, social security numbers, and proof of residence of chief executive officers
- Company bylaws and registration of incorporation
- Business plan, including feasibility study reports, marketing plan, and hiring and operating procedures
- Building title
- Any miscellaneous documents proving adherence to all of the requirements set by the minister of the Department of Culture and Tourism

Casino Regulations

According to the TDL, the casino business is strongly supported by the Korean government to generate attractions for foreign travelers and to maximize tourism receipts along with other segments of the tourism industry. However, the government has set very strict operating policies to control the casino business due to the speculative nature of gambling. All casino operators should obtain approval for the design and structure of casino properties and materials and performance of slot machines and tables from the minister of the Department of Culture and Tourism. Specifically, Article 27 of the TDL states casino operators' responsibilities as follows:

- Casino operators should operate only government-certified casino equipment.
- Casino operators should not modify the casino equipment without approval of the government.
- Casino operation is only allowed in the licensed area.
- Except for the Kangwon Land, no other casino should allow domestic customers to play in the casino.
- Advertisements should not overpromise winnings.
- Casinos should report every financial transaction to the authority.
- Casinos should not allow underage persons (nineteen years old or younger) to gamble.

In addition, Article 28 of the TDL lists casino customers' responsibilities as follows:

- Domestic customers should not enter the casino, except in the Kangwon Land Casino.
- All casino customers should show identification to verify their foreign nationality. Also, all domestic customers must present identification when entering Kangwon Land Casino.
- No minor is allowed (nineteen years old or younger).

The Korean government mandates that casino operators pay the Tourism Development Fund up to 10 percent of gross sales. This money goes toward development of the tourism industry. The government began this fund in December 1972 to build and maintain tourist attractions. Unlike the other segments of the tourism industry, the casino industry has taken on a great portion of the responsibility for developing this fund. The fund should be used for developing monitoring and treatment programs for problem gamblers.

Casino Operating Policy

Korean casino operating policy was developed based upon regulations used by the New Jersey Casino Control Commission in July 1995. With some modifications, a new operating policy was established in October 1999. The modified operating policy consists of eight chapters, including bylaws, an organization chart, structure of facilities, game equipment, operating procedures, regulations for slot machines, accounting procedures, and employees' codes (Ministry of Culture and Tourism Republic of Korea, 2003a). Each casino operator must incorporate all these requirements into company policy.

- Chapter 1 states the need for a mission statement, objectives, and definition of the business. Specifically, the objectives should be clearly communicated between casino employers and employees to generate and maintain a healthy work environment.
- Chapter 2 deals with human resource issues, including the organizational chart; procedures for setting up an executive board of directors and describing their duties; job descriptions and specifications of all positions in the executive office as well as sales, security, accounting, cashier, and database departments. Also, this chapter regulates the operating hours.
- Chapter 3 regulates all types of building codes, including computer database programming and management, layouts of cashier office and count room, and designation and maintenance of restricted areas by adding closed-circuit monitoring systems.
- Chapter 4 controls and maintains the types and quantities of gaming devices, such as tables, roulette wheels, big wheels, dice, and cards.
- Chapter 5 stipulates operating procedures, including admissions control, currency exchange, game rules, limits in the drop box, keys, and counting policies.
- Chapter 6 regulates the operating policies of slot machines in the area of both human resources and equipment. It includes developing the organization chart of the slot department and setting guidelines for installing slot machines and floor configurations, designating the location of coin exchange machines, maintaining slot machine logs, and determining slot wins.
- Chapter 7 deals with accounting policies for all types of financial transactions in the casino, including auditing, bookkeeping, and establishing credit lines.
- Chapter 8 stresses the employees' responsibilities, including dress code, code of ethics, and tipping policies. No employee

should accept tips (except for Kangwon Land Casino), participate in any type of gaming, or have a personal relationship with customers.

A Special Casino for the Domestic Market

The first casino for domestic customers, Kangwon Land Casino, became legally available in Kangwon Province in October 2000 (see Photo 2.2). As in Colorado in the United States, the geographic location of this casino is a rundown mining area that was economically devastated after coal was replaced by gas. This community even once considered building nuclear waste plants to revitalize its economy. After this community repeatedly urged the government to legalize gaming for domestic customers to revitalize dilapidated mining towns, the government legalized a casino in December 1995. The unique aspect of this approval was that only one casino for the domestic market was allowed in Korea.

The initial investment in Kangwon Land Casino was about US$100 million. The central and local governments invested 51 percent and private investors provided the rest of the investment funds. This property was developed in two phases. The first phase involved building a

PHOTO 2.2. Kangwon Land Casino. *Source:* Courtesy of Kangwon Land Casino.

small, temporary casino and the main casino by 2003. The small casino opened in October 2000, included thirty table games and 480 slot games, and was attached to a deluxe hotel with 199 guest rooms. This small casino was planned for a capacity of 700 people, but recorded 3,200 visitors per day, almost five times more than its capacity (Kangwon Land Casino, 2001). The average daily revenue has been recorded as almost US$1 million.

In March 2003, the main casino opened with 132 table games and 960 slot machines. The main casino is also attached to a hotel with 477 guest rooms and a theme park. The hotel earned a five-star rating and targets the family segment as well as high rollers. To attract the family market, the casino has a Las Vegas–style theme park, which has different types of rides and shows. Interestingly, as soon as the main casino opened, the small casino had to close due to the one-casino policy for the domestic market. The small casino has been converted to a golf resort.

The second phase of casino development is associated with a resort. In addition to the theme park, eighteen-hole golf courses and ski slopes are expected to be completed in 2005 and 2006, respectively.

SUMMARY

Many countries have legalized and supported the development of casinos to generate tourism receipts and increase tax revenues. As the proportion of the economic structure invested in casino businesses has increased dramatically, the importance of effective gaming regulations and policies has increased as well.

Although the Korean government recognized the benefits of casinos to the country's economic situation, initially casino regulations were very strict about opening casinos only to foreigners to protect citizens from the negative social impacts. In 1994 and 1995, however, Korea passed a new Tourism Development Law to encourage the tourism industry by including the casino sector and to further deregulate casino-related items in order to establish a casino for domestic customers.

Furthermore, the Korean government amended the TDL in 1998 to ease the hiring requirements and procedures for casino employees and to affect foreign investment policies so that they could better promote casino operations. In addition, a Korean casino operating policy was developed and modified based upon regulations put in place for the New Jersey Casino Control Commission in 1999. The ultimate objective of this policy is to ensure transparent operations by licensees. The policy requires casino operators to submit information, including a mission statement, objectives, and general operating procedures.

The Korean casino industry can look forward to a prosperous future in terms of economic growth. However, a specific gaming control board or commission has still not been established to monitor financial transactions in the industry, even though the Department of Culture and Tourism oversees the application process. The congress is discussing the need for such a specialized unit. The proposed gaming control board will not only monitor casino operations but also control horse racing, cycling races, and lotteries to prevent money laundering, tax evasion, the manipulation of winning probabilities, and so forth. Last, with the Kangwon Land Casino's success in attracting both domestic and international markets, many communities are preparing proposals to amend the TDL to develop casinos in their backyards. Operators and policymakers should clearly understand both the positive and negative impacts of casino development before they make any decisions.

REFERENCES

Kangwon Land Casino. (2001). *Casino visitors and revenues*. Kangwon-do: Author.

Kangwon Land Casino. (2003). *Casino visitors and revenues*. Kangwon-do: Author.

Kangwon Land Casino. (2004). *Casino visitors and revenues*. Kangwon-do: Author.

Korean Casino Association. (2003). *Casino visitors and receipts*. Seoul: Author.

Lee, C. K. (2003). *A long-term strategy for the Korean casino industry*. Seoul: Paradise Walker-Hill Casino.

Lee, C. K., Kim, S. S., & Kang, S. Y. (2003). Perceptions of casino impacts—A Korean longitudinal study. *Tourism Management, 24*(1), 45-55.

Lee, C. K., & Kwon, K. S. (1997). The economic impact of the casino industry in South Korea. *Journal of Travel Research, 36*(1), 52-58.

Lee, C. K., Kwon, K. S., Kim, K. Y., & Park, C. K. (2003). *Understanding of the casino industry*. Seoul: Ilsingsa.

Ministry of Culture and Tourism Republic of Korea. (2003a). *Casino operating policy* (online). Available: http://www.mct.go.kr.

Ministry of Culture and Tourism Republic of Korea. (2003b). *Tourism development law* (online). Available: http://www.mct.go.kr.

Chapter 3

Casino Gambling in Macao: Through Legalization to Liberalization

Glenn McCartney

THE EARLY YEARS: ILLEGAL TO LEGALIZED GAMBLING

In 1557, the isthmus of Macao (the English spelling, with Macau being the Portuguese version), named after the Chinese sea goddess A-Ma, saw the Portuguese being given permission to settle there by the Chinese, although the official documentation was later to be supposedly lost in a fire. It was only in 1887, three centuries later, that China signed an official treaty with Portugal confirming its governing status in Macao (Lamas, 1998). On one of the southernmost tips of China, Macao for the next 300 years became the main and most important trading post between the West and East, in particular China. It represented a strategic gateway, being on the mouth of the Pearl River, an important access point to the godowns and warehouses in the province of Canton. From its outset, it seems that gambling was a favorite pastime for many foreigners and Chinese alike. Although initially illegal, gambling was prevalent throughout Macao as well as Canton. The ancient game of fan-tan, requiring no more than a number of buttons, coins, or stones that are divided four times with a stick and then the number guessed, was one of the more preferred as it was easy to set up and understand (and is still played in some of Macao's casinos to this day).

Early gambling in Macao has been portrayed in a rather negative light, as in reports from the Franciscan friar José de Jesus Maria, who was in Macao in the 1740s and wrote of how the town was plagued with gambling, murder, drunkenness, fighting, robbery, and a long list of other vices (Pinho, 1991). This sentiment was similarly shared by Coates (1966), a writer of several historical books on Macao, who wrote of foreign sailors' antics in the seventeenth century in Macao, saying that there were some who "aggravated the situation by pandering to the sailors, running brothels, drinking and gambling houses for them, soaking them in cheap potent Chinese liquors and robbing them (a favourite trick) when they passed out" (p. 39). Although, in perspective, this had less to do with the number of ships in port, which would have been not more than a dozen, and more to do with the length of time spent there, being between six and eight months (Coates, 1996).

It was also in the mid-eighteenth century that the highest accredited representative to Macao from the Ching Dynasty, Cheung Yue Lam, signed a treaty with the Portuguese representative, Antonio Pereira de Silva, one of the issues being that the Portuguese officers should control gambling. From this, it can be judged that the gambling industry was having a negative effect on public order in the city and was arousing attention even from the Chinese emperor's court.

Up to the 1850s, the Portuguese administration placed no restriction whatsoever on gambling in Macao and the sparsely inhabited islands of Taipa and Coloane, claiming they were respecting Chinese culture, which included the habit of gambling. Interestingly, one of the arguments for the legalization of casinos today is to generate tax revenues and contributions to social and infrastructure projects (Eadington, 1996; Roehl, 1994). In fact, such an argument was used by the governor of Macao, Captain Isidoro Francisco Guimaráes (governor from 1851 to 1863), who introduced a licensing system for gambling houses in Macao to raise much-needed revenue for the Portuguese provinces of Timor and Sohor Islands, which Macao could not afford without gaming revenue (Gunn, 1996). This licensing system was successful from the outset, not only in producing tax revenue, but also in bringing order to gambling in Macao, although the gambling houses were triad controlled, which continued right up to the Macao handover to China in 1999 (Leong, 2002). In the islands, licensing permits were also issued periodically for the popular game of clú-clú (Macanese for the casino game of cussec), and by 1886, sixteen gambling rooms were in operation in the Inner Harbour area and along the

Rua da Felicidade, which were cited as tourist attractions (Pons, 1999).

The timing of the licensing of Macao's gambling houses and the commencement of British rule in Hong Kong in 1842 seems not to be without coincidence. This also signaled the rapid decline of Macao as a trading gateway to China, which it had relied so greatly on for its survival. Because Hong Kong is adjacent to Macao, it has played a key role in the economic success of Macao's casino industry, being the main feeder gaming tourist market until 2002, at that time representing 5.1 million of Macao's 11.5 million tourists. Although Macao's gambling houses had significant visitor arrivals of 4.6 and 5.1 million in 2003 and 2004 respectively, this number was surpassed by the mainland China tourist market with 5.7 and 9.5 million visitors. Macao's total arrivals for 2003 and 2004 were 11.9 and 16.7 million, respectively (Macao Statistics and Census Service, 2005c), thus gambling remains the prime motivation for most of Macao visitor markets. In 1867, the Hong Kong government under Governor Richard MacDonnell briefly tried to emulate Macao, chiefly to stem corruption and bribery throughout the Hong Kong government and police force, by licensing ten public gaming houses. This was to be short lived because of England's dismay and disdain for the large "profits of vice" being generated in Hong Kong (especially as gambling was illegal in England at that time). Gambling houses in Hong Kong were quickly closed down, "bringing back the old (illegal) system of gambling and police corruption" (Nepstad, 2000) and securing Macao a constant flow of willing gamblers from Hong Kong to this day.

PERIOD OF CASINO DEVELOPMENT: LEGALIZATION TO MONOPOLY FRANCHISE

Another major step in the history of Macao's casinos was the granting by the Macao government of the first monopoly rights for casinos in Macao to the Tai Xing Company in 1934. Before giving this monopoly license, the government had considered conceding gaming to a foreign (French) syndicate to pay for a much-needed harbor dredging project in 1883, which was to cost an estimated $2.7 million, which neither Macao nor Portugal could afford. (This dredg-

ing is still done today and is part of the social commitment in the casino contract to "dredge the waterway between Macao, Hong Kong
and the outer islands of Taipa and Coloane to ensure the accessibility
and the unobstructed usage by vessels" [Commission for the First
Public Tender to Grant Concessions to Operate Casino Games of
Chance of the Macao SAR, 2001, p. 19].) With regard to this foreign
syndicate, the scandalized writer Montalto de Jesus (1984) wrote in
1926:

> To carry out the harbour works and other retarded improve-
> ments, eventually a loan was offered by a French syndicate, in
> return for a forty-two years' lease of the gambling monopolies
> and a grant of land for raising hotels, casino and recreation
> grounds. Moreover, the syndicate was to contribute a yearly
> subsidy whereof 50 percent should serve as a sinking fund for
> the loan. But the proposal was pooh-poohed as impracticable,
> and declined as such by local wiseacres. (p. 430)

In the introduction to *Historic Macao* (1984), it is explained that
Montalto de Jesus was later considered a traitor by the Macao
government because he wrote that the Portuguese were incompetent
in meeting Macao's needs and argued that Portugal should give over
the territory to the League of Nations to run, which led to his book being publicly burned in Macao in 1926, when the second edition appeared. It was to be 120 years before foreign companies (with Macao
partnerships) would be awarded casino concessions.

A driving factor behind the first casino franchise was a need to develop tourism, because this guaranteed the future prosperity of the
territory (Gunn, 1996); the only way to do this was to revamp the
gambling industry. It was also an attempt to improve the supervision
and control of the gaming industry. Although the governor had a vision of a Monte Carlo in the East, Macao retained the image of being
a wicked city, with its cocktail of brothels, drugs, and gambling
(Simpson, 1962, cited in Cheng, 1999). Though the Macao Government Tourist Office reputed Macao as having "more churches and
chapels to the square mile than any other in the world" or than the
Vatican (MGTO, 1993, p. 133, cited in Cheng, 1999, p. 158), it was
said to have more gambling tables than Monte Carlo. Even the new

casino concession found it difficult to shake this shady image, with Tai Xing Company's main shareholder, Fu Tak Iam, being kidnapped in 1946 while going for his daily smoke of opium at one of Macao's temples. A huge sum was paid to the captors after the family received one of Fu's ears. A few years later his son was also kidnapped, with the same sinister ritual of sending an ear (Pons, 1999). Pons (1999) goes on to state that Macao suffered through World War II (although taking a neutral stand) with famine and even cholera, although the gambling rooms stayed full, frequented by spies from each warring nation, adding further to Macao's colorful gaming history. Gangster shootouts in the style of Chicago were recorded; even James Bond writer Ian Fleming, after his visit to Macao in 1959 while collecting material for a series of articles he was doing for *The Sunday Times* on "thrilling cities" around the world, wrote that the Central Hotel (the only hotel with a casino) was "the least recommendable place on earth," basing the character Goldfinger on one of Macao's shady underworld figures who dealt in the gold trade (Pons, 1999, p. 121).

In the early 1960s following the death of Fu, a young Stanley Ho decided to take over the gaming industry in Macao, in competition with Fu's heirs. With intensive lobbying of Portuguese authorities and the backing of a powerful list of ten stakeholders, including Eric Fok, Teddy Yip, Stanley Ho, and Yip Hong (these four holding the majority of shares), on January 1, 1962, Sociedade de Turismo e Diversoes de Macau (STDM, translated as Macau Travel and Amusement Company Limited) took over the industry after winning a public tender, the first tender since 1934 (Boletim Oficial de Macau, 1962). Being a privately owned company, STDM has remained relatively secretive in its commercial dealings to this day. Before the first official casino, the Estoril Casino, opened, STDM temporarily transformed a Chinese junk into a floating casino in 1962 (used as scenery for the James Bond movie *The Man with the Golden Gun*), which was later replaced by today's floating Macau Palace. Various economic and social contribution criteria formed part of the concession contract, which was subject to minor contractual revisions and amendments until the end of the casino monopoly in 2002. From a financial undertaking of a set casino tax base of 3 million patacas in 1962, this increased to 10.8 percent of casino gross revenue in 1976, to 25 percent in 1982 (increasing thereafter from 1986 by 1 percent each year until it reached 30 percent), and to the final taxation rate, before the liberalization of the casino industry, of 31.8 percent in 1997. A diverse and comprehensive list of social and infrastructure contributions was also included, ranging from establishing and maintaining (i.e., dredging) waterways, particularly between Macao and Hong Kong, to contributions to social and educational foundations and sharing the costs with the government (50 percent each) on construction projects, such as the Macao Cultural Centre, overseas tourism offices, and a trade office (in Brussels), as well as funding cultural events and shows in Macao.

STDM's control of Macao's gaming industry was considerable, extending beyond the casinos to other forms of legalized betting in Macao, such as pari-mutuel (Macao Jockey Club and Macao Canidrome—greyhound racing), SLOT (a sports lottery with soccer and basketball betting), and Pacapio Lottery (with four betting centers in Macao). A company opened by Stanley Ho during this time was Shun Tak Holdings, with a 5 percent holding in STDM. The importance of this corporation can be seen in its infrastructure investments in Macao. Shun Tak owns one of the world's largest fleets of high-speed jetfoils (and 92 percent monopoly of the seaways between Macao and Hong Kong as well as other Chinese cities); has the sole helicopter service between Macao and Hong Kong; controls stakes in two of Macao's leading hotel properties, Mandarin Oriental and Westin Resort Hotels (although through STDM, Mr. Ho owns virtually every major hotel in Macao); owns the Seng Heng Bank, one of the largest banks in Macao; operates the largest department store; built the 338 meter Macao Tower; runs the Convention and Entertainment Centre; and has controlling interests in other infrastructure projects in Macao.

With gambling generating around 60 percent of Macao's GDP prior to casino deregulation, STDM's significance to Macao and its economy is without question; however, the STDM monopoly, one of the world's most lucrative legal gambling concessions, was to stay in place for only five years after Macao's return to China from Portuguese administration. In 2002, for the first time in Macao's long legal gaming history, concessions were given to three syndicates, with foreign interests. These were SJM (Sociedade de Jogos de Macau, renamed from STDM), Wynn Resorts SA (Sociedade Anónima), and Galaxy Casino SA. In fact, although three concessions were initially awarded, an additional subconcession has created four competing companies. The Venetian held shares in Galaxy Casino SA during the bidding, but after winning a concession, The Venetian became a subconcession of Galaxy Casino's license. The two are now completely contractually independent from each other and have built separate and competing casino properties.

RECENT EVENTS: THE LIBERALIZATION OF MACAO'S CASINO INDUSTRY

It is well supported in casino literature that one of the foremost arguments to justify and introduce casino development, in many gaming jurisdictions worldwide, is as an economic panacea for depleted state coffers (Roehl, 1994; Smith & Hinch, 1996; Smeral, 1998). In Macao, casino liberalization, as well as being a strategy for producing tax and social contributions was also a means for economic restructuring in which casino tax revenues were not solely produced by one concession holder. Looking at gross revenues generated by SJM's thirteen casinos (eleven of which were simply inherited from STDM during liberalization), as well as Galaxy's first casino, Waldo, and Venetian's The Sands, as the number of casinos grew, so did gaming revenues (Table 3.1). Figure 3.1 shows the locations and opening dates of Macao's present eleven casinos. Also included in the figure are the pari-mutuel clubs of the Macao Jockey Club and Macao Canidrome, both owned by SJM. In 1991, only five casinos were operating in Macao, rising to eleven before the liberalization of the casino industry in 2002. The newest casino hall, Pharaoh's Palace (a part of the Legend Club), opened in early 2003, is also owned and operated by SJM.

In a comparison of tax revenue between 1991 and 2004, a substantial increase of more than 360 percent is observed, with the most significant yearly increase in gaming revenue of 44 percent from 2003 to 2004, when the number of casinos increased from eleven to fifteen. (In 1991, only five casinos were in operation.) Even when the casino industry was negatively affected in 1998 and 1999 by the Asian financial crisis, tax revenue still reached 4.86 and 4.39 billion patacas, respectively. The slight decrease in 1996 was due to the high-profile

TABLE 3.1. Macao casino revenue (in million patacas[a]), 1991 to 2004.

Year	Gross revenue	Drop (amount wagered)	Direct tax[b]
1991	8,669	199,185	2,639
1992	11,854	283,684	3,554
1993	13,844	369,243	4,351
1994	15,414	420,504	4,636
1995	17,480	509,840	5,354
1996	16,412	463,823	5,044
1997	17,784	492,740	6,131
1998	14,566	450,017	4,863
1999	13,037	398,015	4,390
2000	15,878	491,960	5,504
2001	18,109	578,830	5,952
2002	21,546	732,613	7,432
2003	27,849	980,940	9,919
2004	40,186	not available	14,150

Sources: Compiled from Commission for the First Public Tender to Grant Concessions to Operate Casino Games of Chance of the Macao Special Administrative Region, 2001; Macao Government Information Bureau, 2004; Macao Gaming Control Board, 2005.

[a] 1 USd = 7.8 patacas.
[b] Before the liberalization of Macao's casino industry, STDM paid a gaming tax of 31.8 percent. Under the new gaming legislation, this has increased to 35 percent. This does not include the significant infrastructure and social contributions, which continue with the new licenses, as well as fixed and variable premiums on the gaming tables and mechanical gaming machines.

triad turf war in Macao at that time, which had a negative effect on tourism arrivals. Gamblers were also seemingly unaffected by the liberalization process. "[T]rue to its reputation as Asia's casino mecca, Macau's gaming industry continued operating non-stop when it changed on Sunday [March 31] from a monopoly to a liberalisation regime at the stroke of midnight" (Bruning, 2002). The only time the twenty-four-hour casinos have ever been closed was in September 1976, when the death of Mao Tse-tung was announced. This seamless liber-

1. Macao Palace Casino, 1962 (Macau Floating Casino)
2. Estoril Casino, 1963, Estoril Hotel (pioneer casino hotel, now closed)
3. Kam Pek Casino, 1963
4. Lisboa Casino, 1970, Lisboa Hotel
5. Jai Alai Casino, 1975 (replacing Estoril Casino)
6. Oriental Casino, 1984, Mandarin Oriental Hotel (formerly Excelsior Hotel; first deluxe casino)
7. Kingsway Casino, 1992, Kingsway Hotel
8. Taipa Casino, 1994, Hyatt Hotel
9. Diamante Casino, 1994, Holiday Inn
10. New Century Casino, 1997, New Century Hotel (renamed Greek Mythology Casino, 2005)

FIGURE 3.1. Locations of Macao's casinos (with year of opening) and pari-mutuel gambling venues.

11. Club VIP Legend, 1999, Macau Pharaoh Hotel (formerly Landmark Hotel; renamed Pharoah's Palace Casino, 2003)
12. Marina Casino, 1999, Pousada Marina Infante Hotel
13. Macau Jockey Club Casino, 2004, Grandview Hotel
14. Sands Casino, 2004 (The Venetian Macao)
15. Waldo Galaxy Casino, 2004, Waldo Hotel (Galaxy Resorts Macao)
16. Casa Real Casino, 2004, Casa Real Hotel
17. Horse racing (Macao Jockey Club), 1980
18. Dog racing (Macao Canidrome), 1963

1. Macao-China border gate (land crossing)
2. Macao Ferry terminal (helicopter and jetfoil use from Hong Kong and China)
3. Macao International Airport
4. Lotus Bridge (land crossing from China)

FIGURE 3.1 *(continued)*

alization process and continuously rising tax generation were aided
by the fact that SJM simply inherited all eleven STDM licensed casinos, including the Lisboa Hotel complex. The outbreak of SARS (severe acute respiratory syndrome) had drastic effects on the tourism
industry internationally in the second quarter of 2003, by which Asia
was particularly hard hit. Although Macao experienced drops in tourism arrivals during this period, in August 2003 SJM was able to report the highest monthly gross revenue on record, 2.8 billion patacas
(Bruning, 2003).

A total of twenty-five types of games are permitted, although not
all are played (Table 3.2). In 2004, baccarat and VIP baccarat represented 90 percent of gross revenue, which has been fairly consistent
over the years. Such statistics are noteworthy, considering that in casino jurisdictions such as Nevada, slot machines are the largest producer of casino gross revenue. Therefore, game mix (table/slot) is
currently a strategic consideration for future design and marketing of
casinos in Macao, for the development of newer casino markets
and/or shifting current gamblers to newer games, for the optimum income generated from the gaming floor area. Some new games have
been introduced, such as stud poker and the lucky wheel, with noteworthy increases in the number of gaming tables, which in 2002 num-
bered 339 rising to 1,092 tables in 2004, and slot machines from 808
in 2002 to 2,254 machines in 2004 (Macao Gaming Control Board,

TABLE 3.2. Casino gross revenue (in million patacas[a]) by game type, 2004.

Game	Gross revenue
Roulette	124
Blackjack	1,176
VIP baccarat	28,916
Baccarat	5,458
Mini baccarat	353
Fan-tan	144
Cussec	1,180
Pai kao	132
Boule	5
Slot machines	622
Mah-jongg pai kao	34
Three-card poker	194
Fish-prawn-crab	1,261
Three-card baccarat	218
Pachinko	8
Tombola	1
Lucky wheel	31
Football poker	2
Stud poker	327
Total	40,186

Source: Adapted from Macao Gaming Control Board, 2005.

[a]1 USd = 7.8 patacas.

2005). However, slot-machine income in Macao's casinos continues to reflect only a small amount of the total gross casino revenue.

Although Macao may not emulate Las Vegas regarding casino table/slot mix, 2004 saw the Las Vegas strip produce US$5.33 billion (American Gaming Association, 2005) while Macao produced US$5.02 billion, thus making it the second largest gambling market in the world. Predictions are that Macao could soon become the world's leading gambling market based on expectations that Beijing will continue to relax travel restrictions from mainland China and that the number of hotel rooms in Macao will continue to increase (Preston, 2005).

Of the gaming tables, most are in fact located in only four of the eleven casino properties: the Lisboa Hotel (42 percent); Jai Alai (15 percent), a standalone property without substantial accommodation; the Legend Club (12 percent), which includes the addition of the first themed casino, Pharaoh's Palace, opened in 2003 with adjacent accommodation (Emperor Hotel) and its own accommodation under renovation; and the New Century Hotel and Casino (9 percent) on Taipa Island. Similarly, over 80 percent of the slot machines are housed within these four complexes.

REGULATION OF THE LIBERALIZATION

In August 2001, Macao's legislative assembly officially passed Law No. 16/2001 (Boletim Oficial da Região Administrativa Especial de Macau, 2001a), the Gaming Industry Framework, which laid out the conditions and process for open bidding for a casino concession in Macao, signaling a significant strategic defining moment in Macao's long gaming history and allowing those with international interests to have a stake in Macao's "dragon head" industry.

When the Macao government set out to regulate Macao's gaming industry, they had several objectives in mind:

> Recognising the strategic social and economic importance of a healthy and sustainable development of the gaming industry, the Macao Government gives great emphasis to liberalisation process that can guarantee the gradual development of its gaming sector into a world-class operation, and at the same time will trigger and/or reinforce the progress of different economic sectors of Macao. (Commission for the First Public Tender to Grant Concessions to Operate Casino Games of Chance of the Macao SAR, 2001, p. 47)

In addition, the Macao government officially stated three specific goals of liberalization:

1. The development of a competitive casino industry that will move to adopt more contemporary practices in casino operations and customer service
2. Providing additional employment opportunities for Macao residents and deriving associated benefits of enhanced economic development and social stability
3. Consolidating Macao's position as the regional center of casino gaming, with an enhanced reputation in its gaming industry for fairness, honesty, and freedom from criminal influence (Commission for the First Public Tender to Grant Concessions to Operate Casino Games of Chance of the Macao SAR, 2001)

Developing and enhancing the casino industry in areas of operation, customer service, and economic development, thereby bringing more employment benefits for local residents, were issues behind the liberalization. However, another key consideration and particular focus was the long-term development of the tourism industry, Macao's economic pillar, which had for so long been dominated by a sole corporation.

The criteria within this regulatory framework were very specific, including the following:

- Macao would have no more than three casino concessions. The duration of each contract would not be permitted to exceed twenty years; upon completion, it could be renewed once or more, with the number of times and length of each extension at the Macao chief executive's discretion.
- Bidding companies should only be casino operators and gaming companies with a capital of at least 200 million patacas. An executive director with permanent Macao residency and owning at least 10 percent of the company capital has to be appointed.
- The concessionaires must pay 35 percent casino tax on gross gaming revenues, and not less than 2 percent of gross gaming revenues to a public foundation for the promotion and development of cultural, social, economic, educational, scientific, academic, and charity projects. An additional 3 percent has to be given to support urban development and construction, promotion of tourism, and social issues.

Taxes on gross gambling revenues in Macao could be judged as high internationally, compared to Nevada's 6.25 percent. Taking into consideration Macao's long gaming history, it was only recently, hastened by the liberalization of the gaming industry, that gaming laws were introduced in Macao regarding such issues as money laundering, licensing of junket operators, and credit arrangements. Therefore, these remain relatively new legal platforms. In addition, an impartial gaming control board has yet to be established. Even under these circumstances (and, at the time, in the absence of laws regulating the licensing of junket operators and credit arrangements), the Macao Casino Concession Committee, set up for the purpose of judging and awarding the three casino concessions, received twenty-one tenders, which came from Macao, Hong Kong, the United States, Malaysia, the United Kingdom, and elsewhere, from some of the world's largest casino corporations, such as MGM Grand, Aspinalls, Sun Entertainment, Wynn Resorts, The Venetian (under the Galaxy Casino banner), and SJM. This showed an appreciation of how economically attractive a foothold in the Asian market was.

As well as satisfying criteria stipulated in the bidding framework, other weighted criteria were used, including experience in running, operating, and managing casinos or related services; a highly profitable investment in the Macao SAR (especially a new concept of investment); and improvement in areas such as job training and recruitment. In all, six weighted criteria were chosen by the government to judge the several tender submissions (Boletim Oficial da Região Administrativa Especial de Macau, 2001b). Three new casino concessions were awarded to Galaxy Casino, Wynn Resorts, and SJM (in that order), who scored some of the highest marks. Fourth to sixth ranking was also given, with MGM Grand (Macau), for example, falling fifth. This was a precautionary measure because, in the event that should any of the concession winners be unable to honor or fulfill the terms and conditions of the contractual agreements, which included completion of the first hotel/casino within four years, the next runner-up would be permitted to step in and take over the casino concession. With these concession criteria, the Macao government has, as before with the STDM casino monopoly, been able to secure a substantial and comprehensive economic package for Macao as a stimulus for the further development of the tourism industry. Although the government may have restricted the casino concessions to three, each concessionaire can grant subconcessions and operate as many casinos and gaming tables as market conditions allow, however, each casino, subconcession, and gaming table must be separately licensed by the government. This has permitted not only Galaxy and The Venetian to operate as separate and competing casino companies, but has recently led to other Macao joint ventures with MGM and SJM (McCartney, 2005).

TOURISM DEVELOPMENT

For a city with a population of 448,500 inhabitants and landmass of 27.3 square kilometers, Macao showed significant tourist arrival statistics of 7.8 million tourists in 1994, increasing within ten years to 16.7 million in 2004 (Macao Statistics and Census Service, 2005c). These figures have far exceeded the World Tourism Organization's (WTO) Tourism 2020 Vision forecasts of 11.2 million visitors to Macao in 2010, with 6.2 million from Hong Kong, 2.7 million from Taiwan, and 0.8 million from China (WTO, 2000). A notable area of visitor growth is from China due to an increase in the purchasing power of the citizens and changes in the visa policy to travel abroad, including the ability to travel to Hong Kong and Macao as independent travelers (rather than as part of a group tour as previously). Chinese tourism is also greatly assisted by the fact that Macao is the only area in the whole of China where casino gambling is legally permitted, with Chinese companies even prohibited from getting involved in Macao's gaming. Thus, since China and Hong Kong do not permit legalized casinos, this "spatially restricted legal location within China ensured Macao has enjoyed a comparative advantage and thus been exceedingly lucrative" (McCartney, 2005, p. 40)

Apart from a decline between 1996 and 1998, tourism to Macao, particularly from mainland China, has increased significantly since 1996. With thirty-nine hotels, thirty-one guesthouses, and a total room count of 9,168 registered with the Macao Government Tourism Office in 2004, average hotel room rates continued to rise since a four year low of approximately US$56 in 2002 (Macau Government Tourist Office, 2004a) to US$68 in 2004 (Macau Government Tourist Office, 2004b). The average occupancy rate in 2004 was at a high of 75.77 percent (in comparison to 55.57 percent in 1994) (Macao Statistics and Census Service, 2005a). Reviewing the average length of stay in the period from 1994 to 2004, the average occupancy rate has remained fairly unchanged, with 1.32 room nights in 1994, a peak of 1.43 in 1998 and 1999, and dropping to its lowest in ten years in 2004 of 1.22 room nights (Macao Census and Statistics Department, 1994; Macao Government Tourist Office, 1999, 2004b). With only 3.96 million of Macao's 16.7 million visitors staying in a hotel overnight in 2004 (Macao Statistics and Census Service, 2005b), Macao is viewed as a day-trippers destination from those coming from Hong Kong or neighboring provinces in China. Although Macao has an international airport, the number of international carriers is small. However, recently low-cost carriers such as AirAsia have started flights from Macao to regional destinations, which may encourage more regional tourism, and thus the potential for longer visitor stay and development of a long-haul tourist market.

There is a growing need for the Macao government to establish a sustained, equitable collaboration of all components of tourism, not only within the new concession holders and governmental bodies but also with all partners in tourism. With a large percentage of Macao residents either directly or indirectly employed in the tourism industry and, therefore, being more dependent economically on the industry, research has shown that this portion of the residents has a tendency to be more positive toward tourism (Pizam, 1978). Although Macao's long gaming history is very much part of the fabric of Macao society, and therefore tolerated, there is also a growing need to observe future resident and tourist interactions, as the new casino concessions develop. Among the tourism impact models, Doxey's (1975) four-stage Irridex model predicts a change from euphoria, welcoming tourists, to complete antagonism, in which tourists are seen as an irritation and a cause of all problems. This is closely related to Macao's capacity to absorb tourism development, or carrying capacity, which as tourism literature suggests revolves around several factors, such as visitor satisfaction, community tolerance, political administration, economic structure, physical structure, and ecological systems (Glasson, Godfrey, Goodey, Absalom, & Van Der Borg, 1997). A particular issue for Macao is the preservation of its heritage and culture, with several sites in Macao having been nominated as a UNESCO World Heritage Site recognition (Engelhart, 2002). Lessons from other rapid casino developments, such as in Colorado, have shown that haste to develop tourism and reap its economic benefits of such will have social impacts (as well as loss of heritage) (Stokowski, 1998). Carmichael, Peppard, and Boudreau (1998) conceptualized in their study of Foxwoods Casino that residents would develop either positive or negative attitudes toward the casino developers (in this case SJM, Wynn Resorts, Galaxy Casino, and The Venetian at present) based on both personal factors (such as employment in the tourism industry or in the casinos) and perceived impacts (social, economic, and environmental). These quality of life and social exchange issues warrant close attention by the developers and the Macao government. As mentioned by McCartney (2005), it is apparent that as Macao's tourism and gaming industry continues to expand in the coming years, Macao's casinos will need to offer benefits beyond just taxation contributions and employment opportunities to positively influence local residents' attitudes.

CASINO INVESTMENT PLANS

Part of the contractual obligations of each casino concession was for license periods commencing in 2002. SJM was awarded an eighteen-year concession (April 1, 2002, to March 31, 2020), with Wynn Resorts SA and Galaxy Casino SA each receiving a twenty-year period ending on June 26, 2022. Each casino concession holder also submitted an investment plan (which was part of the judging criteria) with the amounts of 4.74, 4.0, and 8.8 billion patacas for SJM, Wynn Resorts, and Galaxy Casino, respectively, for the building of the casinos, hotels, and other tourism and resident infrastructures.

SJM produced a comprehensive investment plan for theme parks (Macau Fisherman's Wharf, Ponte 16, and the East-West Cultural Village) and extensions, renovations, and upgrades to its various casino properties, with a focus also on human resource training at its own college, the Macau Millennium College. Although not as detailed, the contract investment plan with the Macao government for Wynn Resorts included a resort hotel and casino opened to the public by December 2006. With the Venetian Macao becoming a sub-concession of the Galaxy Casino, the 8.8 billion pataca investment was shortened from ten years to seven. The Venetian though became the first international concession holder to open a casino complex with The Sands in March 2004 in competition with the SJM casino properties, closely followed by the Galaxy Waldo in July 2004, with plans by Galaxy to have their StarWorld Hotel and Casino open in 2006. However, all casino expansion has taken place to date on the Macao peninsula, with major investments by The Venetian and Galaxy being targeted at the reclaimed Cotai area between Macao's islands of Coloane and Taipa. By the end of 2004, SJM accounted "for more than 80 percent of total gaming revenues in Macau, with the remaining share taken by new overseas gambling licensee upstarts Sands and Galaxy" ("Blowing Vegas Away," 2005, p. 25). Although the new concession holders continue to chip away from SJM's one-time gaming-revenue monopoly, the Macao government has indicated that a maximum number of casinos could be set, with some of SJM's mini-casinos being merged into medium-sized casinos (Leong, 2005), answering concerns over the continual proliferation of Macao's gaming industry.

SUMMARY

Macao's gaming history has evolved from illegal gambling houses at Macao's founding in the sixteenth century to legalization in the nineteenth century, monopoly franchise in the early part of the twentieth century, followed by a second monopoly franchise thirty years later, to liberalization at the turn of the twenty-first century with competition among a few (rather than among many). However, the liberalization, although with limited competition, has created an uneven playing field for the concession holders. Wynn Resorts and The Venetian, with connections in particular to Las Vegas, must adhere to Macao's as well as Nevada's gaming legislation (or risk measures being taken by the Nevada gaming authorities). SJM and Galaxy, with no formal Nevada casino connections, only need to adhere to Macao's laws, a regulatory framework less stringent and pronounced than Nevada's, leaving the Las Vegas concession holders discontented. With this in mind, the Macao government has been gradually discussing and introducing more rigorous gaming legislation. SJM also operates in a culturally familiar market, knowing how to accommodate Chinese gamblers; the labyrinth of junket operators; Macao's sometimes composite web of Chinese, Macanese, and Portuguese cultures; informal working rules; and the business environment. Coupled with these are the initial high investment costs for each new concession holder and the large economic and social contributions upon opening.

As each concession contract is linked to a time frame, the liberalization process carries on. With visions of a Las Vegas in Asia and an Asian version of the strip in the newly reclaimed land of Cotai, Macao also faces an explosion of regional legal casino development from jurisdictions, such as Singapore, which recently legalized the casino industry, lured by the potential net benefits that can be derived from the casinos as tourist attractions yet still discussing policies to minimize the negative social problems that have been attached to casino development. The Philippines and South Korea are also contemplating further growth or upgrade of their own casino industries, as are other jurisdictions, such as Taiwan, Japan, and Thailand, considering casinos for the first time, eager to garner casino tax dollars as an engine and stimulus for tourism development. There is also a patchwork of unregulated illegal and quasi-legal casinos in Asian countries, such as Indonesia, Cambodia, and Thailand. In Asia, the floodgates of casino debate and governmental investigation have finally fractured. Macao presently maintains the competitive edge and position in the region, with a virtual monopoly and comparitive advantage within China (and therefore access to one of the world's largest populations and growing economies), assisted by its experience from a long gaming history, with the liberalization process aimed at enhancing and developing the casino and tourism industry to a further level. Strategically, this can be a ticket to success in Asia's lucrative, and recently, fragmenting casino market; but with the expected regional casino growth, there is a need to keep the liberalization process, and the objectives behind it, moving forward.

REFERENCES

American Gaming Association. (2005). State of the States: AGA survey of casino entertainment 2005. Available online at: http://www.americangaming.org/assets/files/uploads/2005_State_of_the_States.pdf.

"Blowing Vegas Away." (2005, January). *Macau Business*, p. 25.

Boletim Oficial da Região Administrativa Especial de Macau. (2001a, September 24). No. 16/2001, pp. 1027. Macau: Imprensa Oficial.

Boletim Oficial da Região Administrativa Especial de Macau. (2001b, October 29). No. 26/2001, pp. 1242. Macau: Imprensa Oficial.

Boletim Oficial de Macau. (1962, July 14). No. 28. Macau: Imprensa Oficial.

Bruning, H. (2002, April 5). Dice keep rolling during seamless changeover. *South China Morning Post*, p. 13.

Bruning, H. (2003, September 5). Macau casinos see record $2.8b month. *South China Morning Post*, p. 1.

Carmichael, B. A., Peppard, D. M., & Boudreau, F. A. (1998). Megaresort on my doorstep: Local resident attitudes toward Foxwoods Casino and casino gambling nearby Indian reservation land. *Journal of Travel Research, 34*(Winter), 9-16.

Cheng, C. M. B. (1999). *Macau: A cultural janus*. Hong Kong: Hong Kong University Press.

Coates, A. (1966). *Macao and the British, 1637-1842, Prelude to Hong Kong*. Hong Kong: Oxford University Press (China).

Commission for the First Public Tender to Grant Concessions to Operate Casino Games of Chance of the Macao SAR. (2001, November). *Information memorandum*. Macao: Author.

Doxey, G. V. (1975). A causation theory of visitor irritants, methodology and research inferences. *Proceedings of The Impact of Tourism, Sixth Annual Conference* (pp. 195-198). San Diego: Travel and Tourism Research Association.

Eadington, W. (1996). The legalization of casinos: Policy objectives, regulatory alternatives, and cost/benefit considerations. *Journal of Travel Research, 34*(Winter), 3-8.

Engelhart, R. (2002). *The management of world heritage cities. Evolving concepts: New strategies*. Paper presented at The Conservation of Urban Heritage: Macao Vision, International Conference, Macao.

Glasson, J., Godfrey, K., Goodey, B., Absalom, H., & Van Der Borg, J. (1997). *Toward visitor impact management: Visitor impacts, carrying capacity and management responses in Europe's historic towns and cities* (pp. 43-63). Avebury: Ashgate.

Gunn, G. C. (1996). *Encountering Macau: A Portuguese city-state on the periphery of China, 1557-1999*. Boulder, CO: Westview Press.

Lamas, R. W.-N. (1998). *History of Macau: A student's manual*. Macau: Institute of Tourism Education.

Leong, S. (2005, January 14). Francis Tam indicates max limit of 19 casinos for Stanley Ho. *Macao Post Daily*, p. 3.

Leong, V. M. (2002). The "Bate-Ficha" business and triads in Macau casinos. *QUTLJJ, 2*(1), 83-96.

Macao Census and Statistics Department. (1994). Tourism statistics. Macao: Author.

Macao Gaming Control Board. (2005). Statistics. Available online at: http://www .dicj.gov.mo/EN/Estat/estat.htm#n4.

Macao Government Information Bureau. (2004). *Macao yearbook 2004.* Macao: Author.

Macao Government Tourist Office. (1993). *Macau travel talk* (No. 133). Macao: Author.

Macao Government Tourist Office. (1999). Macau travel and tourism statistics. Research and Planning Department. Macao: Author.

Macao Government Tourist Office. (2002). *Statistics 2002.* Macao: Author.

Macao Government Tourist Office. (2004a). Macau travel and tourism statistics. Research and Planning Department. Macao: Author.

Macao Government Tourist Office. (2004b). Visitor arrival statistics, December 2004. Research and Planning Department. Macao: Author.

Macao Statistics and Census Service. (2005a). Hotel occupancy rates by classification of establishments. Available online at: http://www.dsec.gov.mo/index.asp? src=/english/indicator/e_tur_indicator.html.

Macao Statistics and Census Service. (2005b). Tourism statistics, *e-publication.* Available online at: http://www.dsec.gov.mo/index.asp?src=/english/pub/e_tur _pub.html.

Macao Statistics and Census Service. (2005c). Visitors' arrivals by place of residence. Available online at: http://dsec.gov.mo/index.asp?src=/english/indicator/ e_tur_indicator.html.

McCartney, G. J. (2005). Casinos as a tourism redevelopment strategy—The case of Macao, *Journal of Macau Gaming Research Association,* Issue 2.

Montalto de Jesus, C. A. (1984). *Historic Macao* (3rd ed.). Hong Kong: Oxford University Press.

Nepstad, P. (2000). *Revealing the heart of Asian cinema.* Available online at: http://www.illuminatedlantern.com/cinema/features/gambling.html/.

Pinho, A. (1991). Gambling in Macau. In R. D. Cremer, *Macau city of commerce and culture: Continuity and change* (2nd ed., pp. 247-257). Boulder, CO: Westview Press.

Pizam, A. (1978). Tourism impacts: The social costs to the destination community as perceived by its residents. *Journal of Travel Research, 34*(2), 3-11.

Pons, P. (1999). *Macao.* Hong Kong: University Press.

Preston, H. H. (2005). Gambling firms place their bets on China. *International Herald Tribune.* Available online at: http://www.iht.com/articles/2005/02/11/your money/mbet.html.

Roehl, W. S. (1994). Gambling as a tourist attraction: Trends and issues for the 21st century. In A. V. Seaton, C. L. Jenkins, R. C. Woods, P. U. C. Dieke, M. M. Bennett, L. R. Maclellan, & R. Smith (Eds.), *Tourism: The state of the art* (pp. 156-168). New York: Wiley.

Simpson, C. (1962). *Asia's bright balconies.* Sydney: Angus and Robertson.

Smeral, E. (1998). Economic aspects of casino gaming in Austria. *Journal of Travel Research, 36*(4), 33-39.

Smith, G. J., & Hinch, T. D. (1996). Canadian casinos as tourist attractions: Chasing the pot of gold. *Journal of Travel Research, 34*(Winter), 37-45.

Stokowski, P. A. (1998). Community impacts and revisionist images in Colorado gaming development. In K. J. Meyer-Arendt & R. Hartmann (Eds.), *Casino gambling in America: Origins, trends and impacts* (pp. 137-148). Elmsford, NY: Cognizant Communication Corporation.

World Tourism Organization. (2000). *Tourism 2020 Vision, East Asia and Pacific, 3.* Madrid: Author.

Chapter 4

Gambling in Japan

William N. Thompson

This chapter examines gambling in Japan. The focus is upon the game of pachinko and the many pachinko parlors in the country. Some attention is also given to the lottery and to pari-mutuel betting on various kinds of races.

Gambling is illegal in Japan. The law (or Keiho) since as long ago as 1882 strictly prohibits gambling. The current law derived from the 1882 statute was passed in 1907. The Gambling Keiho, sections 185 and 186, still maintains that "a person who gambles shall be punished by a fine," and that "a person who indulges in gambling as a habitual practice shall be punished with penal servitude for not more than three years." However, the law does have an escape clause, "provided that, this shall not apply when the bet of a thing is made only for momentary amusement" (cited in Tanioka, 2000, p. 81).

The laws passed were certainly promulgated in response to very widespread uncontrolled gambling that thrived in Japan a century ago. Courts have ruled that the laws were correct, as they pointed out that along with gambling came "family destruction," a corruption of "public morals," and a "lower motivation to work" (see Tanioka, 2000, p. 85).

Gambling remains illegal in Japan, and yet upwards of 50 million people have played pachinko games, with 30 million playing regularly. Japan has 15,255 pachinko parlors. The gamblers make annual wagers of 27.807 trillion yen (US$235.7 billion) and lose 3.059 trillion yen (US$25.9 billion). The parlors employ over 300,000 workers and have over 3.2 million pachinko machines, in addition to 1.6 million pachisuro machines—similar to a standard slot machine.

For this chapter, the author used a mid-2003 exchange rate of US$1 = 118 yen.

The pachinko parlors with these two types of machines command revenues equal to 4 percent of the Japanese gross domestic product. Fully 23 percent of Japanese leisure dollars are spent in the parlors (Lubarsky, 1995; Sibbitt, 1997; Tanioka, 2003; Kiritani, 2003).

The Japanese also lose 2.285 trillion yen (US$19.4 billion) annually at other gaming activities including the lottery, a sports lottery, horse races, bicycle races, motorboat races, and motorcycle races. The national lottery has annual sales of 1.070 trillion yen (US$9.1 billion) with player losses of 567 billion yen (US$4.8 billion), or 53 percent of the annual sales, making the game the biggest in the world. On a per capita basis, the Japanese lose twice as much money to gambling than citizens of the United States.

There certainly must be exceptions to the law prohibiting gambling. These exceptions, sometimes in legislation, sometimes due to administrative interpretations, and sometimes in tolerated loopholes, are discussed in turn as each type of game is examined (Tanioka, 2000, 2003).

PACHINKO: MY INTRODUCTION TO THE GAME

In 1995, I was the guest of the Japanese Pachinko Association. I gave speeches to groups, and I toured the pachinko parlors of Tokyo, Kawasaki, and Kyoto. After observing games in several parlors, I was invited to play. First, I was motioned to a machine where I inserted 400 yen (US$3.40) and I received a plastic card (a prepaid card). I was then directed to a pachinko machine that had a large sign saying in English as well as Japanese characters, "reserved for Dr. Thompson." I had never played pachinko before, but I was assured that players developed fine skills that permitted them to win frequently. I obviously did not have those skills. I inserted the plastic card, and I saw my card's value reduced to zero, as 100 balls came into an area where they could be played. Actually, I had not purchased the balls. Rather, I had rented their use, a fiction maintained to assure authorities that I was not "gambling" (see Bybee, 2003, p. 270).

I twisted a circular handle with my right hand, shooting several balls upward on the surface of the vertical pachinko board (see Photo 4.1).

PHOTO 4.1. Pachinko machines.

The balls fell and bounced off of nails one by one down to the bottom and into a groove that took them away; each ball played being a loser. Then, one or several balls went downward without being deflected by the nails and fell into a special hole. A little set of slot machine–like reels started spinning, and one, two, and then three bars lined up in a row. Balls started pouring out of the machine and into baskets beside my playing stool. The balls just gushed forth. Indeed, I could tell that I was a winner. A big-time winner.

I asked my hosts what I should do next. They said I should gather up the baskets of winning balls and have them weighed. The balls were placed on a scale and a printer on the scale recorded the number of winning balls and printed a ticket for me. I was then directed to take the ticket to a prize booth. The booth was a small gift store within the pachinko parlor. It had cigarettes, cartons of beer, bottles of wine, cosmetics, toys, transistor radios, tape recorders, CD players, music tapes and compact discs, travel cases, shirts, jewelry, and many more

items. Each was marked with a value. I looked at my ticket and fig-
ured I could take a CD player, but then I wondered about customs and
how much room I would have in my suitcase; so I asked about receiving a cash payout. I was told that that was totally forbidden. I certainly could not receive money inside a pachinko parlor.

However, I was told that I might wish to exchange my ticket for a
plastic plaque that contained a little chip of gold. I was told that this
would be a valuable gift to have, and that perhaps someone might
even wish to buy it from me. I exchanged my ticket for the plaque
with gold. My hosts then pointed to a back corner of the shop. I saw a
little sign with an arrow pointing down a rather dingy hallway. I went
with them down the hallway and outside of the parlor. We walked
a few feet down an alleyway and found ourselves in front of a building, called the kankin, the size of a small garage with a stucco wall
(see Lubarsky, 1995). In the center of the side of the building, there
was a little slit about six inches high and twelve inches across, with
a small countertop at the bottom of the opening. I was told I should
slide the plaque into the slit. I did so, and I heard a voice mumbling
something I could not understand. I waited about thirty seconds
and cash bills were pushed in my direction. I took them and counted
them, 6,000 yen, or about US$50. Skill, or should I say beginner's
luck?

My next stop on the tour happened to be the vice squad headquar-
ters of the Tokyo police department. My hosts had arranged for me a
visit to the deputy police chief to share my views on gambling with
him, so I did. I indicated that the game could be run with much more
efficiency, integrity, and operational security if the machines themselves could be structured to simply pay the customer in cash the
value of the winnings. This was a point of view my hosts wanted me
to support, and I did. I had an entirely logical rationale, which I will
share in a moment. However, as the deputy police chief heard my
words being clearly translated, he held up his hand firmly as if to say
emphatically, "No!" Albeit the Japanese are very reticent about ever
using the actual word *no.* Along with the gesture, he spoke. The trans-
lation into English was also very clear. "Gambling is illegal in
Japan!"

WHAT IS GAMBLING?
DEFINITIONS AND FICTIONS

Although in the United States we accept a common law that defines gambling as including three elements, the elements carry different meaning in Japan. First, we find that gambling contains an act of consideration, which is putting forth something of value as a bet or wager. Second, gambling involves some act of risk or chance—at least an act containing a major element of chance. Third, the outcome of that act of chance determines if one is a winner or loser; in the case of a winner, the player will receive a prize that is worth more than the item of consideration—the amount of the bet or wager.

There is no law specifically regarding pachinko in Japan, but there is a broad 1948 Entertainment Establishments Control Law that pertains to matters such as licensing of amusement halls, age limits on admissions, and hours of operation. The law authorizes regulations by national as well as local public safety commissions, but enforcement is done by the local police authorities. Regulations generally prohibit providing entertainment as well as serving food and alcoholic beverages in parlors. More important, there are understandings—in the context of the English and American common law we would say these are legal fictions—in many but not all of the local jurisdictions regarding exactly what is allowed.

Pachinko is tolerated as an amusement-only game due to certain conditions required by the police as well as the public safety commissions. In recent years, the Tokyo police have insisted that all new parlors have to use cash cards for the machines if they wish to be licensed. No money is placed in the machine. This became a requirement because the overall machine use can now be monitored through the card-distributing machines. The police can thereby track parlor revenues. The card was instituted because pachinko parlor operators had gained the reputation of being the largest tax evaders in the country. But the use of cards also reflects a notion that one is not gambling because one is not putting money in the machines (Sibbitt, 1997).

Another fiction says that the style of play involves skill to a large extent. Therefore, as luck is not a major factor, the game is not gambling. Professor Ichiro Tanioka of Osaka Commerce University accepts this notion in his book *Pachinko and the Japanese Society*. He writes, "if I must choose, I would say pachinko is a game of skill. A skilled pachinko player examines thoroughly the machines before choosing his own to play. Skilled players check the number, angles, and positions of the nails that influence the paths of the shot balls. They also possess special shooting techniques" (Tanioka, 2000, p. 20; Bybee, 2003, p. 270).

The skill is essentially external to the game. Once playing starts, the machine will treat each ball the same. Although Tanioka believes that players use shooting techniques, others now discount this, as the latest machines are computerized; the balls, while being shot upward at varying speeds, all fall at essentially the same speed after they hit the top of the board. The skill of playing pachinko, then, is basically the same skill as figuring odds at a craps table. There are good-odds bets and bad-odds bets. This management of odds, along with general gambling money management, can indeed affect outcomes.

Nonetheless, many players do believe that pachinko is a skill game and that they can gain the upper hand in play. The twisting of the handle gives an illusion of control, much as a video poker game gives a player an illusion of control as the player can choose to hold or discard specific cards displayed. There certainly is some manner of skill in selecting machines. Obviously, the machine I was directed to play had a placement of nails that facilitated a win. I daresay that part of my machine must have been rigged in my favor. I did not stay at my machine after I played. I was off to get my cash prize. Had I stayed inside the parlor, I am sure I would have noticed an "out of order" sign being placed on the machine. Then after hours, when the parlors close from midnight until eight in the morning (the amusement law says "sunrise"), the machine would have been "adjusted" to meet the standards of others in the parlor. The regulations are ambiguous regarding how and when a machine may be "fixed."

Some players claim that they always win. Although this is highly unlikely, some may do very well. Indeed, over time, some may be winners. But are they really? The next point suggests that they may be telling themselves a fiction. The fact that the parlor can only give the player merchandise prizes helps the police to maintain the fiction that there is no gambling. The little booth in the small building in the alley

next door, the kankin, was owned by a separate party. It was uncon-
nected with the management of the pachinko parlor. It was indeed a
separate profit center. The trouble with the arrangement was that the
money exchange operation was totally ignored by the police. It was
also the part of the process that was vulnerable to an intrusion by organized crime elements—the yakuza. I was amused that each parlor
had a single money exchange booth nearby. The booth would only
make money exchanges for specific parlors.

Players play to win money. A survey found that 96 percent of the
players who won prizes actually converted them to cash (Sibbitt,
1997). The existence of the money exchange service also provided a
means by which a player could be hooked into believing he (or sometimes she) was a skilled, expert player who always won.

For a cost of 400 yen (US$3.40), I purchased 100 pachinko balls (4
yen for each ball). If after play I was left with 120 balls, I would indeed be a winner. The balls were worth 480 yen (US$4.10). Right?
Wrong! I would get a certificate stating that I won 120 balls. That certificate could be exchanged for a music tape or a pack of cigarettes,
each of which might retail for 480 yen (US$4.10). I won. Well, sort
of. The item, however, would cost the parlor (wholesale) only 300
yen (US$2.50). The parlor won. But then, I wished to have cash. My
little piece of gold plastic plaque was taken to an exchange where I
would be given perhaps 336 yen (US$2.80), a discount of 30 percent.
But then I wanted cash, so I did not complain. In fact, if I am a player,
I will know the process. Indeed, I know it so well that if I win a jackpot, I will remain in the parlor and keep betting the winnings. Only
when I wish to go home, or it is closing time, do I seek a cash payout.
On the other hand, if I have a big win, I am not at all upset with the
discounted rate; after all, I am a winner.

The plaques are exchanged back to the parlors at a price assuring
that both the parlor and those in the exchange business are winners
(see Bybee, 2003; Bybee & Thompson, 1999). Bybee (2003) indicates that a third party is brought into the equation and that party buys
the prizes from the kankin and resells them to the parlor. This is a further step taken to assure that the parlors are totally out of the cash exchange business. But of course, it is simply a further exercise of fiction that permits the police to turn their eyes the other way.

The rationale I wished to present to the police was simple. With a cash payout, the opportunities for organized crime incursions into the pachinko business would be greatly reduced. Also, the players' false beliefs that they can always be winners would be reduced, and hence an incentive that moves many into habitual and even compulsive play would be reduced. They could directly see that most of the time they will be losers. I made a point or two, but I was silenced. The police would not listen to me. But then, I am sure that the association knew that. I had some assurances that they were not connected to organized crime, and my arguments, such as they were, would let the police know that they did not wish to be connected to organized crime. That was the point I was making on their behalf. I do not think they wanted to change the system. After all, they make a large part of their revenues out of the exchange system. It was the best way they could consistently beat the winners.

WOULD PACHINKO WORK ELSEWHERE?

The pachinko association and other entrepreneurs in the business have often asked me if their product could be used by casinos in the United States. They also asked if new full-service casinos could be developed in Japan around pachinko. My answers to them are disappointing. The pachinko machine is not played as a social recreation or leisure-time activity in Japan. It is played by people who really think they can make money at it. For this reason, it cannot be a casino game. I will elaborate on Japanese culture and pachinko in a moment.

First, the machine in its present structure could not be licensed in American casinos. Operators (and presumably others) can open the machines (and do so regularly) and adjust the face of the machine (change locations of nails) so that more or fewer prizes will be awarded to players. It is suggested that operators could do so according to the size of their crowd. If it is a rainy day and people are staying home, they may make it easier to win jackpots. Word of mouth may reach the stay-at-homes who will then venture out to play. Others suggest that some machines are fixed to give out more prizes when crowds are large, as the parlor is then making more money; plus, many more people will observe the jackpot and carry forth the news.

In either event, the ease of fixing the machine would render it insecure and not licensable in commercial casino venues of the United States and most other countries as well. The face of the machine would have to be sealed.

Second, the machine structure involves steel balls going into and out of the machines with some rapidity. Large halls have to use conveyer belts for the balls. Monitoring ball supplies is a major task. No commercial casinos would be willing to take on the task. If the machines were to be viable in commercial casinos, the balls would have to remain fully within the machines at all times. Meters could record winnings or the number of balls remaining available for play. And winnings would either be in cash or in printed tickets coming out of the machine. On the good side, the removal of the money exchange would help players realize that they cannot be regular winners, but these features would also make the machine much less exciting for players. But then some players might still feel that their use of the shooting handle could affect the payout from the machines.

ADDICTIVE QUALITIES OF PACHINKO

Although it is not a security feature, government licensing boards and public safety commissions should be concerned that the machines appear not to be used mainly for leisure recreation, but rather are heavily used by habitual players who play more for money than for fun. A false sense of having skill leads to a belief that one can win. Pachinko also offers a chance for people to escape lives of loneliness or stress. Some parlors have special areas just for women players. They come in the daytime to escape monotonous household routines. One parlor had individual refrigerators so that women could bring their groceries with them into the parlor after shopping (Kiritani, 2003).

Players become lost in the activity of turning the handle, watching the balls fly, and listening to the monotonous noise of the parlor. Indeed, the game is called *pachinko* because the balls go "pachin, pachin, pachin" as they bounce around the machine. It has a special allure for many (see Lifton, 1964).

People who cannot find many enjoyments in life may seek to find enjoyment in the notion that they are experts and winners at games. The pachinko game shares several qualities with video poker machines, which are very popular around the world. Both machines require solitary play. A person must pay attention if he or she believes the game involves skill. He or she must watch the screen or the face of the game and either select cards carefully or turn a handle in a precise manner. The pachinko player (as well as the video poker player to a degree) must seek out a machine that is favorable to winning (in the case of video poker, a machine with a good payout table). Playing these games is serious business. A person cannot play and socialize at the same time. A person cannot play and hold a conversation at the same time. Players become isolated. Through their interaction with the machine, they become part of the machine.

Psychiatrist Durand Jacobs counsels many problem gamblers. He finds common traits among many video poker addicts that we could probably also find among habitual pachinko players. The players he counsels often are in a trance as they play. They lose track of time, thinking hours of play are really only minutes. He finds that many players take on the identity of other people while they play, in most cases people they admire, and that at least half of video poker addicts have out-of-body experiences while they play. Escape is their game. For many pachinko players, escape is also their game (Jacobs, 1986).

In the case of pachinko, certain rules encourage compulsive behaviors. Parlors cannot serve food to players; there can be no drinking; and there is no live entertainment. These items make casinos more attractive as entertainment venues; the items also serve as devices to divert someone from compulsive play—they interrupt the activity and give the players a regular reality check on their behavior. So too does the presence of friends offering conversation.

The term *pachinkoholism* is now widely in use, as many Japanese are concerned that the machines represent a social danger. There have been many highly publicized cases of children being abandoned at home or in cars while parents played. Children have been kidnapped or suffocated from heat in cars because of this neglect. Other cases of robberies abound as a result of people losing money to machines. Most pachinkoholism victims are poor, simply because the machines appeal mostly to blue-collar workers and to poor and idle people (see Sibbitt, 1997).

A study in the mid-1960s found that the parlors were pervasive in the "Doya-Gai" or skid row districts of Tokyo and other big cities. Very poor people were hooked. Carlo Caldarola (1968-1969) reported that many of these poor residents sold blood in order to have funds to live. For 400 cc of blood, they would receive 800 yen (the 1960 value of yen was much greater vis-à-vis the dollar than today). His survey found that these poor souls would spend on average 60 yen to eat, 150 yen for a flop house, 160 yen for drinks, 15 yen for bus transportation, and 400 yen (half the total) for pachinko.

Of growing popularity in the pachinko parlors is the pachisuro machine, which is similar to a three-reel slot machine found in casinos all over the world. The pachisuro machines do have "nudge" features that allow a player to hit a button and have a specific reel spin again, and then hit the button and stop the spinning. This feature appears on European-style slot machines, and it can give the player an illusion of control that is another fiction. However, this feature makes play somewhat complicated, and it does give an advantage to a player who is familiar with it. It creates among players another incentive to pay close attention to the machine and to forget any friends who might have accompanied them to the parlors.

These reasons make pachinko (as well as pachisuro) an unlikely candidate for use in a major casino environment, whether in Japan or elsewhere. If casinos come to Japan, they will be structured more like Las Vegas casinos than like pachinko parlors, and they will feature Las Vegas casino games, not pachinko.

A BIT OF HISTORY—A LOT OF AMBIGUITY

Pachinko became popular in Japan for unique reasons that keep pachinko play essentially only in Japan, to a large degree. The game of pachinko is a spin-off of games developed in the United States in the 1920s. The American game was played with a board at an angle tilt. Balls, typically marbles, were shot upward (actually outward) and fell down a slope into areas where they would be judged to be winning or losing balls. Over time, the game was developed into what are now called pinball machines by companies such as Bally's. The pinball machine is essentially a horizontal machine that requires an area of six to eight feet in length and three or four feet in width. The game surface has a slight incline, but a heavy spring propels a ball with such speed that it quickly falls downward into various slots that record points.

The game idea came to Japan in the 1930s, where it was adapted to the lack of space in commercial amusement centers. The board was made vertical, and the machine required only two feet of lateral space. At first, the game was played only for amusement. It became very popular but was discouraged during the war years as the machines required parts and supplies that were needed in the war effort. The machines were also seen as devices that would waste valuable time that should be spent in other pursuits (see Thompson & Bybee, 2001).

After World War II, new incentives made pachinko popular once again. It is important to realize that the time of its rise as the major gambling device in Japan was a time when the American army occupied Japan and when government policymaking was essentially controlled by General Douglas MacArthur. There were certain shortages and surpluses. Japan had had an active manufacturing sector during the war. Several companies found their factories destroyed, but they also found that an essential element in their machinery, the ball bearing, was not destroyed. They had millions of ball bearings, but nowhere to use them. These manufacturers created a demand for something that was otherwise useless to them. They started making pachinko machines to specifications that would use many of the ball bearings (see Sibbitt, 1997; Lubarsky, 1995).

They also began to finance halls for pachinko play. The American army supported the moves. Indeed, American forces became very close to certain manufacturing elements in the population. Any productivity was seen as good. People were getting jobs. Stability was returning to a "new" Japan. That someone was getting rich in the process did not bother an occupying force from a country that promoted entrepreneurship. Also, amounts of items people wanted or needed were limited, things like chewing gum and chocolate on the one hand, and soap and home cleaning materials on the other hand. The pachinko game became a device for rationing these products. Who got the products? The winners of the pachinko games.

As more and more consumer goods became available, the mechanisms for awarding prizes changed, and the cash exchange process came into play. The process also offered a way for crime elements to come into the picture. The pachinko machines developed their internal slot machine features as the parlors proliferated. Parlors began to increase in size; by the 1980s and 1990s, each hall had an average of 250 machines (pachinko and pachisuro). The game's popularity remains high; however, as the Japanese economy has hit difficult times, the number of parlors and revenues from the games have decreased (Tanioka, 2003).

The American occupying forces did not intervene as the yakuza crime organizations interjected their presence into the operations as owners and elements controlling the prize system. Yakuza operatives had demonstrated a high degree of nationalism during the war. Indeed, many of their leaders were designated as war criminals for their misdeeds. Yet the Americans somehow admired their entrepreneurial spirit, and indeed applauded their capitalistic drive, especially when they directed their supernationalism against Communist elements of the population. The yakuza thrived on goods obtained from the U.S. military, and they helped break up strikes that interfered with the rebuilding of Japan (see Gragert, 1997).

The early and current rules of the game have been fraught with ambiguity. At what point does pachinko become gambling? When must an existing parlor have a prepaid card system? How many steps must there be in the cash-prize exchange system? What refreshments can be given to players at the machines? This ambiguity is heightened because there is no clear law on pachinko. This reality has many consequences. A system exists and is working, and major changes could upset the system in many ways that are unknown; so the system persists. Police know when to look the other way, but parlor owners also know that they should "take care" of the police. They do so with small favors, with bribes, and with employment after police retirement.

Another consequence of having no clear law regarding pachinko is that pachinko businesses cannot get capital funds from banks or from the stock market. The lack of a strong legal foundation makes pachinko businesses unacceptably risky. For this reason, the yakuza, just like the mob in early Las Vegas, has provided capital for some projects. Overall, however, the parlors remain small. This makes them good mom-and-pop family businesses. As they operate on the margins of legality, they attract certain business outcasts. Among these are Koreans living in Japan but not enjoying the full blessings of Japanese citizenship. Eberstadt (1996) wrote of an unintended consequence of this situation as he examined the flow of Japanese money to North Korean government authorities through these and other Korean businesspeople in Japan.

OTHER FORMS OF GAMBLING IN JAPAN

The Lottery

The postwar years also found political approval (by the new National Diet and of course by American forces) of other gambling. In all these cases, gambling was specifically authorized in legislation as an exception to the 1907 law. The legislation absolved all parties to gambling of blame. This was in accordance with Keiho Article 35, which states, "no person shall be punished for an act in accordance with laws and ordinances or in carrying on lawful or proper business." In each case, the new national legislation was adopted for economic reconstruction and development purposes (Tanioka, 2000, p. 85).

Lottery legislation was enacted in 1948. A mixture of government units, national, regional, and local, have come together with banks to operate the lotteries over the past fifty years. The Dai-Ichi Kangyo Bank and its subsidiaries have a leading role in the sale of tickets today. The lottery products mirror those sold in all other lottery jurisdictions of the world.

It is interesting that the major lotto games typically do not give a single super-large prize of billions of yen, but rather offer many prizes in the category of 100, 200, or 300 million yen (US$1 to 2 million). Seventy-seven such prizes were awarded in one game. In 2001, perhaps in anticipation of the coming World Cup soccer matches, which were played in Japan and Korea, a Toto football lottery began (LotteryInsider.com, 2003).

Horse Racing

The Keiba Ho, or horse racing law, was put on the books in 1948, as was legislation for motorboat racing, the Mota Bota Kyoso Ho. In 1950, the Kogata Jidosha Kyoso Ho or motorcycle racing law was passed, while the Jitensha Kyoso Ho or bicycle racing law was passed in 1951. These laws allow betting in racing facilities as well as off-track parlors that exist in many prefects of Japan (Tanioka, 2000, 2003).

The horse racing operations are owned by the government, as are all the other racing venues. Horse racing tracks may be operated by either the national government or by one of the forty-seven prefectures (regional governments). National racing constitutes about 85 percent of the market. In 2001, players wagered 4.058 trillion yen (US$34 billion), with the tracks holding 1.014 trillion yen (US$9 billion) (Tanioka, 2000, 2003).

The racing event of the year is the Japan Derby. This one race commands more single-day betting than the total combined bets taken on the Kentucky Derby, Preakness, and Belmont Stakes. In 1999, US$474 million was wagered on the Derby and the Tokyo track where it was run drew a live crowd of 173,340 (Haukebo, 1999).

Motorboat Racing—Only in Japan

Japan is the only venue in the world with regular ongoing wagering on motorboat racing events. Although the twenty-four water race-courses in Japan are government owned, as is the mechanism for conducting betting, one man, Ryoichi Sasakawa, was given control over operations in 1951, a control maintained until he died in 1995. He organized all the racing events, and he collected all the revenues. Also, 13 percent of the hold from the wagers was directed to the Nippon Foundation, over which he exercised total control. Sasakawa's son, Yohei, is now the director of the foundation (Prideaux, 2001; Tanioka, 2000).

With wagers of approximately 1.3 trillion yen (US$13 billion), the racecourses hold 325 billion yen (US$2.7 billion). The foundation keeps 42 billion yen (US$350 million) per year. The twenty-four racecourses offer 4,205 racing days a year, each event drawing an average attendance of 15,000 (The Japan Association for International Horse Racing, 2002).

The motorboat races are conducted on racecourses that are 600 meters long. Racecourses have two long straightaways and two turns. The boats make a flying start at the end of one straightaway. Usually the boat that can best maneuver the first turn can achieve a lead that it never gives up. The excitement of the race, then, is in its first 300 meters. The boats go around the racecourse three times for an 1,800 meter race. Most races last only two minutes. The boats are provided for the drivers, with a lottery drawing for each race. The only thing besides skill that the driver brings to the race is his personal propeller (Prideaux, 2001).

Motorcycle Racing

The smallest share of the pari-mutuel racing pie is taken by motorcycle racing. Revenue declines in recent years have prompted private business interests to underwrite the sport. Municipalities that have the six racecourses have seen dwindling profits for their local charities (Kittaka, 2002; Tanioka, 2000). The six tracks had 729 racing days in 2001, with an average attendance at each event of 6,000. Bettors placed wagers of 172 billion yen (US$1.5 billion), and the tracks held 43 billion yen (US$364 million) (The Japan Association for International Horse Racing, 2002).

Bicycles Around the Velodrome

Bicycle racing began in an effort to rebuild a bicycle industry that was a critical element in postwar transportation. Under the new wagering system, races began in Kokura in 1948. The first race drew 55,000 spectators, and the popularity of the sport increased. The legislation authorizing the wagering came following the sport's rather rocky start. Several riots occurred at tracks (velodromes) when incidents, such as false starts or miscounted laps, occurred and people lost wagers. The law established a strong regulatory association to head off campaigns to abolish the sport.

There are now forty-nine velodromes in Japan. In 2001, there were 3,759 racing dates with events drawing an average attendance of 4,000. Each track is an oval from 330 meters to 500 meters long.

Races are typically 2,000 to 2,500 meters long (Price, 2000; Tanioka, 2000). In 2001, bettors put down 2 trillion yen (US$17 billion), with the velodromes holding 300 billion yen (US$2.5 billion). Much of the profit is now designated for sports charities (The Japan Association for International Horse Racing, 2002).

SUMMARY AND FUTURE DEVELOPMENTS

Gambling is a healthy industry in Japan. It is the leading leisure activity of the land, in terms of revenues. However, recent economic declines have not spared the industry. Also, gambling venues are found throughout Japan; therefore, most of the wagering is by local residents. Gamblers are not entertainment driven; too many look to gambling as a way to make money. Gambling is most healthy when it is seen as entertainment, and gambling is most helpful to an economy when it draws tourists. Therefore, attention is being and should be given to the development of a casino industry (with standard casino games) for Japan. In recent years, entrepreneurs as well as government authorities in several prefectures have been exploring the possibility of having a series of casinos spread across Japan. Fifteen prefectures have been selected as possible venues. Such gaming could be beneficial if it were tied to a variety of entertainment experiences such as music and shows, fine restaurants, spas, pools, and recreation. It would be most beneficial if the casinos were located in places remote from the core of large cities. The facilities should be attached to hotels and convention centers, and casinos should try to find markets not served by pachinko parlors, as they should not be established as competitors who might ruin current businesses.

Casinos will come only if there is a change in national law. It is unlikely that casinos will come very soon, as there still is a reluctance to embrace the reality that confronted the shocked policeman in the movie *Casablanca*—"You mean there is gambling going on here?"

REFERENCES

Bybee, S. (2003). *Evidence of a serendipitous career in gaming.* Boston: Pearson Custom.

Bybee, S., & Thompson, W. N. (1999). Japan. In A. Cabot, W. Thompson, A. Tottenham, & C. Braunlich (Eds.), *International casino law* (pp. 518-520). Reno, NV: University of Nevada Institute of Gambling Studies.

Caldarola, C. (1968-1969). The Doya-Gai: A Japanese version of skid row. *Pacific Affairs, 41*(4), 511-525.

Eberstadt, N. (1996). Financial transfers from Japan to North Korea: Estimating the unreported flows. *Asian Survey, 36*(5), 523-542.

Gragert, B. A. (1997). Yakuza: The warlords of Japanese organized crime. *1997 Annual Survey of International and Comparative Law, 4*(Fall), 147-178. San Francisco, Golden Gate University, School of Law.

Haukebo, K. (1999, November 14). Think racing is the rage in Japan. *Louisville (Kentucky) Courier Journal.*

Jacobs, D. (1986). A general theory of addictions: A new theoretical model. *Journal of Gambling Behavior, 2*(Spring), 15-31.

The Japan Association for International Horse Racing. (2002). *Japan Racing Journal, 10*(1). Available: http://www.jair.jrao.ne.jp/journal/v10n1/main.html.

Kiritani, E. (2003). Pachinko—Japan's national pastime. *Mangajin, 34.* Available: http://www.mangajin.com/mangajin/samplemj/pachinko.htm.

Kittaka, K. (2002, June 3). Toward rebirth: "Keirin" bicycle and motorcycle racing to introduce private business resources. *IIST World Forum.* Available: http://www.iist.or.jp/wf/magazine/0089/0089_E.html.

Lifton, R. J. (1964). Individual patterns in historical change: Imagery of Japanese youth. *Comparative Studies in Society and History, 6*(4), 369-383.

LotteryInsider.com (2003, October). The lottery industry news site. Available: http://www.lotteryinsider.com.

Lubarsky, J. (1995). Pachinko hits the jackpot. *Intersect Japan.* Available: http://www.commerce.usask.ca/faculty/links/Japan_CIBS/pachinko.htm.

Price, M. (2000, September). Old sport in new bottle. *Rediff.com.* Available: http://www.rediff.com/sports/2000/sep/02cycle.htm.

Prideaux, E. (2001, July 19). Japan's motorboat races: Through propella. *Sake drenched postcards.* Available: http://www.bigempire.com/sake/boat.html.

Sibbitt, E. (1997). Regulating gambling in the shadow of the law: Form and substance in the regulation of Japan's pachinko industry. *Harvard International Law Journal, 38,* 568-582.

Tanioka, I. (2000). *Pachinko and the Japanese society: Legal and political considerations.* Osaka: Osaka University of Commerce.

Tanioka, I. (2003, May). *Gambling in Japan.* Paper presented at the Twelfth International Conference on Gambling and Risk Taking, Vancouver, Canada.

Thompson, W. N., & Bybee, S. (2001). Japan and pachinko. In W. N. Thompson (Ed.), *Gambling in America: An encyclopedia of history, issues, and society* (pp. 202-205). Santa Barbara, CA: ABC-Clio.

Chapter 5

Gaming in Southeast Asia

Paul D. Bromberg

INTRODUCTION

This chapter provides an overview of legal gaming in Southeast Asia. Its primary aim is to gather a broad range of information from a variety of sources to present an accurate picture of the legal forms of gaming presently taking place in Cambodia, Indonesia, Laos, Malaysia, Myanmar, Singapore, Thailand, and Vietnam (Figure 5.1) and the authority under which it takes place. In each country, research has been undertaken to determine the legality of casino gaming, the types of existing gaming establishments, and the nature and scope of gaming regulation and control, if any.

In addition to conducting research, over the last three years, field visits and numerous interviews with a wide range of sources, including various local and foreign government officials, casino operators, and vendors and members of the hospitality profession, have also been conducted. This chapter presents a synthethis of findings.

Copies of relevant laws were obtained and translated into English, where possible. However, in some of the countries researched, the political and legal structures were found to be not very sophisticated. The rule of law is uncertain and, in some instances, laws relating to gaming prohibitions have been ignored with the tacit consent of the government.

It should also be pointed out that international gaming standards simply do not exist in most of the countries reviewed in this chapter. There are no gaming commissions and few government resources or efforts are dedicated to the control of casinos. Yet gaming activities exist with the knowledge and authorization of the various governments.

FIGURE 5.1. Southeast Asian countries.

Compared to the development and expansion that has taken place in the U.S. and European gaming industries in the past ten years, the gaming industry in Southeast Asia is still very much in its infancy. As governments and the casino industry gain experience, there is reason to remain optimistic that we might yet see the growth of a mature, responsible industry, adhering to international standards of regulation and control.

CAMBODIA

Status of Legal Gaming

The promulgation of Legal Decision No. 39-SSR on May 4, 1995, resulted in the closure of all kinds of gambling places not otherwise authorized by the government. A 1996 law titled The Law on the Suppression of Gambling and a Government Circular, dated July 23, 1996, banned all forms of gambling in Cambodia, including video games, and gave the Ministry of the Interior the responsibility for enforcing the law. However, there is a notable exception to this law. All of the banned games can be played *if authorized by the government.* Casinos can be approved and licensed to operate by the government acting through the prime minister. Another law enacted on July 22, 1999, provided guidelines for the operation of casinos, which are only to be open to foreign nationals and not Cambodian citizens.

Existing Gaming Establishments

As a result of this exception, the government has issued casino licenses to various companies. As of December 2002, the government had issued twenty-one casino licenses, of which seventeen are actually operating while the remaining four have been granted but remained unopened. The casinos are spread around the country as follows: seven in Poipet, four in Sihanoukville, two in Pailin, and one each at Koh Kong, Osmach, Phnom Penh, and Svay Rieng. Several new applications have been received and are being considered by the prime minister at this writing.

Casinos are supposed to be located not less than 100 kilometers from the capital, Phnom Penh. Consequently, most of Cambodia's casinos operate along the country's border with Thailand and cater almost exclusively to Thai patrons. The glaring exception is the floating Naga Casino in Phnom Penh itself, which appears to cater only to tourists. Table game play is the major activity of the gamblers visiting all these properties, but it appears as though slot machine play is increasing, and each casino typically operates 100 to 150 slot machines.

Regulatory Control

Gaming is strictly controlled by the national government, and licensing decisions come directly under the prime minister's auspices. The government does not appear to have any standards by which it evaluates casino projects or integrity requirements for owners or operators. Licenses are negotiated individually and are essentially a contract between the government and the operator/owner. There is no transparent process, so the cost of obtaining a license is open to speculation. The license itself covers all casino operations, equipment, and machinery. There do not appear to be any governmental restrictions on casino size or the number of slot machines and table games.

A casino license is issued by the central government, after which the local authorities in the jurisdiction where the casino is to be established are notified. The local government, army units, and police may support the investor and provide assistance with security, local employment, and immigration matters.

Gaming Control Agencies

Utilizing the French system of gaming control as its model, the government in 1999 assigned the Ministry of the Interior to oversee all casinos operating in Cambodia. The Ministry of the Interior then assigned the General Information Department to handle this task. The General Information Department has six to eight officers working independently in each casino. They are the equivalent of inspectors in U.S. casinos. These officers receive occasional training from their French counterparts and work together with local security guards hired by the casino operator. Their main functions are to observe what is happening in the casinos, to bar Cambodian citizens from entering and playing in the casinos, to observe the level of business, and to prevent anyone from making trouble.

Enforcement Programs

There are no specific gaming enforcement programs in Cambodia. The 1999 law provides various powers to the General Information Department to monitor casino operations and to enforce operators' compliance with the terms of their contract to operate a casino.

INDONESIA

Status of Legal Gaming

Gambling and all gaming activities are strictly illegal in Indonesia, according to the law Crimes Against Decency, Chapter IX, Second

Book Regulating Crime of the Criminal Code, dated November 6, 1974. This law articulates the philosophy that gambling is "against religion, morality and the state ideology 'Pancasila,' that it is dangerous for society, the state and the nation."

Illegal Gaming

Research by the University of Indonesia's Institute for the Study of Social Institutions indicated there were thriteen large illegal gambling dens operating in Jakarta in 2001-2002, with a daily turnover of between 2 billion rupiah (US$200,000) and 10 billion rupiah (US$1 million) each (Junaidi, 2002a). The illegal gambling industry is dominated by ethnic Chinese and non-Muslims, who pay protection money to organized crime syndicates and the military. They also comprise the majority of high-stake gamblers.

The illicit gambling industry actually receives all but official sanction. Operations range from deluxe establishments for high rollers to *togel*, the numbers game popular in the *kampung* (local neighborhoods). The most popular forms of gambling include card games and slot machines.

There would likely be considerable opposition to legalizing gambling from the powerful vested interests that currently control the illegal gambling industry. A study by the University of Indonesia reported that police officers in Jakarta receive at least 150 million rupiah (US$15,873) from one casino a night as protection money (Junaidi & Kasparman, 2002).

Prospects for Legalization

Some Indonesian parliamentarians argue that legalizing gaming and taxing revenues would provide significant benefits for the impoverished state. Consequently, legalizing gaming in some form has been under discussion since 2001 in the Indonesian legislature. Bali, the predominantly Hindu tourist destination, has been touted as a possible location for a legal casino. However, journalists as well as legal and government sources canvassed during the research for this chapter advised that there is little prospect of gaming being introduced to Bali in the near future, even if it is legalized. Instead, should the Megawati government repeal the 1974 antigaming law, the Seribu Islands (or Thousand Islands) north of Jakarta would likely be given first consideration for any legal gaming project.

In April 2002, Jakarta City Governor Sutiyoso stated that his administration wanted to build the infrastructure for casinos in the Seribu Islands. However, the approval and acceptance of the ulema (Muslim clerics) and the city council would be required before proceeding. Sutiyoso acknowledged that gambling could not be banned completely. Therefore, it would be better to open a legal gambling center. However, the Indonesian Ulema Council rejected the idea of opening any casino (Junaidi, 2002b). It appears that the ulema and the Islamic political parties pose the greatest obstacle to gaming ever being legalized in Indonesia. Most apparently prefer the present status quo.

LAOS

Status of Legal Gaming

No specific laws govern or prohibit gaming or gambling in the Lao People's Democratic Republic. However, Article 22.1.3 of the law Regulations on the Management of Hotels and Guesthouses dated July 7, 1997, specifically prohibits gambling in these types of facilities.

Gaming is, in fact, treated like any other commercial business although it is considered a sensitive subject. The government does not wish to be seen to encourage gambling among the population, which is predominantly poor and Buddhist. Consequently, Lao nationals are not permitted to gamble, though gaming projects in specific instances are legal. Illegal gambling is mostly of a low-level local nature in Laos and is not highly organized.

Existing Gaming Establishments

The one existing legal casino, the DanSaVanh Casino, is located about sixty kilometers from the capital Vientiane. It is owned and operated jointly by the Laotian Ministry of Defense (Army) and the Syuen Group of Malaysia. Given its remote location, it is difficult to identify the casino's target market. The resort has 200 rooms and a nine-hole golf course. It is reportedly crowded only on weekends and holidays; but during a visit in mid-2002, a few Thai and Chinese patrons were observed. Most of the patrons appear to prefer table play, although the casino does operate 150 old or reconditioned slot machines.

The government would reportedly consider other resort projects with gaming facilities, but the location would have to be better situated to attract new investors. Several slot rooms also exist in five-star hotels in Vientiane for the exclusive use of foreign guests or visitors.

Regulatory Control

The Ministry of Information and Culture in Vientiane oversees all gaming activities in Laos. All foreign gaming investments are decided at the national government level and cannot be approved at the provincial or local government level. Foreign investments, including the development of resorts and hotels, are governed by the Law on the Promotion and Management of Foreign Investments, dated March 14, 1994. This law is the basis upon which gaming facilities can be incorporated into resort or hotel projects. The contract between the government and a foreign investor can provide for a gaming facility. This would appear to contradict the Regulations on the Management of Hotels and Guesthouses discussed earlier.

Enforcement Programs

No specific gaming enforcement programs exist. There are license requirements and a ban on advertising gaming activities. Visits are made irregularly to the casino or slot room by the police or officials of the Ministry of Information and Culture to ensure that the premises and machines are fully licensed and that Lao nationals are not being allowed admission. Beyond that, there are no compliance programs, although the right to inspect and audit hotels and presumably gaming facilities in hotels is included under the Regulations on the Management of Hotels and Guesthouses.

MALAYSIA

Status of Legal Gaming

Under the Betting Act, 1953 (Act 495), Common Gaming House Act, 1953 (Revised 1983, Act 289), Pool Betting Act, 1967 (Act

384), and the Lotteries Act, 1952 (Act 288), all gambling activities in Malaysia are illegal, except for those permitted under the law, such as gambling at any legal turf club, licensed casino, and licensed public lottery. Gambling is also against Islamic teachings and is illegal under Section 90 of the Syariah Criminal Offences Enactment No. 3, 1995. (It should be noted that the Syariah law governs Muslims only.)

Existing Gaming Establishments

The Genting Highlands casino, which opened in 1969, is the only licensed casino operating in Malaysia. It is open to non-Muslims only, and most of the patrons are ethnic Chinese. The property comprises a hotel with 692 rooms, an entertainment complex offering live programs, and a casino that is open twenty-four hours. The casino features 3,140 slot machines and 426 table games, including roulette, keno, baccarat, blackjack, and French dice.

In addition, the Berjaya Group has obtained licenses to operate 250 slot machines for guests at its Bukit Tinggi Resort and twenty slot machines for guests at its Tioman Beach Resort. Prime Minister Mahathir Mohamad reiterated in early 2003 that these slot licenses were meant for non-Muslims only and that his government would not license a second casino (Yoong, 2003).

Regulatory Control

The Ministry of Finance controls all forms of gaming in Malaysia. In addition to the aforementioned resorts, the Berjaya Group has been licensed by the Ministry of Finance to run the Malaysian lotto.

UNION OF MYANMAR (BURMA)

Status of Legal Gaming

Under the Gambling Law of 1986, gambling is illegal in Myanmar. However, foreign-invested hotels may apply to have gaming rooms, with slots or gaming tables, included in their investment license at the time of application. Only foreign nationals are legally permitted to gamble at these locations.

Existing Gaming Establishments

Currently, five licensed gaming rooms are operating or about to start operation in Myanmar, all of which are targeted primarily at Thai patrons. Two large casinos are also operating in Minelar, in the Shan State Special Region No. 4 on the Chinese border. These casinos primarily cater to Chinese patrons and are not licensed by the central government.

The luxury Andaman Club located at Victoria Point, Myanmar, just off the coast from Ranong in southwest Thailand, comprises a 205-room hotel and a gaming room offering roulette, baccarat, blackjack, "sickbo," and about 200 slot machines. Most of the patrons are flown in from Bangkok. In contrast, Regina Entertainment Hotel and Golf Club and Golden Triangle and Paradise Resort, located just over the northern border with Thailand, cater to less well-heeled patrons and offer numerous table games and some slot machines.

Slot machines are common in entertainment and video game arcades in major cities, but all games are for prizes only, not cash. These entertainment arcades operate in a gray area as there do not appear to be any formal regulations governing their establishment or operation.

Regulatory Control

No specific agency is involved in gaming control because there is no real control of gaming taking place in the country. The Ministry of Tourism is responsible for the hotels where licensed gaming rooms are permitted. Yet permission to operate a gaming room in a hotel is granted at the national level. Local authorities are only responsible for border immigration regulation and other local infrastructure functions, such as land lease and external security.

Enforcement Programs

There are no enforcement programs in Myanmar for investors, employees, or vendors. Ministry of Tourism officials may inspect the hotel premises but do not routinely check on the gaming rooms.

REPUBLIC OF SINGAPORE

Status of Legal Gaming

According to the Betting Act (Chapter 21), Betting and Sweep-stake Duties Act (Chapter 22), Common Gambling Houses Act (Chapter 49), and Private Lotteries Act (Chapter 250), all gambling activities in Singapore are illegal. The exceptions are charity draws, Toto and Singapore Sweep lotteries, and on-course betting on horse-racing at the Singapore Turf Club. Legislation is presently being drawn up to allow the operation of two new casinos (see below), and is expected to be enacted by the end of 2006. A Casino Regulation Division has also been set up under the Ministry of Home Affairs. Gambling cruise ships also operate from Singapore, but gambling is not allowed to take place until the ships reach international waters.

Prospects for Legalization

On April 18, 2005, the government announced that they would allow two casino Integrated Resort (IR) projects to be developed in Singapore. They received nineteen bids from inter-national operators, and expect to choose the winning bid for the Marina Bay IR by May 2006 and the winning bid for the Sentosa IR by September 2006. The total investment value of the two IR projects is US$9 billion, and the first IR is expected to open in 2009.

THAILAND

Status of Legal Gaming

All gaming is prohibited in Thailand, with a few exceptions. The Gaming Act, initially enacted in 1935 and amended several times since, provides a list of twenty-eight games including hilo, dice, baccarat, slot machines, and others that cannot be licensed without specific cabinet approval and a royal decree. The only legal forms of gambling that currently exist are the bimonthly lottery run by the Government Lottery Office and horse racing run every week by the Royal Turf Club in Bangkok.

Illegal Gaming

Many forms of illegal gambling, including gambling dens, an underground lottery, and betting on the results of European football matches, are extremely widespread throughout Thailand. In the mid-1990s, illegal gambling and other illegal activities may have constituted as much as 20 percent of Thailand's gross domestic product (Phongpaichit, 1998). By 2002, the money channeled through gambling amounted to almost 40 percent of the local economy (Sanandaeng, 2003). Research by Chulalongkorn University determined that gambling in Thailand has become much more widespread and that between 500 and 800 billion baht passes through illegal gambling businesses per annum (Phongphaew & Piriyarangsan, 2003). It is generally understood that the police and military indirectly operate illegal gaming facilities throughout the country, along with powerful local organized crime groups.

Prospects for Legalization

Thai governments historically have been opposed to gaming, but it appears that public opinion has changed, due primarily to the emergence of casinos on Thailand's borders with Cambodia, Myanmar, and Laos. The outflow of huge sums from the local economy to these new casinos as well as traditional gambling destinations, such as Genting Highlands in Malaysia, Macao, and Australia, has become a major political issue. The present government has decided to try to reverse the situation and at the same time increase its own revenue streams through legalization of the underground lottery and possibly casinos.

As Thailand already has a very sophisticated tourism infrastructure, some politicians see casinos as a way to encourage the development of new resorts and attract even more visitors. Although some academics and politicians have expressed concern that legalizing gambling could lead to more social problems, advocates of legalization argue that it would result in increased government revenue and increased scrutiny of financial transactions. To date, there has been little organized or public opposition to legalization of gaming.

It is unlikely that the government would consider having a casino in Bangkok. Phuket, an internationally renowned tourist destination, is also unlikely to be the location of a casino initially, due to the large Muslim population and the fact that it is already the wealthiest province in Thailand. Northern locations, such as Chiang Mai, are unlikely to be considered initially due to their proximity to the Golden Triangle and tainted drug money. Consequently, the tourist city of Pattaya on the eastern seaboard has emerged as the most likely candidate to host a casino.

Thai Prime Minister Thaksin Shinawatra will probably make the final decision about legalization of gaming. He is on record as stating that if casinos are to open legally, they must be well regulated and possibly part of a large-scale entertainment complex (Tunyasin & Saengthongcharoen, 2003).

Regulatory Issues

Regulation will very much depend on the commitment of the government. It was apparent from many interviews with government officials at various ministries in May 2002 that there is agreement on the need to regulate gaming, but little thought has been given to specific issues relating to licensing, operational oversight, the collection of gaming taxes, and other related issues.

VIETNAM

Status of Legal Gaming

Gaming is a very sensitive topic for the Vietnamese government. With the exception of the state lottery, all forms of gambling by Vietnamese nationals are completely illegal. There does not appear to be much prospect for change in the near future as Vietnam is a very poor country, and the government does not wish its citizens to "waste" their time and money on gambling.

In addition to two licensed casinos open to foreign customers, five-star joint venture hotels are now legally allowed to apply for licenses to operate slot rooms for their foreign guests. Vietnam also has authorized lotteries at the national and state levels. Lottery revenues are allocated to public infrastructure projects.

Existing Gaming Establishments

The two licensed casinos in Vietnam both cater exclusively to foreigners. Other companies have discussed the development of casinos in conjunction with hotel projects. However, the government seems reluctant to approve any new casino projects in the foreseeable future.

The Doson Casino, located ten kilometers from Haiphong, is a joint venture between Stanley Ho of Macao and Haiphong Joint Venture International Tourist Corporation. Most of the patrons are Chinese nationals, and the gaming and dining areas appear to be not well maintained. The appearance and ambiance of the casino, not surprisingly, are similar to those of many casinos presently operating in Macao.

The Lai Lai Hotel in Mong Cai, on the border with China, opened in 2000. It is a US$10 million hotel and resort joint venture project between Hong Kong Profit Come Enterprise Development Company and Hai Min Import and Export Company. All of the patrons are Chinese nationals and are mainly offered table games.

In addition, a total of approximately 500 slot machines are presently operated in slot machine parlors at the Hanoi Horison Hotel, Guoman Hotel, and Fortuna Hotel in Hanoi, as well as the New World Hotel, Hotel Equatorial, Caravelle Hotel, and Omni Hotel in Ho Chi Minh City. These parlors are open only to hotel guests and not to Vietnamese nationals.

Regulatory Control

Gaming is controlled at the national level with input from the local level. All gaming issues are overseen by the Ministry of Culture and Information, which is responsible for overseeing all aspects of "healthy culture." The Ministry of Planning and Investment handles all licensing matters for gambling projects. The Ministry of the Interior (the police) in fact controls all aspects of daily life in Vietnam. Without their tacit approval, no casino or slot room can operate.

A casino project can only be approved at the national level, by the Ministry of Planning and Investment and the Ministry of Culture and Information, and requires the support and approval of the general secretary of the Communist Party. Without ratification by the Vietnamese Communist Party, no gaming project can be authorized. Locally, the People's Committee is responsible for and must give approval to each local project in its jurisdiction.

Enforcement Programs

There are no specific gaming enforcement programs in Vietnam. Strict licensing requirements are in place for the few existing gaming operators. Strict licensing means that gaming establishments cannot operate without the approval of the government; however, it does not mean or imply that any suitability checks will be made. Visits may be made irregularly to the licensed casinos and slot rooms by the police or officials of the Ministry of Culture and Information to ensure that Vietnamese nationals are not being allowed entry and to verify that the number of slot machines matches the number listed on the license.

REFERENCES

Junaidi, A. (2002a, April 16). The illegal gambling business generates huge money. *Jakarta Post,* City News.

Junaidi, A. (2002b, April 12). Sutiyoso prepared to build island casino. *Jakarta Post,* City News.

Junaidi, A., & Kasparman. (2002, April 22). Hot debate on gambling cools the business. *Jakarta Post,* City News.

Phongpaichit, P. (1998). *The illegal economy and public policy in Thailand.* Thailand: Chulalongkorn University.

Phongphaew, P., & Piriyarangsan, S. (2003). *The role of Thai frontier casinos in Thai society.* Thailand: Chulalongkorn University.

Sanandaeng, K. (2003, February 4). The itch for legal gambling. *Bangkok Post,* Commentary.

Tunyasin, Y., & Saengthongcharoen, J. (2003, January 29). Sonthaya upbeat about casino. *Bangkok Post,* City News.

Yoong, S. (2003, July 10). Casino controversy. *Bangkok Post,* Outlook, p. 3.

SECTION II:
OPERATION

Chapter 6

Essentials of Effective Regulation: Suggestions for Asian Gaming Jurisdictions

Fredric E. Gushin

INTRODUCTION

It is now obvious that gaming was one of the major worldwide growth industries in the 1990s and that this growth continues into the first decade of the new century. Legalized gaming has existed in Nevada for over seventy years and in New Jersey for over twenty-five years and has been expanded to most of the states in the United States. In Asia, casino gaming has been legalized for over forty years in Macao and over thirty years in Malaysia, and has been proliferating throughout Southeast Asia for the past ten years.

Both the governments that legalize casinos and the casino industry face challenges as a multitude of jurisdictions legalize gaming activities. The challenge for government is to put into place effective controls to oversee gaming activities and to maintain the will to regulate the industry for public benefit. There is a direct nexus between effective regulation of the gaming industry and the long-term success of casinos. As gaming opportunities continue to expand internationally, the international gaming industry will be challenged to maintain the high standards of integrity that allowed casino gaming to expand this far, this fast. For reasons discussed in this chapter, jurisdictions that create effective regulatory controls will not only protect themselves but also provide a strong foundation for international investment in casino hotel resorts.

This chapter focuses on standards that gaming jurisdictions should consider in regulating and controlling casinos. In just about every successful jurisdiction that has legalized casino gaming, that activity is highly regulated. The elements of effective casino regulation include various operational controls and licensing of those companies and individuals who participate in the gaming industry. The goal of licensing is to ensure that only those companies and individuals who meet the standards of the particular jurisdiction receive a gaming license, that organized criminal elements are kept out of the ownership and operation of the casino industry, and that unqualified companies and individuals do not receive a casino license. Additionally, from an operational perspective, the goal of casino regulation is to ensure that all monies are accounted for, the casinos are not used to launder money, and the games are run fairly.

PUBLIC POLICY

Public policy is the underpinning of casino regulation. Governments contemplating the legalization of casinos should generally consider and clearly articulate the reasons why casino gaming is being legalized. The basic reasons for legalization typically include job creation, revenue generation, economic development, and the building or enhancement of an existing tourist industry. The goals and objectives are not mutually exclusive and are oftentimes complementary of each other. Jurisdictions contemplating the legalization of casinos will need to address basic issues including how many casino licenses should be issued, whether an exclusive license should be issued and what exclusive means in the particular jurisdiction, and how best to achieve the policy goals desired.

Many jurisdictions have also incorporated into their gaming legislation public policy goals the regulation and oversight of gaming, including some or all of the following:

1. Strict regulation of the industry, including detailed provisions pertaining to licensure, ongoing regulation, and taxation.
2. Framing the granting of a casino license as a privilege that can be revoked by the government if circumstances so warrant

rather than as a right or entitlement. In this way, the holder of the license is placed on notice that it must conform its conduct to certain standards.

3. Creation by the enabling legislation of an independent agency to oversee gaming activity. Alternatively, the oversight of gaming should be placed in an agency or cabinet department with sufficient authority to effectively regulate gaming activity. In either event, the regulatory agency should have law enforcement powers and should be isolated, to the extent possible, from the political whims of the day. The powers typically granted to regulatory agencies include the following:
   * Investigation of the qualifications of casino applicants
   * Issuance of casino licenses and permits
   * Promulgation of regulations
   * Investigations of violations of gaming laws and regulations
   * Initiation of regulatory compliance actions
   * Continuing reviews of casino operations
   * Financial and operational audits of casino operations
   * Hearings and adjudication of licensing and other cases
   * Collection of fees and penalties

4. An all-encompassing and continuing obligation of individuals and companies who want to participate in gaming activity to disclose information to the appropriate regulatory agency. A subcomponent of this category is that companies and individuals applying for a casino or vendor license should be required to pay all costs associated with the conduct of their background investigations. This requirement allows the regulatory agency to perform its functions in a way that will emphasize the integrity aspects of regulation and reduce the absolute need to conduct these sometimes-complex investigations with cost as the only basis for completing the investigation.

5. A fairly strict code of ethics, under which regulatory agencies and senior government officials should operate so that actual and perceived conflicts of interest can be avoided and regulatory decisions can be made on the basis of merit.

CASINO LICENSING

One of the fundamental methods to preserve the integrity of casino gaming is an effective and comprehensive licensing process. Licensing standards are designed to allow regulatory agencies to perform these functions and maintain public confidence in the integrity of the process.

Culturally, in Asia, individuals and companies are not necessarily forthcoming with information and it is difficult to determine true beneficial ownership of privately held companies. Despite these attitudes, companies and individuals applying for licensure should be required to fully and accurately disclose information to regulatory agencies.

Licensing standards are commonly divided into affirmative and disqualification criteria. Many jurisdictions require that applicants for a casino, vendor, and employee license demonstrate qualifications for licensure. For example, an affirmative demonstration of good character, honesty, and integrity for a designated period of time prior to licensure is a common feature of the licensing process. Generally, a demonstration of financial stability, responsibility, and integrity relating to financial solvency, viability, and honesty in business dealings is also required.

Disqualification criteria permit a casino regulatory body to deny a license even if the affirmative criteria have been met. Failure to provide information, failure to reveal material facts, or supplying false or inaccurate information are generally independent bases to deny licensure. However, not every failure to disclose information may lead to a licensure denial. For example, a failure to disclose must generally be willful or show a conscious disregard for the regulatory process; an inadvertent failure to disclose a nonmaterial fact would not usually mandate automatic disqualification. Other disqualification factors typically relate to criminal conduct and convictions. Conviction of certain offenses, generally felonies or first- or second-degree crimes, within a specific period of time, usually ten years preceding the date of the casino application, results in automatic disqualification. Disqualification is also usually mandated if an applicant is a career offender, a member of a career offender cartel, or an associate of a career offender cartel. Involvement in the illegal drug trade would also be a basis for denial.

The licensing standards safeguard against infiltration of organized crime or other undesirables through the ownership or management of a casino. Qualification standards ensure that all individuals who have control or influence over the corporate structure of a casino licensee satisfy minimum standards for licensure.

The scope of the licensing process is important to note as well. Typically for casino entity licensing, the individuals who are required to file application forms include members of the board of directors, company officers, and key employees.

Similar standards typically are applied to companies that engage in business activities with casinos and for casino employees. Corporations and their boards of directors, major stockholders of the casino companies, financial sources, casino service industries, and casino employees are subject to licensure. Once a casino applicant receives a license, the licensee remains under government scrutiny, and its operations are subject to review, audit, and regulation.

These standards are used by most gaming jurisdictions, but their interpretation can differ among jurisdictions. Nevertheless, the basic goal of barring organized crime and undesirables from the industry remains a universal goal of credible gaming jurisdictions. Strict licensing standards and their implementation have been successful in frustrating hidden casino ownership and ensuring that only qualified individuals are licensed and employed in the casino industry.

OPERATIONAL CONTROLS

Once a casino applicant has been licensed, it is important to monitor and regulate casino operations. Elements of effective casino control typically relate to the following:

1. Adoption and implementation of accounting and other internal controls
2. Generally uniform rules of the games
3. Effective oversight by casino supervisors
4. Internal controls for slot machines
5. Viable surveillance
6. Regulatory oversight

The first element of effective control in casino operations relates to a system of accounting and other internal controls designed to safeguard casino assets. To the extent possible, such a system establishes accountability of casino revenues and pinpoints areas and individuals responsible for such funds during the gaming day.

The second aspect of casino control relates to having uniform and defined rules for each game offered by the casino. Uniform substantive rules of the game permit casino supervisors and regulators to identify any deviations, which may indicate cheating or tampering with the games. The third aspect of casino control relates to internal controls associated with gaming equipment, including cards, dice, dealing shoes, and casino software.

The next aspect of casino control relates to slot machines. Electronic games are unique and subject to unique forms of tampering and cheating. Effective controls over slot machines start with the testing of the slot machines by an independent laboratory to determine the randomness of the gaming-related computer chips and to determine whether the payouts are fair. The next step includes an aggressive inspection program to ascertain whether tampering has occurred. A final step relates to the verification of slot machine jackpots to make sure they are legitimate.

The next aspect of casino control relates to the clandestine surveillance of gaming operations by management and regulators. Surveillance personnel act as a check and balance over casino personnel on the gaming floor and provide an independent level of review and observation. The surveillance department should operate independently of the management of the casino and should report to the casino entity's board of directors or audit committee. The final element, which ties the five previous aspects together, relates to an effective regulatory process. As noted, regulatory agencies should have full authority to conduct reviews, audits, and observations of all aspects of a casino's operations.

CONCLUSION

Clearly, these standards represent new controls that have not historically been widely applied in Asia. However, other industries, including financial and nonbanking institutions, throughout Asia have had to implement comprehensive compliance and know their customer controls, partially in response to the tragic events of September 11, 2001, in New York and to prevent money laundering.

Full disclosure, verification of information, and comprehensive casino controls may be controversial in parts of Asia. Some will argue that the so-called Asian culture mitigates against full disclosure or the implementation of casino controls. Although culture is important in any jurisdiction, it should not be used as a justification to issue casino licenses to otherwise unqualified individuals or to launder money in casino facilities.

Casino gaming can be a tremendous tool to create jobs, increase tax revenues, and act as a catalyst for resort and hotel development. It is, however, no panacea for public ills. The model of regulation described herein has proven to be effective for casino operations in many countries and regions, including the United States, Australia, and Western Europe. It serves to create public confidence in casino gaming and has led to the investment of billions of dollars in physical facilities and the creation of tens of thousands of jobs. There is no reason why the same goals and objectives could not be realized throughout Asia.

Chapter 7

Casino Licensing Investigations

William R. Kisby
William O'Reilly

The casino industry has seen worldwide growth over the past ten years, in part because casino gaming is perceived by law enforcement and the general public as being respectable. Legalized gaming has demonstrated that it can provide revenue to government, create jobs, and act as a catalyst for economic development. In Asia, advocates of casino gaming have used the themes of job creation, increased revenue, and development as the rationale to expand casinos.

Achieving these broad policy goals is premised upon establishing a viable regulatory control structure for gaming. The underlying foundation of successful gaming is that those who own and operate casinos should be subject to suitability standards to ensure that statutory standards for integrity and good character are achieved. In addition, companies engaging in business with licensed casinos and those who work in casinos should be subject to qualification as well. Gaming regulators make these determinations through conducting background investigations. This chapter discusses the investigative process and highlights cases that we have worked on over the years.

It is the responsibility of government to set licensing standards and conduct background investigations. As set forth in more detail in Chapter 6, this starts by establishing effective gaming regulations and their implementation by regulators. The purpose of these regulations is to ensure the integrity of the entire regulatory process because those who are licensed will have satisfied certain standards. Moreover, strong and clear regulations relating to licensing serve to level the playing field in that all casino licensees will have met suitability standards. Just as important is the governmental will to regulate and to enforce its own regulations.

In our international investigations over the years, we have seen unsuitable companies and individuals moving into jurisdictions that do not have licensing systems in place and into jurisdictions that do not conduct meaningful background investigations. Some jurisdictions around the world are still issuing casino licenses and even Internet gaming licenses upon the payment of fees and do not conduct any significant background investigations.

In casino jurisdictions in North America, Europe, and Australia, gaming legislation typically requires regulatory agencies to conduct background investigations before a casino license can be issued. No credible gaming jurisdiction wants to find itself in the position of having licensed a company and then be blindsided by another jurisdiction finding that same company or its principals unqualified or unsuitable based on information it did not have or develop properly.

THE APPLICATION PROCESS

This chapter discusses the need for government to have a process in place that provides a meaningful way to determine the suitability of casino applicants. This process starts with having an application form that solicits necessary information to make this determination. The philosophy behind this process is that full and complete information must be provided so that determinations about suitability can be made. In Asia, the custom sometimes is not to disclose and to be secretive about personal information, including financial information. This cultural barrier has to be overcome.

Applicants for casino entity licensing, vendor licensing, and employee licensing should always be required to complete an application form supplied by the government agency responsible for casino control. Typically, the nature and scope of information requested through the application form vary depending upon the applicant's level of employment and whether the applicant is applying to own or operate a casino. Typically, an individual would be required to complete a personal history disclosure form; a business entity would have to complete a business entity disclosure form. These application forms request personal information, family history, financial history including bank account information, and educational background. The application forms also request information relating to criminal record, civil litigations, business holdings, licensing in other jurisdictions, and a variety of other information. The applicant is also requested to affirm the information and is placed on notice that omissions, misinformation, or untrue information may lead to a denial of the license applied for. The purpose of these questions is to provide information to regulators so that an assessment of character, integrity, financial stability, and business ability can be made.

In the case of key employees, major stockholders, officers, or directors of an entity seeking licensure, the application forms typically request tax returns and other personal financial information. The applicant's other business dealings should generally be disclosed and the beneficial ownership of other companies in which the applicant has an interest should also be disclosed.

As a result of the proliferation of legalized gaming, the International Association of Gaming Regulators has devised a multijurisdictional application form that is gaining increasingly wide usage. This application form adopts the concepts described previuosly and meets the disclosure requirements mandated by many gaming jurisdictions. Jurisdictions such as New Jersey, Nevada, and Great Britain have adopted these forms and have developed a short supplement requesting additional information as needed.

The application form generally provides a blueprint for the agency that is required to conduct a background investigation. Once submitted by the applicant, regulators typically check the application for completeness and omissions before they are forwarded for investigation.

Release Authorization

A release authorization should accompany each application that is filed by any applicant for any type of casino license. The release authorization is signed by the applicant and permits the disclosure of information about the applicant to third parties, such as gaming regulators or their agents.

Release authorizations are essential in getting third parties to cooperate during the course of the background investigations. For example, with a valid release authorization, the background investigations will be able to pierce the so-called corporate veils that may exist in offshore companies. Investigations are crucial in obtaining critical financial information relative to the applicant. In addition, release authorizations can and should be used to obtain information from other governmental authorities and regulators. A release authorization is also important to secure credit reports relative to the applicant.

In some cases, even with a release authorization, information may not be made available. In that situation, the applicant should be requested to provide the necessary information, as the applicant always has the burden of proof to secure proven suitability. In the event certain information is held by a third party who is reluctant to supply it, the applicant should be asked to contact the third party to authorize the third party to provide the needed information.

INVESTIGATIVE PROCESS

The first step in any investigation is to conduct a variety of database checks regarding the applicant. As noted previously, the provision of false, inaccurate, or misleading information or the omission of information can be a basis to deny any application. Typically, the following database checks should be undertaken in every application:

Media check
Civil litigation check
Bankruptcy check
Criminal record check
Credit check

Once all of the database checks have been completed, an investigator reviews the application form and compares the results of the information disclosed with what the databases revealed. In addition, the applicant should usually be interviewed and given an opportunity to clarify information in the application form and perhaps be given one last opportunity to provide information.

However, in some Asian jurisdictions, privacy laws may inhibit non–law enforcement agencies from gathering information. For example, in Hong Kong and Singapore, it is illegal for non–law enforcement investigators even to ask for criminal record information. In other countries, records are kept in a computerized format, making some of these basic searches very cumbersome.

In many instances in conducting international investigations, it is crucial to retain investigative consultants or agents who can pave the way for these types of investigations. This would especially be the case in Asian jurisdictions where language barriers and cultural differences clearly exist. The conduct of due diligence and casino investigations internationally is much different from that in the United States. All of these elements have to be factored into the investigation. However, under no circumstances should culture or values ever be used as a justification or excuse for criminal activity. An attorney working with the regulatory agency to evaluate the information should review the results of the investigation.

OPERATOR, VENDOR, AND EMPLOYEE INVESTIGATION

Operator Licensing

Entities that seek to own or operate casinos are typically publicly traded corporations, partnerships, or entrepreneurs. Background investigations on these companies and their stockholders, directors, and officers form the foundation of casino control. The investment community is generally reluctant to lend funds to projects that are located in jurisdictions that do not seriously regulate casino gaming. Moreover, raising capital is that much more difficult in jurisdictions that do not have a stable political environment, that have unacceptably high levels of corruption, and that have a seemingly ineffective or arbitrary approach to the enforcement of gaming regulations.

Since every jurisdiction is unique, gaming regulations should be drafted to be not only comprehensive and effective, but also reasonable for the jurisdiction where they are to be enforced. The New Jersey and Nevada gaming regulations are excellent starting points for all jurisdictions to study when drafting gaming regulations. These regulations have undergone years of scrutiny, legal challenges, and modifications, which have been proven effective in blocking the infiltration of organized crime ownership of casinos. In these jurisdictions, the casino industry is viewed as a legitimate business and industry in the eyes of the financial community, in addition to a majority of the citizens in communities where casinos are located.

In many cases, the applicants for casino licensure may be publicly traded companies who are well-known and are required to file corporate disclosure forms and financial statements with governmental bodies in jurisdictions where they conduct business. These companies are rather transparent and generally require less time to investigate than private companies. Private companies generally require closer scrutiny and more extensive investigations with the utilization of trained financial investigators to determine the true beneficial ownership of these entities and trace the cash flow of these companies from the initial investment through their day-to-day operation. Furthermore, investigation will focus on the business practices and any criminal associations that the company or its principals may have or have had in the past.

The following represents an example of an investigation of an individual and his company who sought a casino license.

Investigation of the applicant in one jurisdiction revealed that the address the applicant utilized was in fact a mail drop, with no bricks-and-mortar presence. Further initial investigation disclosed that this individual lied on his application form about his educational background and failed to adequately disclose and explain all of his criminal and civil litigation history. As a result of these failures to disclose, regulators decided to expend additional resources to verify other information in the application form. The theory was that if the applicant lied about his educational background, something else might be inaccurate or false. In addition, a financial investigation revealed that the applicant could not prove by clear and convincing evidence his financial stability and that his business practices involved violations of liquor laws. Upon further investigation, it appeared as though the applicant may have been involved in various frauds, which had the effect of increasing his net worth. In fact, his net worth and the net worth of his businesses were inflated. Finally, the applicant was not able to disclose any viable source of funds for the casino project being pro-posed. As a result, serious questions were raised about the company's suitability and the suitability of the sole owner of the company.

Vendor Licensing

Regulators not only have to be concerned that casino operators are investigated thoroughly, but also should address the issue of ancillary businesses that provide goods and services to casinos. When casino gaming came to New Jersey after the passage of the referendum in 1976, the then head of organized crime in the Philadelphia/South Jersey area, Angelo Bruno, was reported to have said, "I don't want to own a casino, I want to control the ancillary industry thereby indirect-ly controlling the casino."

As a result of the first twenty-five years of legalized casino gaming in New Jersey, it has been documented by federal and state law en-forcement that organized criminal elements have attempted to infil-trate the casino industry through junkets, various service industries including construction companies, and labor unions. It should also be noted that, in New Jersey, all ancillary businesses are investigated by the New Jersey Division of Gaming Enforcement once the vendor conducts US$75,000 worth of business with one casino during a cal-endar year or US$250,000 with two or more casinos. In the state of Nevada, there is less emphasis on vendor licensing; however, Nevada regulators have a "call forward" system, which allows gaming au-thorities to require vendors to submit to a licensing investigation if regulators receive information of a derogatory nature concerning the company or its principals. Many other jurisdictions in the United States and internationally do not conduct any due diligence on ven-dors, and this becomes the underbelly of the industry susceptible to internal corruption and organized criminal infiltration.

Even with stringent regulations and vendor investigations, orga-nized crime continues to attempt to infiltrate these service industries periodically. An example of ancillary infiltration by organized crime can be found in the infiltration of Union Local 54 (hotel-bartenders' union) in New Jersey. In that case, the president of the union was on the payroll of organized crime. Regulators took action to clean up the union and remove corrupt officials. Another example is the result of a two-year New Jersey State Police sting operation into the junket industry, code named Operation Eagle. The results of this investigation disclosed the control of sixty-five junket agents in twenty-five states, who were paying off organized crime to operate junkets in certain casinos in New Jersey, Nevada, the Bahamas, and the Dominican Republic. This investigation ultimately led to a racketeering indictment of seventeen individuals and seven corporations. Two of the seventeen individuals were captains (capos) in the Bonanno and DeCavalcante crime families.*

It has been well documented that when organized crime cannot directly own a casino operation, they resort to infiltration into the ancillary businesses through corruption, commercial bribery, or extortion. The same will hold true in Asia as well as any jurisdictions contemplating the legalization of casino gaming. Jurisdictions considering the legalization of casino gaming need to assess how they are prepared to combat organized crime and sophisticated organized criminal groups involved in casino-related scams. This assessment and ability of law enforcement to combat organized crime is crucial.

Employee Licensing

Employees who work in gaming-related positions in casinos are generally licensed based on their specific functions. The level of authority and discretionary supervision the employee may have usually determines the level of investigation. For example, an individual working as a security guard in the casino is not typically investigated to the same level as a casino supervisor or shift manager. Furthermore, a floor employee will not be investigated to the same level as a key employee of the casino.

When investigating lower-level employees, the concern is generally related to verification of information on the application form, criminal record history, and honesty issues. The duties of some employees require them to work on the casino floor and to work with

---

*Kisby, W.R. (1985). Testimony of William R. Kisby, New Jersey State Police in 1985, before the President's Commission on Organized Crime in the portion of the testimony concerning Organized Crime and Gambling. (Available from the President's Commission on Organized Crime, Record of Hearing VII of June 24-26, 1985, in New York City, New York, through the Federal Document Research in Hearing, Washington, DC.)

chips and casino credit, or in other sensitive money-handling positions. Therefore, these employees should be investigated more thoroughly. These individuals' investigation would include a criminal history search in addition to a personal credit profile, civil litigation history, bankruptcy, and media checks to ensure they do not have a problem that may impact on the casino, since they will be involved in the integrity of the games or handling the cash flow of the casino operation. The key employee investigation would also include an extensive personal financial investigation, which would consist of the disclosure of three years of tax returns and net worth statements to determine financial stability, since they will be in supervisory and decision-making positions.

A CASINO LICENSING CASE

We would now like to apply what we have been discussing to a casino licensing case that was investigated and prosecuted in Tinian. By way of background, it is important to set the scene and in the process provide an overview of gaming in Tinian, explain why Tinian was an attractive locale for Japanese organized crime known as the yakuza, discuss the inherent difficulties that any small, isolated jurisdiction may have in effectively regulating gaming, and review the investigation and casino licensing case of ASA Development and Investment Corporation.

Tinian is a part of the Commonwealth of the Northern Mariana Islands (CNMI). It is probably most famous in military history as the site from where the Enola Gay left to drop the atomic bomb on Hiroshima in 1945. Today, CNMI consists of three islands, namely Saipan, Rota, and Tinian. Up until 1976, these islands were trust territories of the United States. In 1976, the United States and the CNMI entered into a covenant, which made CNMI a commonwealth of the United States. Although U.S. laws generally apply, specific exemptions were carved out as a result of the negotiating process for commonwealth status. For example, land can be owned only by people of Chamorro or Carolinian heritage; customs and immigration were left under the control of CNMI rather than the U.S. government; the U.S. minimum wage does not apply; and citizens of the commonwealth are not subject to U.S. individual, corporate, or business taxes. Although these elements have helped develop the islands, they have problems for law enforcement and serious opportunities for the yakuza.

Saipan is the capital and is also the business, social, and political hub of the commonwealth. In the early 1990s, CNMI had about 25,000 citizens, of which 2,200 lived in Tinian. There are an additional 20,000 to 25,000 foreign workers, mostly from the Philippines and China.

Economically, the major industries of CNMI at that time were tourism and garment manufacturing. On the tourism front, the commonwealth was doing quite well. Saipan is only 90 miles from Guam and both jurisdictions attracted about 1 million tourists a year in the early 1990s. Over 1 billion people are within an eight-hour plane ride to CNMI. Tourists are attracted primarily from Japan and Korea. The tourism boom of the 1980s spurred hotel construction, golf courses, shops, restaurants, and an active nightlife. However, with the 1991 economic slowdown in Asia, CNMI suffered an economic slowdown as well.

Based on a lack of funds and experience, the Tinian Gaming Commission did not seek qualified applicants when it was first established and recruited applicants in 1990 and 1991. Rather than devoting resources to recruiting well-known casino companies, the commission advertised for casino applicants in the local newspaper, and seven local companies applied for a casino license. In at least three applications, preliminary investigation and intelligence reports documented yakuza efforts to penetrate ownership. Tinian was viewed as a vehicle for the yakuza to become involved in a legitimate business. In addition to casino ownership, the opportunity to skim casino funds, and the operation of lucrative junkets, the yakuza saw Tinian as a vehicle to launder money. Most important, doing business in Tinian gave the yakuza a backdoor entry into the United States and would facilitate their ability to secure U.S. passports. In CNMI, the U.S. government does not control immigration and customs. All of this made Tinian an irresistible lure that was impossible for the yakuza to ignore.

ASA was a casino applicant that sought to build a US$300 million casino hotel project in Tinian. The investigation of the applicant took ten months and involved both background and financial investigations. We want to emphasize that the facts of the case are matters of public record based on oral testimony and documentary evidence introduced at the hearing held in 1992. This case highlighted how the yakuza attempted to penetrate casino ownership.

After a comprehensive investigation involving the background of ASA and its key personnel as well as a financial analysis of the project, a report recommending the denial of this application was issued. The basic reasons for the denial recommendation were the conclusion of the investigation that the applicant and its 92 percent stockholder and chief executive officer, Yukimiro Asai, was a front for the yakuza; that he attempted to deceive the commission in the application form; that he lacked honesty, good character, and integrity; that both Asai and ASA lacked financial stability and integrity; and that ASA and Asai lacked sufficient business ability and casino experience to be issued a license.

During the hearing on this case in January 1992, regulators put together information that highlighted the case against ASA. For example, regulators presented a report prepared by our expert on the yakuza outlining the typical activities of the group. Next, regulators attempted to develop a profile of someone who might be willing to act as a front for the yakuza. Although there is no foolproof litmus test for yakuza associates, there are certain measures which, taken collectively, might be indicative of such behavior.

1. Yakuza associates are invariably engaged in financial management as owners of businesses, in formal banking, or in some form of stock or as commodity dealers.
2. They frequently have criminal records, although these records may be for minor infractions, and may or may not be related to traditional yakuza activities.
3. They maintain impressive business operations as fronts in order to conceal possession and movement of illegal funds from law enforcement and other scrutiny.
4. They tend to entertain a great deal and to favor luxurious accommodations.
5. Their business dealings and the records they keep are rarely straightforward.
6. They often operate though attorneys, accountants, political figures, and others.

Regulators then attempted to apply the facts of this case to this profile to demonstrate the yakuza involvement of the applicant. This was accomplished in a number of ways. First, in 1979, Asai had been arrested and convicted of loan sharking. This was a typical low-level yakuza activity in the 1970s and early 1980s. In fact, Asai had been collecting loans made to individuals who otherwise might not have been qualified to receive those loans, and he was keeping exorbitant commissions of up to 50 percent of the loan amount. In effect, this began a pattern establishing someone who was all too willing to act for and on behalf of yakuza organizations.

Asai's primary business since the mid-1980s was to negotiate with property owners for the sale of their land to third parties. These negotiations were often equivalent to intimidation and this activity was also typical of yakuza actions in the early 1980s. One of the significant yakuza activities is gunrunning. Guns are strictly prohibited in Japan, and gunrunning into Japan is almost always associated with the yakuza. Regulators were able to show Asai's association with convicted gunrunners. These associations occurred in the Philippines where gun buying and selling activities often take place and from which guns are then smuggled into Japan. Regulators were able to identify several witnesses from the Philippines who observed Asai with gunrunners and who were prepared to testify to that effect. Other witnesses placed Asai with yakuza members negotiating to bring women to Japan for the sex industry.

Asai and the other major stockholder in this case represented on their personal application forms that they had a net worth of US$50 million and US$300 million, respectively. In fact, after a thorough review of their finances, it was determined that their combined net worth was less than US$6 million. They had intentionally overstated their assets to appear to be respectable businessmen. For example, the financial investigations revealed that Asai claimed land as his own which he had never owned, that he claimed land which had been sold (in one instance within a week before he filed his application form), and that he claimed holdings that were in the name of some of his corporations as his own. All of this was done to inflate his assets.

Asai claimed US$82,000 annual income on his Japanese income tax forms but had made personal loans in one year in excess of US$800,000 to friends and associates; he drove a Rolls-Royce automobile; he traveled with an entourage to Saipan, the Philippines, and elsewhere; and his lifestyle far exceeded his reported income. On cross-examination during the hearing, Asai's financial advisor tried to explain away these inconsistencies by stating that perhaps that was one year's income. He explained that this was an aberration and that perhaps in previous years Asai had a larger income. Because the financial investigation was thorough, regulators were able to produce documentation that showed Asai's reported income to be only US$82,000 in each year. The applicant's own financial advisor could not explain how Asai could maintain his lifestyle on US$82,000 per year. The prosecution believed that Asai understated his income to avoid paying Japanese income taxes.

Asai and his associates attempted to portray themselves as wealthy and respectable businessmen when they were not. For example, on the application forms, Asai swore and had notarized statements about his net worth and the net worth of the companies he controlled. On the application form, they reflected total assets of US$138 million. Only through comprehensive financial investigation did regulators learn that the liabilities of the companies exceeded the assets and the companies had an overall negative net worth. Such being the case, how could this applicant raise the capital to finance a US$300 million casino hotel from legitimate sources?

Through strong financial analysis, regulators were able to show that Asai had money wire transferred to Saipan from Japan. In total, Asai transferred some US$12.7 million dollars to Saipan. US$1.7 million of those funds could not be accounted for and regulators speculated that the applicant used that money to support his lifestyle over an eighteen- to twenty-four-month period and embezzled those funds from his investors.

Overall, because of the thorough investigation, regulators were successful in applying the facts of the case to the profile of the yakuza associate. The picture we created was of an individual who was all too willing to front for and be controlled by the yakuza as long as he made money in the process. Ultimately, the commission denied the ASA casino license. They did so because the investigation was thorough and the evidence was overwhelming and uncontested by the applicant.

Gaming is proliferating throughout the world. It was one of the growth industries of the 1990s. Casino gaming is a serious business and difficult to control. The regulatory process can be expensive. However, effective, thorough, and professional investigations are a strong tool to ensure that those seeking to own or operate casinos maintain high-integrity standards. With a strong governmental commitment, emerging jurisdictions can keep organized crime and other undesirables out of the industry.

Chapter 8

Accounting, Internal Controls, and Casino Auditing

Kevin O'Toole

The concept of accounting and internal controls in any business enterprise is commonly accepted as the primary means by which the enterprise ensures that its assets are properly safeguarded and its financial records are accurate and reliable. Internal controls are generally designed to provide reasonable assurances that

1. transactions are performed only in accordance with management's authorization;
2. transactions are recorded to allow proper preparation of financial statements and to provide accountability for assets;
3. access to assets is permitted only in accordance with management's authorization; and
4. exsting assets are periodically compared to recorded assets and differences are addressed.

In the gaming industry, internal controls take on an even greater significance because of the risks inherent in the nature of the business. For example, in most businesses, revenue is measurable and is recorded in accounting records when the product is delivered or the service is performed. In casinos, however, the revenue transactions occur continuously at table games or in slot machines, but the measure and record of that revenue do not occur until hours later when the drop is collected and counted. Because there is no contemporaneous record of each revenue transaction as it occurs and because large quantities of cash are used, casino operations are susceptible to a greater risk of loss from employee or customer dishonesty. It is therefore incumbent upon management to reduce these greater-than-normal risks by establishing and maintaining an effective system of accounting and internal controls. Such a system should provide for authorization, accountability, and safeguarding of revenue and assets while at the same time recognizing the concept of reasonable assurance at reasonable cost. That is, the cost of control should not exceed the benefits to be derived.

In most of the major gaming jurisdictions worldwide, regulators have generally adopted, through regulations, minimum accounting and internal control standards. Casino licensees or companies awarded a gaming franchise are required to prepare and implement accounting and internal control procedures, which meet minimum standards defined by regulation. In New Jersey, for example, casinos are required, as a condition of their licensing and operation, to submit a comprehensive description of their system of internal procedures and administrative and accounting controls in accordance with regulations (see New Jersey Administrative Code, Title 19, Chapter 45). In Nevada, gaming operators must meet minimum internal control standards as set forth in Regulation 6. Similarly, the National Indian Gaming Commission, the federal agency that governs Indian gaming in the United States, requires Indian gaming facilities to establish, implement, and enforce minimum internal control standards. In all of these jurisdictions, the minimum control standards not only address accounting controls in traditional gaming areas such as table games, slot machines, cage operations, and the count rooms, but also include administrative and management control requirements, such as reporting lines, the table of organization, financial reporting, auditing, and record retention.

A gaming operation's system of accounting and internal controls should include standards related to the casino's organizational structure. Fraud, embezzlement, and other misappropriation of funds can be minimized, or even eliminated, if job descriptions are written to avoid incompatible functions and tables of organization are structured with a chain of command that facilitates independence among departments and clearly identifies areas of responsibility. Some general principles that an effective system of accounting and internal controls should include are as follows:

1. The reporting line for each department head should ensure an appropriate level of independence. For example, the head of the surveillance department and internal audit department should not report to the chief operating officer. Rather, to ensure independence, the reporting line should be directly to the chief executive officer, an independent audit committee, or an independent regulatory authority.
2. A supervisor's area of responsibility should not be so extensive that it is impractical for one person to monitor.
3. Transactions involving a significant exchange or transfer of funds should include representatives of two independent departments or be monitored directly by a supervisor.
4. No employee should be in a position both to commit an error or perpetrate a fraud and to conceal the error or fraud in the normal course of his or her duties.
5. The chain of command should be clearly defined to hold accountable managers and supervisors for actions or omissions within their areas of responsibility.

This chapter reviews two significant, interrelated topics that provide the foundation for an honest, efficient casino operation. As noted, accounting and internal controls establish those standards of operation that a casino operation must follow. These standards encompass a broad spectrum of topics, but, stated briefly, these topics relate to cash, gaming checks, and gaming equipment integrity. Casino auditing relates to the daily, monthly, and annual process whereby a person or persons independent of the gaming operation evaluates the level and scope of compliance with the accounting and internal control standards.

ACCOUNTING AND INTERNAL CONTROLS

Gaming jurisdictions worldwide recognize the importance of accounting and internal controls. Accounting and internal controls serve to ensure the integrity of gaming operations in the broadest sense. These standards of operation accomplish the following:

- Safeguard assets
- Ensure accuracy in the reporting of revenues and expenses
- Mandate effective audit trails

Accounting and internal controls are generally developed and written by the gaming operation. More specifically, the accounting or finance department of the gaming operation generally takes the lead role in this process. Once the accounting and internal controls are developed and written, most jurisdictions require that the gaming operation submits the accounting and internal controls to the regulatory authority for review and approval. In addition, a time frame is often imposed to ensure that the regulatory authority acts expeditiously to accomplish its task of review and approval.

Protecting the Casino Cage

Accounting and internal control standards always mandate that a gaming operation constructs, on or immediately adjacent to the gaming floor, a central location for the banking functions associated with the casino. This central location is generally referred to as the casino cage. Accounting and internal control standards for the casino cage further mandate procedures that focus on two areas: (1) physical security of the casino cage, and (2) accounting controls within the casino cage.

Physical Security of the Casino Cage

The casino cage shall be designed and constructed to provide maximum security for the substantial assets that are housed within the casino cage. To accomplish the objective of maximum security, gaming regulators generally require the following:

- The casino cage must be constructed as a fully enclosed structure except for openings through which items such as gaming chips, checks, cash, promotional coupons, records, and documents can be passed to service the public and gaming tables.
- The casino cage must be equipped with manually triggered silent alarms at each cashier drawer location, with the system con-

nected directly to the monitoring rooms of the surveillance and security departments.
- The entry and exit system to the casino cage must be a double door system, often referred to as a mantrap system, whereby a person cannot exit through the second door until the first door is securely locked.

In addition, the casino cage is a restricted access location. Accounting and internal control standards should require that a log be maintained with the names of all persons authorized to enter the cage.

Accounting Controls Within the Casino Cage

In addition to the physical security measures pertinent to the casino cage, an effective system of accounting and internal controls mandates that the casino cage be physically segregated by personnel and by function. Four accountability centers exist within a casino cage: the main bank, the chip bank, the check bank, and the front window cashier banks.

Each accountability center within the casino cage has specialized functions. The chip bank services the gaming tables through table fills and table credits. The check bank maintains custody and control of negotiable instruments presented by gaming patrons to enable those patrons to obtain funds to gamble with. The front window cashier banks are utilized to service gaming patrons who present gaming chips in order to exchange them for coins or currency. The main bank within the casino cage receives the funds from the count rooms, engages in exchanges with the other casino cage banks, and prepares the daily deposit and the overall cage reconciliation forms.

Protecting the Table Games

The integrity of table game operations is constantly at risk. So long as a casino's doors are open to the public, some percentage of its patrons will attempt to cheat or swindle. In addition, to protect the assets of the gaming operation, steps should be taken to identify card counters and to neutralize their ability to win big. Sound accounting and internal controls designed to protect table game operations in-

clude standards that cover table game equipment, table game revenue, and table game supervision.

Table games are generally organized into a *gaming pit,* which consists of a configuration of multiple gaming tables. The first component of internal controls pertaining to the gaming pit is to secure the
pit with access-control stanchions. Inside the gaming pit are the playing cards, the dice, table inventories of gaming chips and coins, and
computer terminals utilized by pit clerks and table game supervisors.
A gaming pit is a restricted casino area and only authorized personnel
should be allowed to enter the gaming pit.

Table Game Equipment

Accounting and internal controls pertaining to playing cards and
dice begin from the point in time that the warehouse or receiving
clerk is notified that unopened boxes of cards or dice have arrived on-
site. A security department representative, often accompanied by a
regulator, should respond to the receiving area to escort the unopened
boxes to a predesignated card and dice storage room. Once there, the
playing cards and dice should be preliminarily inspected and recorded in a master inventory log. The master inventory log tracks all
incoming and outgoing decks of playing cards and sets of dice. At
least once a day, the table games department, along with a security
department representative, removes the required amount of cards and
dice needed in the gaming pits for that gaming day. These items are
then transported to and secured within the gaming pit.

Table Game Revenue

When a gaming table is open for play, numerous financial transactions occur that are not evidenced by documents. Each wager placed by
a patron and the outcome of that wager (win or lose) are not recorded
on any document. This presents a challenge to the casino auditor. How
is table game revenue calculated and how is that calculation audited by
the casino's accounting department or by external accountants?

The answer to this question lies, in part, in the concept of inventory
controls. Stringent inventory controls exist in a properly operated casino to account for the inventory of gaming chips that comprise the

table float. The inventory of gaming chips at a gaming table is referred to as the table float because it constantly fluctuates. Each time a patron's wager wins, gaming chips leave the table float to pay the winning wager, and each time a patron's wager loses, gaming chips are added to the table float when the losing wager is collected by the dealer.

Table game revenue is calculated per gaming table per a specified period of time, generally per shift. If a casino operates twenty-four hours per day, the day is generally divided into three eight-hour shifts: day shift, swing shift, and graveyard shift. The formula for calculating table game revenue per shift is as follows:

1. Ending inventory of gaming chips at table X at close of shift,
2. +, drop box receipts from table X,
3. +, table credits from table X,
4. −, table fills from table X,
5. −, beginning inventory of gaming chips at table X at beginning of shift,
6. =, table game revenue for table X for that particular shift.

Each step in the process to calculate table game revenue, as set forth in the formula, includes accounting and internal control standards that must be strictly followed to ensure that all table game revenue is properly secured and accounted for.

Table Game Supervision

As a general rule, most gaming jurisdictions include in their accounting and internal controls a mandate that gaming pits be adequately staffed with table game supervisory personnel. Standards of operation that identify the levels of supervisory personnel and the scope of their authority are particularly evident in the area of table game operations. Table game supervisory personnel, with authority equal to or greater than those being supervised, are an essential part of the overall control of table game operations.

The casino's closed-circuit television system, monitored by the surveillance department, is not the only tool available to protect table game revenue from cheating and swindling activities. The concept of

people watching people is an equally important control device to reduce the dangers of illegal practices and methods in the conduct of table games.

All table games in a casino are watched by several levels of supervisors. In most cases, this involves floorpersons, pit bosses, and shift
managers. In the game of craps, due to the fast-paced action and multiple types of wagers, an additional supervisor, the boxperson, is sta-
tioned at each craps table to provide the first level of supervisory
oversight. Table game supervisory personnel have organizational and
administrative responsibilities as well, but their primary role is to
watch the table games to ensure that both employees and patrons are
not compromising the integrity of table game operations.

Protecting the Slot Machines

The percentage of total gaming revenue that is attributed to the operation of slot machines now approximates 70 percent or more in
many U.S. jurisdictions. Protecting that enormous stream of revenue
as well as maintaining the highest level of confidence in the integrity
of the slot machines themselves requires strong and effective accounting and internal controls. Preliminarily, it should be noted that
the phrase *slot machine* is somewhat limiting in today's casino industry. Given the rate at which manufacturers are producing different
types of machines that generate gaming revenue, the statutes, regulations, and gaming compacts drafted in recent years are utilizing the
phrase *gaming machine* to capture a broader spectrum of technology.

Standards for protecting slot machines and other types of gaming
machines focus on procedures in two areas: (1) the collecting, counting, and recording of slot machine revenue; and (2) the safeguarding
of slot machine game programs to ensure fairness to the gaming
public.

Collecting, Counting, and Recording of Slot Revenue

Whenever assets are taken out of, or put into, a gaming machine,
standards of internal control should apply. For traditional slot machines, drop box pickup procedures are necessary to remove accumulated coins or tokens from the machine. At a minimum, the security

department and hard count team should jointly process the unlocking of the slot cabinet, the removal of the drop bucket, and the placing of an empty drop bucket in the slot cabinet. When all drop buckets are removed from the slot machines, they are transported to the hard count room. Calibration standards should be in place to ensure that hard count scales are accurate within a narrow set of parameters.

Safeguarding Slot Machine Game Software

A gaming operator must maintain the public's confidence in the integrity of the games. With respect to slot machines, this means ensuring the fairness of the game. Fairness of slot machines can be achieved through a combination of the following: (1) establishing and maintaining fair payout percentages for each gaming machine, (2) testing game software prior to implementation on the gaming floor, and (3) establishing and maintaining effective accounting and internal controls to ensure that gaming machines are not tampered with or otherwise compromised in any way.

Fair payout percentages. In some jurisdictions, fair payout percentages for slot machines are mandated by legislation. For example, the state of New Jersey mandates an 83 percent payout percentage for all slot machines. More common, however, are jurisdictions that permit the gaming operation to establish fair payout percentages that must meet a standard of reasonableness.

Testing game software. The testing of slot machine game software prior to its implementation is fast becoming viewed as essential to the fairness of slot machine operations. Independent testing laboratories have been established to provide these services to gaming equipment manufacturers and governmental entities. Some major U.S. jurisdictions, such as New Jersey and Nevada, maintain their own governmentally operated testing lab. Furthermore, a growing number of gaming operations maintain a group of technicians within the information technology department, slot operations department, or internal audit department who perform testing of game software on an in-house basis.

Internal controls over game software. To ensure that slot machine game software is not tampered with, the use of security seals is generally recognized as an effective internal control procedure. A security seal should be placed over all slot machine game program eproms (erasable programmable read-only memory; computer chips), or other equivalent game software media. In addition, the game software circuit board or logic board should be locked or physically sealed within the gaming machine. On at least an annual basis, security seals should be checked to determine if there has been any attempt to tamper with them.

CASINO AUDITING

All businesses that sell goods or perform services, whether for profit or not for profit, should be subject to auditing. Auditing seeks to provide an acceptable level of confidence that a business, and in particular the financial transactions of the business, is conducted with honesty and integrity. Auditing serves to deter and detect theft, embezzlements, scams, or other misappropriation of assets.

The casino industry in particular requires effective auditing because it is a cash-intensive business and a significant number of transactions occur without documentation. A transaction at a gaming table is undocumented when a patron buys in for gaming checks, when a wager is made, when the dealer collects a losing wager, or when the dealer pays out a winning wager. Many transactions at the casino cage involving gaming patrons are also undocumented. When a patron redeems gaming checks for cash, generally no document is created. As previously stated, in this cash-intensive business, the need for auditing is paramount.

Auditing requirements for a casino operation should include aspects of both internal and external auditing. With respect to internal auditing, large casinos maintain an internal audit department; small and midsized casinos often retain outside companies to conduct compliance audits of casino operations. Irrespective of whether the compliance audits are undertaken in-house or through an outside company, the following list includes the types of audits that should be performed on an annual basis:

- Table games
- Slot machines
- Credit issuance and collections
- Complimentary services

- Cage
- Casino software
- Anti–money laundering controls

Persons who perform the internal audit function within a gaming operation must be independent of the departments subject to audit. Independence is obtained through the organizational reporting relationship, as the internal audit department should not report to management of the gaming operation. Rather, the internal audit department should report to the chief executive officer regarding matters of administration and daily operations and should report to an independent audit committee or independent regulatory authority regarding matters of policy, purpose, responsibility, and authority.

With respect to external auditing, most jurisdictions that have authorized casino gaming mandate that casino operations have annual financial statements audited in accordance with generally accepted auditing standards and performed by a qualified independent certified public accountant. An external audit includes examining, on a test basis, evidence supporting the amounts and disclosures in the financial statements. An external audit also includes assessing the accounting principles used and significant estimates made by management, as well as evaluating the overall financial statement presentation.

Audited financial statements prepared annually are often accompanied by the independent certified public accountant's report on material weaknesses in accounting and internal controls. A material weakness is defined as "a condition in which the specific control procedures, or the degree of compliance with them, do not reduce to a relatively low level the risk that errors or irregularities in amounts that would be material in relation to the financial statements being audited may occur and not be detected within a timely period by employees in the normal course of performing their assigned functions" (Statement on Auditing Standards No. 30, "Reporting on Internal Control" [July 1980] [AICPA, *Professional Standards,* Vol. 1], paragraph 62). External auditors work closely with the internal auditors in preparing this report on material weaknesses. The external auditors conduct compliance testing of selected documents, interview selected gaming employees, observe selected gaming employees as they perform their duties, and conduct unannounced observations of various activities, including the collection of drop boxes and the counting and recording of currency and coins in the soft count and hard count rooms.

In conclusion, accounting and internal controls are the primary procedures used to protect the integrity of casino funds and games and are a vitally important part of properly regulated gaming activity. A critical measurement of compliance with these accounting and internal controls is obtained through the process of casino auditing, performed through the objective evaluation of both internal auditors and external accountants.

Chapter 9

Nonnegotiable Chips: Their Use and Cost

Andrew MacDonald
Sean Monaghan

This chapter discusses the use of nonnegotiable chips as an instrument in calculating commissions paid to VIP or international premium players at casinos. The majority of programs operated in Australia and East Asia for premium players are based on turnover and incorporate the use of nonnegotiable chips. Like many industries, casinos reward patrons for visiting their property. The level and type of rewards paid to casino customers can vary greatly depending on the policies of the property, the type of game played, the amount wagered, and the preference of the player.

Casinos pay the highest level of rewards to those players who are prepared to gamble the greatest amount of money. Rewards paid to premium players typically are a combination of complimentary privileges and commissions or rebates. Complimentary privileges can include airfares, transfers, accommodation, food, beverage, and entertainment. Monetary commissions paid back to players can be calculated based on either the front money brought to the casino or, more commonly, on the extent of play undertaken at the casino. Commissions paid based on the extent of play can in turn be paid according to the level of turnover (calculated in terms of theoretical win) or on the amount actually lost by the player.

NONNEGOTIABLE CHIPS

Nonnegotiable chips are a useful addition to a casino's armory of promotional tools. They offer a simple and effective way of tracking

play and are readily accepted, if not demanded, by Asian junket operators. The preference for using nonnegotiable chips is twofold:

1. Nonnegotiable chips allow junket operators and players to accurately track their individual playing activities; they know the
   system works and that it is fully verifiable by themselves.
2. Nonnegotiable chips provide an additional element of entertainment not possible under rebate-on-loss programs. This additional element is created by the fact that commissions based on
   turnover ensure payments are made whether the player loses or
   wins on any particular visit to the casino. Players view this as a
   leveling of the playing field, whereas for the casino it becomes
   irrelevant as the casino operation will achieve a theoretical win
   rate over a given period of activity and given level of turnover.

An understanding of the fundamentals behind the use of nonnegotiable chips is essential if a casino operator is to achieve a suitable balance between a commission payment to junket operators or players
and an acceptable net operating margin. A simple tour through the
systematic process may assist in understanding what nonnegotiable
chips are and how they are used:

1. Junket group arrives at the casino.
2. Deposited front monies are converted into nonnegotiable chip
   purchase vouchers (also known as check credits in some casinos). This is recorded on a nonnegotiable chip purchase voucher
   schedule at the casino cashier.
3. Nonnegotiable chip purchase vouchers are used to buy nonnegotiable chips at the gaming table (usually baccarat).
4. Junket players wager nonnegotiable chips during the course of
   play.
5. Winning wagers are paid in cash (negotiable) chips with the
   nonnegotiable chips remaining as the original wager.
6. Losing wagers are taken by the dealer/croupier and placed in the
   table float.
7. Nonnegotiable chips can only be exchanged for nonnegotiable
   chips.
8. Once the players have exhausted their nonnegotiable chips, they
   take their cash chip winnings and exchange them for nonnego-

tiable chip purchase vouchers at the casino cashier. This exchange is noted in value and added to the player's/group's individual nonnegotiable chip purchase voucher schedule.

9. When the junket group departs, the nonnegotiable chip purchase voucher schedule is totaled and all remaining nonnegotiable chip purchase vouchers are deducted as well as any nonnegotiable chips held. This provides a value for turnover upon which commission is paid. All chip purchase vouchers and chips are converted to a cash equivalent or deducted from personal checks held with a new check value written out.

The commission payment is therefore calculated essentially on the loss of nonnegotiable chips over the period. A common saying that holds some validity is, "Once through the cage equals twice over the tables." What this means is that actual turnover may be calculated using a ratio of 2:1 if nonnegotiable turnover is known. For example, given that baccarat is a fifty-fifty game (excluding ties) and assuming that the bet distribution is $50,000 banker and $50,000 player, then after a single hand the casino will be in possession of a single $50,000 chip and turnover will be equal to $100,000.

Hence, once through the cage, twice across the table. This helps some people understand why on a game such as baccarat, where the house advantage is around 1.25 percent, casino operators are prepared to pay commissions of around 1.5 to 1.8 percent or even higher on nonnegotiable chips. The house advantage can be viewed as being twice as much as normal due to the ratio of actual versus nonnegotiable turnover being 2:1. Thus, baccarat could be viewed as having a house advantage of 2.5 percent on nonnegotiable play or, conversely, the nonnegotiable commission percentages could be halved to bring them back into line with actual turnover. Either way, the same result is achieved.

MATHEMATICAL RATIOS: A SIMPLE GEOMETRIC PROGRESSION

We now consider this more mathematically and find a formula that more aptly defines the ratio. To entirely convert nonnegotiable chips to zero in a theoretical sense, one would have to continue to play until exhaustion. If the theoretical return were obtained after each bet, we would have an equation as follows:

Wager	Residual amount following wagering
1	p
p	p^2
p^2	p^3
p^3	p^4
p^4	p^5
. . . etc.	

where p is the probability of the wager winning. The total amount wagered in this series would equal:

$$1 + p + p^2 + p^3 + p^4, + \ldots, pn$$

This would provide the ratio of actual amount wagered to nonnegotiable losses. This is in fact a simple geometric progression with a solution that may be found in numerous mathematical textbooks. That solution is:

$$R = 1/(1 - p)$$

where R = ratio.

What, then, of nonnegotiable chips and baccarat? In this case, the probability of the wager winning (p) is equal to 0.4932 for player and 0.5068 for bank based on relative probabilities (which is correct given that ties have no effect on nonnegotiables). Thus

$$\begin{aligned} R &= 1/(1 - p) \\ &= 1/(1 - 0.4932) \text{ for player} \\ &= 1.97 \end{aligned}$$

or

$$\begin{aligned} R &= 1/(1 - p) \\ &= 1/(1 - 0.5068) \text{ for bank} \\ &= 2.03 \end{aligned}$$

If equal amounts were bet on both player and bank, then p would equal 0.5. R would then equal $1/(1 - p) = 1/0.5 = 2$.

What about other noneven payoff games such as roulette? Using single-zero roulette for our example, p would equal the following. Straight-ups:

$$p = 0.027$$
$$R = 1.028$$

Dozens and columns:

$$p = 0.324$$
$$R = 1.480$$

Even chances:

$$p = 0.486$$
$$R = 1.947$$

As shown, the ratio of actual turnover to nonnegotiable losses is not fixed, but rather is a function of the probability associated with the individual game and the particular wager placed. Thus, our truism, "Once through the cage equals twice over the tables" is roughly valid only for even-chance games with a low house margin. If nonnegotiables are played solely on straight-ups on roulette (for example) the ratio is much closer to one.

How is this additional information of use? When constructing commission programs using nonnegotiable chips, it is essential to understand the cost of the program. Let us look at several simple examples and assess this in table form. Baccarat: (equal play on player and bank); edge: 1.26 percent.

Theoretical turnover	= 2 × cage turnover
Casino tax	= 20 percent win (example only)
Theoretical win	= edge × turnover
	= 1.26 percent × (2 × cage turnover)
	= 2.52 percent × cage turnover
Theoretical win (after tax)	= 2.52 percent × cage turnover
	− 20 percent (win)

Win after tax   = 2.016 percent × cage turnover
                                  = 2.016 percent per turn

REVENUE CALCULATION COMPARISONS FOR VARIOUS GAMES AFTER TAX

From the information in Table 9.1, it is possible to calculate the effect of offering various commission percentages. If commission was set at, for example, 1.5 percent of nonnegotiable turnover, then the net edge for the various games can be calculated as shown in Table 9.2.

Nonnegotiable Chip Use on Roulette

Although some casino operators have shown a reluctance to use nonnegotiable chips on games such as roulette, clearly this discussion should dispel it. Of course, if the group prefers to play roulette for no commission or at a reduced cash chip rate, so much the better. Conversely, by not allowing nonnegotiables to be played on roulette, an important segment of the market may not be tapped and, by neglect, casino operators and managers are encouraging players to play lower-margin games.

TABLE 9.1. House edge of various games.

Game	Wager	Edge (%)	Theoretical turn: cage turn	Edge per turn (%)	Edge less tax per turn (%)
Baccarat	Player	1.36	1.9732	2.6836	2.1468
	Banker	1.37	2.0276	2.3723	1.8978
	Tie	1.26	2.0000	2.5200	2.0160
Blackjack	Even	2.70	1.9470	5.2569	4.2055
Roulette	Even chances	2.70	1.9470	5.2569	4.2055
	Straight-ups	2.70	1.0280	2.7756	2.2205
	Dozens/ columns	2.70	1.4800	3.9960	3.1968

TABLE 9.2. The effect of offering commission.

Game	Wager	Edge per turn (%)	Edge less tax per turn (%)	Commission (example only) (%)	Net (%)
Baccarat	Player	2.6836	2.1468	1.5	0.6468
	Bank	2.3723	1.8978	1.5	0.3978
	Tie	2.5200	2.016	1.5	0.5160
Roulette	Even chance	5.2569	4.2055	1.5	2.7055
	Straight-ups	2.7756	2.2205	1.5	0.7205
	Dozens/ columns	3.9960	3.1968	1.5	1.6968

Could this be initiated quickly and simply into a casino already offering nonnegotiable junket programs and commissions? Yes. The stroke of a pen would do it, subject to appropriate regulatory approvals being obtained. The rates of commission, method of calculation, and operating procedures would remain unchanged.

OTHER METHODS OF EXPLANATION

Let us now look at other potential methods of explanation of nonnegotiable chip usage. This may assist those not comfortable with the mathematics or those wishing to explain simply to casino staff.

Consider the game of baccarat. The player buys in for two units at the cashier and is provided nonnegotiable chip purchase vouchers. These are taken to the gaming table and two units are purchased. One unit is placed on player, the other on bank. Player is the winning result and thus bank loses (–1 nonnegotiable unit). Player is paid in cash chips.

The player then takes this cash chip unit to the casino cashier cage and converts it into a nonnegotiable chip purchase voucher of one unit. The player returns to the table and converts the chip purchase voucher to a nonnegotiable chip and again wagers one nonnegotiable unit on player and one nonnegotiable unit on bank. This time bank wins and the player is paid 0.95 of a unit in cash chips and loses one nonnegotiable unit. If the player now leaves, we have the following:

Initial deposit	= 2 units
Subsequent deposit/conversion	= 1 unit
Total	= 3 units
Retained final nonnegotiable unit	= 1 unit
Nonnegotiable turnover	= 3 – 1
	= 2 units
Actual turnover	= 4 units (2 units × 2 decisions)
Loss	= 0.05 unit (cash out 1 unit non-negotiable + 0.95 unit cash)
Ratio of actual turnover to non-negotiable turnover	= 4/2 = 2
House advantage	= 0.05/4
	= 1.25 percent of actual turnover
House advantage	= 0.05/2
	= 2.5 percent of nonnegotiable turnover

This calculation reasonably represents the theoretical and probabilistic processes involved. The same scenario can be followed through for single-zero roulette, again using a full-cycle approach.

Initial deposit	= 37 units
Cover all numbers and zero on roulette table	
Loss in nonnegotiables	= 36 units
Gain in cash chips	= 35 units
Retained nonnegotiables	= 1 unit
Actual turnover	= 37 units
Nonnegotiable turnover	= 36 units
Actual loss	= 1 unit
Ratio of actual to nonnegotiable turnover	= 37/36 = 1.028
House advantage	= 1/37 on actual turnover
	= 2.70 percent

House advantage	= 1/36 on nonnegotiable turnover
	= 2.78 percent

Thus, another way of expressing the ratio of actual turnover to nonnegotiable turnover rather than $R = 1/(1 - p)$ is:

1 + retained nonnegotiables / loss in nonnegotiables

in a full cycle.

GLOSSARY

buy-in/front money: Customer deposit at the casino cage used for gaming purposes in place of a line of credit. The customer plays at the tables as if using a line of credit, which will be applied against the deposit.

commission-based play (also referred to as VIP and international play): Play from customers where a commission is paid to secure the activity, typically for customers with more than US$25,000 initial buy-in.

complimentary: Also known as a comp, enables free use of casino services, such as hotel rooms or restaurants. Complimentary privileges are offered to patrons as part of incentive programs based on play volume/activity.

drop: For table games, refers to the total amount of currency and chip purchase vouchers, complimentary bet vouchers, and so on.

hold percentage: Refers to the percentage calculated by dividing the win by the drop. Calculated by individual table as well as by game type, day or shift, and period to date. Used by casino management as a key performance indicator.

junket: A group of players who travel to the casino specifically for the purpose of gaming. The travel is prearranged through a junket operator.

junket operator: The individual who is responsible for organizing junket trips. Usually an independent agent, who negotiates a commission for players of the junket group and is paid a commission by the casino based on turnover activity of the junket group.

theoretical win: The theoretical casino win based on turnover and house edge. The house edge is calculated based upon the actual mix of games.

turnover: Total amount wagered, also known as handle.

SECTION III:
GAMING AND SOCIETY

Chapter 10

Social Impacts of Gambling in Australia

Nerilee Hing

The unprecedented growth and expansion of gambling in Australia in the past two decades—particularly casino and machine gambling—have been accompanied by a range of impacts, both social and economic. This chapter provides an overview of these impacts and notes that, in Australia, most attention has been given to one particular social impact of gambling—problem gambling and its associated costs. Given its dominance in current policy debates in Australia, problem gambling is the major focus of this chapter. After identifying what problem gambling is and the range of impacts it has, the chapter explains why it has emerged as an important social issue in Australia, and details the range of remedies that governments and gambling providers have pursued. Following a public health approach to problem gambling, many gambling providers have implemented a variety of responsible gambling measures to improve harm minimization and consumer protection in gambling. This chapter identifies these measures and some opportunities and challenges facing gambling providers in implementing them and in achieving outcomes that effectively address problem gambling.

THE IMPACTS OF GAMBLING

The impacts of gambling apply to various parties. Some apply directly to people who work in gambling industries; some apply indirectly to people who work in other industries; some affect those who partake in gambling activities and the people they interact with; while other impacts operate at the community-wide level (Productivity Commission, 1999). The first and only Australian national enquiry into gambling (Productivity Commission, 1999) compiled the following listing of impacts of gambling:

- *Impacts within the industry.* These include income and job satisfaction for gambling employees, rent for gambling venue owners, profits (or sometimes losses) for investors, and taxes for governments.
- *Impacts on other industries.* Gambling boosts jobs and profits in related industries that supply the gambling industry's needs (e.g., gaming machine manufacturers or the horse racing industry) or receive flow-on boosts because they complement gambling (e.g., taxis and restaurants that gain customers). However, the gambling industry competes with other industries for the consumer dollar, so gambling impacts the jobs, profits, investment, and taxes paid in those industries.
- *Impacts on gamblers.* It requires time, money, and concentration to gamble; gambling can cause feelings from great joy to great despair for some people; and gambling may affect the day-to-day mood of some people who now get out of the house to patronize gambling venues where previously they may have stayed at home instead.
- *Impacts of problem gambling.* Where problem gambling occurs, it affects the gamblers concerned and sometimes also their families, friends, work colleagues, employers, governments, welfare agencies, and the police, court, legal, and prison systems.
- *Impacts on the community.* Gambling can impact the nature and feel of community life through, for example, the services provided by community clubs from gambling revenues; the nature and provision of entertainment venues and recreational activities and the type of interaction people in the community experience; people's general feelings about the community they live in; and people's behavioral norms and social ethics and, through them, the way people act in relationship to others in all aspects of life.
- *Impacts on people's interests and activities.* The growth of gambling has provided a new or heightened source of interest and action for some individuals, the media, consultants, lobby groups, government bodies, policy advisers, ministers, and parliaments.

Clearly, some of these impacts of gambling are primarily economic in nature and are addressed in Chapter 11. Of the impacts that are primarily social in nature, problem gambling and its impacts have captured the most attention in Australia. Thus, the remainder of this chapter focuses on problem gambling and how various stakeholders are now grappling with ways to reduce the costs of problem gambling while retaining the recreational benefits of gambling.

PROBLEM GAMBLING IN AUSTRALIA AND ITS IMPACTS

A definition of problem gambling that has gained wide acceptance in Australia is "the situation when a person's gambling activity gives rise to harm to the individual player, and/or to his or her family, and may extend into the community" (Australian Institute for Gambling Research, 1997, p. 106). The Productivity Commission (1999) estimated that approximately 1 percent of the adult Australian population (around 130,000 people) had severe problems with gambling, while an additional 1.1 percent (160,000) had moderate problems, making a pool of approximately 290,000 problem gamblers, or 2.1 percent of adult Australians.

As the definition suggests, the impacts of problem gambling can be widespread. Focusing on the personal consequences of problem gambling, Lesieur (1996) cited depression, insomnia, intestinal disorders, anxiety attacks, cardiac problems, high blood pressure, migraines, suicidal tendencies, and other stress-related disorders as typical problems in more advanced stages. He noted that the gambler's family can also bear the costs, particularly the financial burden. Added debt may mean fewer family expenditures, overdue bills, utilities cut off, belongings repossessed or sold, or the family left homeless. Spouses often are harassed by bill collectors and may experience insomnia, stress-related problems, and suicidal tendencies. The gambler's lies and deception compound marital problems, contributing to family dysfunction and increased likelihood of child abuse and neglect. In the workplace, lateness, absenteeism, extended lunch hours, and leaving work early are common occurrences, while people may misuse company time by gambling on the job, or through irritability, moodiness, and poor concentration. They may borrow from work colleagues, seek advances on paychecks, or embezzle from the company. After exhausting savings, rent money, and lines of credit, they may resort to illegal activities, including loan fraud, check forgery and bouncing, embezzlement, and other white-collar crimes, which in turn pose criminal justice, court, and bankruptcy costs (Lesieur, 1996). Provision of services to assist problem gamblers and their families can be added to these community costs. Taking these widespread types of impacts into account, the Productivity Commission (1999) found that for each person experiencing gambling problems in Australia, at least five others in the community are likely to be affected.

Although these estimates indicate that the number of problem gamblers represents a very small minority of the Australian population, national survey data suggested that problem gamblers comprise around 15 percent of regular, nonlottery gamblers. Further, their losses account for approximately 30 percent of gambling industry revenues and over 40 percent of machine gaming revenues, or about $3.6 billion per year. This represents average gambling losses for problem gamblers of around $12,000 per head or 22.1 percent of household income (before tax) (Productivity Commission, 1999).

Because of the scope and severity of its impacts, problem gambling has become an important social issue in Australia, one requiring consideration as a public health problem rather than a problem confined to a small number of unfortunate individuals. The following discussion provides further explanation for the increased acceptance of this view in Australia.

THE RISE OF PROBLEM GAMBLING AS A SOCIAL ISSUE IN AUSTRALIA

Many factors can be identified that have catalyzed the rise of problem gambling as a social issue in Australia, reflecting concern for its social impacts:

1. A change in the conceptualization of problem gambling. Pathological, compulsive, addictive, excessive, and problem gambling are terms used to describe frequent, uncontrolled gambling causing harm (Caldwell, Young, Dickerson, & McMillen, 1988). Although historically the behavior has been viewed primarily as an individual affliction related to a mental disorder, an

addiction, or excessive behavior, more recently it has been conceptualized as a behavior that leads to social and individual harm (Australian Institute for Gambling Research, 1997). This has nurtured a public health approach to problem gambling in Australia.

2. Shifts in government policy on gambling. In Australia, gambling policy, regulation, and taxation are state government responsibilities. Although these governments generally agree on the broad objectives of gambling policy as maximizing revenue, minimizing social impacts, ensuring product integrity, and deterring criminal involvement (Productivity Commission, 1999), it is their prioritization of these sometimes conflicting objectives that have influenced the emergence of problem gambling as a social issue. What has been observed in Australia is a general move toward prioritizing the economic returns from gambling over minimizing its social impacts. Thus, market stimulation, expansion, and competition have characterized government policy on gambling since the 1970s (McMillen, 1996).

3. Increased expansion and commercialization of gambling. Gambling expenditure in Australia continues to escalate, providing robust returns to gambling providers, such as casinos, hotels, and clubs (Tasmanian Gaming Commission, 2002; Productivity Commission, 1999). Many providers have capitalized on gambling's apparent immunity to fluctuating economic conditions and sympathetic government policies by adopting an expansionist approach. This has resulted in easy access to gambling, particularly continuous forms; a proliferation of gambling options; and aggressive marketing. These factors have heightened public concern for gambling-related problems and calls for more socially responsible provision of gambling.

4. Heightened pressure from lobbyists for reforms that address the social impacts of gambling. Until the early 1900s, opposition to gambling was framed mainly in the moral arguments advanced by the churches and conservative middle classes (Sylvan & Sylvan, 1985). However, with increased secularization, more liberal social attitudes, and the institutionalization of gambling as a culturally acceptable leisure activity, arguments against gambling have focused increasingly on its social impacts and have

emanated from a wider variety of stakeholders, more often advocating restriction and control than abolition. Stakeholders calling for gambling reform have increasingly focused on problem gambling and its harmful social effects as their major concern, placing responsibility squarely on the shoulders of governments and gambling operators, with gamblers often depicted as victims of irresponsible, predatory practices.

The many developments in Australia have collectively drawn attention to problem gambling as a serious social impact of gambling, one requiring recognition as a public health issue. As explained next, the increased acceptance of this view point has prompted calls for better harm minimization and consumer protection measures in the provision of gambling.

A PUBLIC HEALTH APPROACH
TO PROBLEM GAMBLING:
THE ROLE OF HARM MINIMIZATION
AND CONSUMER PROTECTION

It is apparent that problem gambling now tends to be defined in Australia in terms of its social impacts, rather than its underlying medical causes or psychological processes. This view recognizes that the impacts from gambling are contextually based according to factors such as income, gender, life cycle, traditions, and social norms and values (Australian Institute for Gambling Research, 1997). The Productivity Commission (1999) also supports this view, with these findings:

- Problem gambling is generally not regarded as a mental illness for the bulk of the people who are affected by it, but some will need clinical assistance to resolve their problems.
- Problem gambling is not only about people with severe problems or those needing counseling help. It is very important to see problem gambling as a continuum—with some people having moderate problems and others more severe ones.
- Public policy is appropriately directed at those who need help to resolve their problems, those whose lives are adversely affected

without needing clinical or counseling intervention, and those who are at risk of developing problems.

- Problem gambling should be seen as a public health issue. The goal is not to eliminate all gambling problems, but to reduce risks in a cost-effective manner.

This redefining of problem gambling places unprecedented pressure on governments and gambling providers in particular to implement policy, management, and marketing strategies to address problem gambling. Thus, a public health approach to dealing with problem gambling is now favored, one that emphasizes the need for harm minimization and consumer protection strategies in gambling, rather than just the provision of assistance to gamblers once they have developed problems.

GOVERNMENT RESPONSES TO PROBLEM GAMBLING

The emergence of problem gambling as a public health issue in Australia has prompted a shift toward government policy frameworks and regulations that focus on more responsible provision of gambling through better harm minimization and consumer protection. However, approaches taken by the governments of the six states and two territories in Australia generally have been diverse and fragmented, reflecting varying levels of commitment to reducing the negative social impacts of gambling. These approaches can be grouped into categories of legislation, funding, provision of direct services for problem gambling, research, and community education about gambling.

Legislation for Responsible Gambling

To advance consumer protection, all Australian state governments have legislated minimum returns to players, outlawed underage and credit betting, and established substantial monitoring and control systems in all jurisdictions (McMillen, 1996). Beyond these requirements, however, there is substantial variation. For example, New South Wales (NSW) is the only Australian jurisdiction that has introduced responsible gambling acts and regulations that apply to all gambling sectors in that state. The Gambling Legislation Amendment (Responsible Gambling) Act 1999 of New South Wales has the expressed purpose "to amend certain Acts to minimise the harm associated with the misuse and abuse of gambling activities (and) to promote the responsible conduct of gambling activities" (p. 1). It introduced regulations for gambling-related advertising and inducements, management and staff training in responsible gambling, display of problem gambling signage, provision of product information, placement of automatic teller machines (ATM) and electronic funds transfer at point of sale (EFTPOS) facilities, and removal of legal impediments to self-exclusion.

In other states and territories, acts and regulations prescribing responsible gambling measures apply to only one or a limited range of gambling sectors in that jurisdiction. This has resulted in different requirements for different types of gambling. For example, in Queensland and the Australian Capital Territory, responsible gambling obligations are more stringent for casinos than for hotels and clubs. In South Australia, the situation is reversed. Mandatory obligations for Totalisator Agency Boards (TABs) and lotteries are typically less demanding than those for gaming machine venues.

Other jurisdictions are taking a staged approach to legislating more responsible gambling measures. For example, in Victoria, the Gaming Machine Control Act 1991 VIC requires gaming machine venues to allow self-exclusion, to comply with certain rules pertaining to machine gaming competitions, to adhere to special requirements for restricted areas, to locate ATM and EFTPOS facilities outside gaming areas, and to prohibit provision of cash for gaming purposes from credit card or charge transactions. The Gambling Legislation (Responsible Gambling) Act 2000 of Victoria then extended these requirements to embrace its objective of "fostering responsible gambling in order to minimise harm caused by problem gambling" and "accommodate those who gamble without harming themselves or others" (p. 1) The act froze the number of gaming machines in Victoria, provided for the determination of maximum numbers of gaming machines on a regional basis, restricted twenty-four-hour licenses, required applications for new gaming licenses to address economic and social impacts on the local community, provided for the views of municipal councils to be considered regarding placement of gaming machines in that district, established the Gambling Research Panel, and provided for regulations on gambling-related advertising and provision of player information. A further stage of reform in mid-2001 required clocks to be installed on all gaming machines and natural lighting in gaming machine venues.

A further variation can be observed in Queensland, where the government has supported the development of a voluntary code of practice for gambling providers, rather than stringent regulation. Nevertheless, a legislative approach may follow if the voluntary code is not widely embraced.

Funding

Most Australian state and territory governments either impose a levy on certain gambling sectors, usually casinos, hotels, and clubs, to raise funds for specific community projects, including those that address problem gambling, or they fund problem gambling services from a percentage of gambling revenues. The exceptions are Western Australia and South Australia, which rely on voluntary contributions from industry.

Direct Services for Problem Gambling

Although general community, health, welfare, financial, and legal services in Australia sometimes deal with problem gambling, specific problem gambling services have been established relatively recently (other than self-help groups such as Gamblers Anonymous and Gam-Anon). Governments and industry in most jurisdictions fund two types of problem gambling support services (Productivity Commission, 1999):

1. A network of problem gambling counseling and support services; in all states except New South Wales, a geographically based network has been established called Break Even to provide free counseling to gamblers, their families, and friends.
2. A twenty-four-hour help line to provide immediate crisis counseling, an information and referral service, and ongoing support.

Problem Gambling Research Programs

Many Australian governments direct a proportion of industry levies to research on gambling, typically into areas such as its social and economic impacts, the effectiveness of harm minimization measures, and the efficacy of problem gambling treatment approaches. For example, the NSW Casino Community Benefit Fund regularly invites grant applications for research into the social and economic impact of gambling on individuals, families, and the general community. A different approach is taken by the Victorian Gambling Research Panel, which develops an annual research program and then tenders out the projects involved. The Queensland Research and Community Engagement Division of Queensland Treasury operates both a tender system and a grant application process.

Community Education

Broad-based education programs aim to minimize harm from gambling through education about responsible gambling strategies and the risk factors, symptoms, and effects of problem gambling. Comprehensive community education strategies have been implemented only in the Australian jurisdictions of Victoria and Queensland. Victoria has had three television, radio, and billboard campaigns, each evaluated and linked to impacts on its telephone hotline and other services (Wootton, 1996). The more recent Responsible Gambling Community Awareness Campaign in Queensland has the key message of "Don't let gambling control you" with the tagline "Gamble responsibly" to reaffirm and reinforce the responsible gambling behaviors that most gamblers already utilize. These messages are reflected in a series of innovative advertisements targeting regular gamblers, focusing on the mainstream population aged eighteen to thirty-four. The campaign materials are displayed in licensed venues, newspapers, buses, taxis, bus shelters, radio, and cinema, with specialist messages developed for universities (Queensland Treasury, 2005). Victoria is also developing gambling education guidelines for primary and secondary schools, while the Queensland government has introduced two modules into the school curriculum—Gambling with Health: Building Communication Skills, and Gambling: Minimising Health Risks (Productivity Commission, 1999). In other states, community education has been limited mainly to the work of Break Even officers who liaise with industry, community health and welfare agencies, and the general community to raise awareness (Anglicare, 1996).

In summary, government initiatives to address problem gambling have increased in recent years. Although these efforts are laudable, most Australian state governments rely on gambling revenues for around 12 percent of their taxation base (Productivity Commission, 1999), and so are unlikely to introduce measures that will substantially reduce gambling revenues. Instead, the onus has been on gambling providers to introduce responsible gambling measures at the venue level.

INDUSTRY RESPONSES TO PROBLEM GAMBLING

Many jurisdictions, gambling industry sectors, and gambling providers have introduced responsible gambling programs and codes of conduct in recent years. A comprehensive audit (Hing, Dickerson, & Mackellar, 2001) identified and examined thirty voluntary responsible gambling codes operating in Australia in 2001. This section identifies and comments on the range of responsible gambling practices found in these codes, grouped according to how they address the public health objectives of harm minimization and consumer protection.

Harm Minimization Measures

Consumer Education

Consumer education involves alerting consumers to the risks of problem gambling and advice on gambling responsibly. Some types of information advocated include what problem gambling is; that problem gamblers are people of all ages, sexes, and backgrounds; its signs (such as chasing losses and loss of control); its risk factors (such as depression or stress); its consequences (such as poverty, job loss, relationship breakdown); and advice on where to obtain help (Productivity Commission, 1999). However, current industry efforts focus mainly on providing contact details for problem gambling support services, with warning messages and checklists of problem gambling indicators sometimes included. This information typically is contained on posters, brochures, and wallet cards located in gambling areas, toilets, and near ATM and change facilities. Such messages could also be incorporated into gaming machine screens, but this practice is uncommon. Limited problem gambling information is available at most TAB and lottery outlets.

Problem Gambling Warnings

Where used by gambling providers, these tend to be much less hard hitting than those used in other public health campaigns (Productivity Commission, 1999). Some slogans used in Australia include "Bet with your head, not over it"; "Your best bet is the one you can afford"; "Be a winner, just play for fun"; and "Have fun, but play it safe." In raising awareness of safety issues in gambling, there appears to be considerable scope to learn from measures adopted in other public health areas and for research into the efficacy of alternative messages, media, slogans, and placement of problem gambling information.

Access to ATMs and EFTPOS

Because ready access to funds from venue-based ATMs and EFTPOS can contribute to harm arising from gambling, there are grounds for restrictions on multiple withdrawals and on withdrawal amounts from venue-based ATMs, and ultimately an outright ban (Productivity Commission, 1999). In some Australian jurisdictions, ATM and EFTPOS facilities by law cannot be located in gambling areas within casinos, clubs, and hotels. In others, some venues have voluntarily removed ATMs and EFTPOS from gambling areas, while other codes of practice encourage this as a voluntary measure. ATMs in many venues allow only the withdrawal of cash from savings or checking accounts. The National Australia Bank has removed its ATMs from gambling venues as a harm minimization measure.

Restrictions on Check Cashing

Although there are some mandatory restrictions on check cashing in gambling venues, some gambling providers have pursued voluntary restrictions. However, even among the voluntary Australian codes that restrict check cashing, very few impose an outright ban in the venue, with considerable variation in the other restrictions imposed. For example, some industry codes do not allow any checks to be cashed in gambling areas; some restrict the cashing of third-party and multiple checks; and others set a daily monetary limit.

Check Payment of Winnings

Partial payment of large wins by check is mandatory for some gambling providers in Australia, as both a harm minimization and a security measure. Others have voluntary policies in place. Some provide for venue operators to encourage patrons with large wins to have a cooling-off period and take payment by check. Others establish a limit, often between A$1,000 and A$2,000, above which all winnings are paid by check or electronic transfer.

Reality Checks

Prominent display of clocks within sight of people gambling can help people keep track of the time spent gambling and provide a reality check. Outside the Australian jurisdictions where this is mandatory and in TABs where this is an essential business practice, some gambling providers voluntarily display clocks in gambling areas. Others have windows and natural lighting also to help people keep track of time while gambling.

Encouraging Breaks in Play

Some gambling venues must, by law, close for at least a few hours each day. By not providing food, drink, and change service to gaming rooms, venues also encourage players to take breaks in play.

Precommitment Strategies

Precommitment stategies operate where players can nominate betting limits per session, per week, or for some other period of time. Although such measures have had limited use in Australia, restricted mainly to some online gambling operations, advances in technology and the emergence of cashless gaming using smart cards provide further opportunities for gamblers to make enforceable decisions on expenditure before they start gambling.

Restrictions on Staff Gambling

Staff working in gambling venues may represent an at-risk group of patrons. Although staff are prohibited by law from gambling in their workplace in some Australian jurisdictions, casinos, clubs, and hotels in most others voluntarily prohibit gambling by staff in their venues.

Restrictions on Gambling by Intoxicated Persons

Clearly, intoxicated persons have diminished capacity for informed consent in their gambling decisions. The liquor licensing acts in Australia prohibit service of intoxicated persons in licensed venues, which many gambling venues are. Many voluntary responsible gambling codes suggest procedures for assessing intoxication and refusal of service.

Self-Exclusion

All Australian casinos, clubs, and hotels with voluntary responsible gambling programs have self-exclusion procedures. These generally involve a written contractual agreement between the venue and patron, and direction to problem gambling support services. Most are operated in-house, although some take a sectorwide approach. For example, self-exclusion from hotels and clubs in Victoria allows patrons to self-exclude from a range of self-nominated venues. Another variation is the minimum time period for self-exclusion. Some programs leave this to the patron's discretion, while others nominate a minimum period, often three to six months. Although self-exclusion can be a useful adjunct to other measures by encouraging problem gamblers to confront and act on their problems and by facilitating access to counseling and support services (Productivity Commission, 1999), it has a number of inherent weaknesses—it relies on recognition of a problem by the gamblers, limiting effectiveness for those in denial; self-excludees can circumvent exclusion from one venue by going to another; it can be difficult for venues to monitor and enforce; where breaches of self-exclusion incur fines, this compounds financial problems typically experienced by problem gamblers; it requires legal impediments to be removed such that the gamblers, not the venue, are liable for breaches; it requires venues to provide patrons information about this option and how it works; and it requires incentives for venues to enforce and promote the measure (Productivity Commission, 1999).

Direct Counseling

Some large gambling venues provide direct counseling for patrons, through either retaining counselors on staff or arrangements with counseling services to provide crisis intervention.

Consumer Protection Measures

Product Information

To optimize informed purchasing decisions, basic information that gambling operators might provide for consumers includes information on the price of different forms of gambling where this is not already transparent, expressed as odds of winning, loss rates, and the likelihood of key payouts; and information on how games work and the most frequent misunderstandings about them (Productivity Commission, 1999). Nearly all Australian gambling operators provide some product information for players, but this varies from simply providing game rules to patrons on request, to comprehensive brochures explaining different bet types, game options, and odds of winning. There is scope to learn from approaches used for other public health issues that have assessed the most effective content and media for relaying product information and the extent to which this changes purchasing behavior. At present, no such research has been conducted for gambling products.

Responsible Advertising and Promotions

Although advertising and promotion of gambling are constrained by trade practices legislation, they have been criticized for being weakly controlled and ignoring whether gambling warrants special treatment beyond that applied to most other products. There may be grounds for tighter advertising controls where information reinforces false beliefs about winning or the way that gambling technologies work and for all gambling advertising to incorporate risk warnings about the product (Productivity Commission, 1999). Many responsible gambling codes of practice in Australia provide guidelines for responsible advertising, while some are a specific advertising code of ethics. Typical inclusions are legal compliance; target audiences age eighteen years and over; good taste in advertising to not offend community standards; no false, misleading, and deceptive advertising; and no association between gambling and alcohol. However, a major weakness in these codes is that many of their provisions require voluntary compliance.

Consumer Complaints Mechanisms

Regulatory bodies in all Australian jurisdictions have responsibilities in handling consumer complaints. However, questions have been raised over their effectiveness, particularly where these are not independent of government (Independent Pricing and Regulatory Tribunal of NSW, 1998; Productivity Commission, 1999). Although these are essentially regulatory issues beyond the responsibility of gambling providers, venues can inform consumers of avenues for complaints. Many voluntary codes in Australia remind gambling providers of these avenues, and some venues display signage to inform consumers.

Privacy Mechanisms

Although gambling providers are regulated by general privacy legislation applicable to all traders, some face additional requirements.

Some responsible gambling codes in Australia reinforce these legislated requirements to safeguard player information and the publicity of prizewinners. However, in the context of increased data collection from technologies such as player cards, and also from Internet and phone betting accounts, and with the more common usage of exclusion schemes, which by necessity must be relayed to staff in gambling venues, player privacy mechanisms could warrant additional attention in responsible gambling codes of practice.

THE EFFECTIVENESS
OF RESPONSIBLE GAMBLING MEASURES

Having outlined some approaches taken by industry in responsible gambling programs in Australia, an obvious question is, how effective are they? This section considers this question in terms of three types of effectiveness that might be measured—the effectiveness of the implementation of the programs, their effectiveness in changing gamblers' behaviors, and their effectiveness in reducing problem gambling. This analysis is consistent with models of evaluating public health programs in general, which identify three types of evaluation—process evaluation, impact evaluation, and outcome evaluation (Hawe, Degeling, & Hall, 1990). The following discussion considers the effectiveness of responsible gambling programs in Australia in terms of these three aspects.

Process Evaluation: Effectiveness of Program Implementation

Process evaluation measures the success of a public health program in providing and delivering what was planned (Hawe et al., 1990). That is, it evaluates how successfully the program has been implemented. Because many responsible gambling programs in Australia are voluntary and have been developed by industry associations rather than individual gambling providers, the processes used to publicize these programs, disseminate program materials, train management and staff, and generally support program implementation are vital to optimizing compliance rates among the gambling venues. Some typical support mechanisms in such programs include steering and advisory committees, mechanisms to facilitate community liaison, management and staff training, and the provision of implementation manuals, responsible gambling signage, and other supporting collaterals.

Although the aforementioned audit of responsible gambling codes in Australia (Hing et al., 2001) found that most had support of this kind, a major difficulty for these voluntary programs is providing incentives for compliance or disincentives for noncompliance. Where a code applies to only one venue, such as a casino, management can monitor compliance in ways similar to monitoring compliance with other organizational policies. However, where a code has been developed for whole sectors or states, compliance mechanisms are limited, with industry associations and steering committees having few powers to enforce such measures. Where compliance rates are monitored, these usually are based on a self-auditing system, rather than an independent process evaluation.

Impact Evaluation: Effectiveness in Changing Gamblers' Behaviors

Impact evaluation assesses whether the public health program has brought about the desired change in the behavior of the target group and whether it has achieved the desired reduction of contributing risk factors associated with the health problem (Hawe et al., 1990). Thus, this type of evaluation of responsible gambling programs would assess whether and to what extent the implemented measures have led to gamblers adopting more responsible gambling behaviors, such as not spending more than they can afford, not gambling for longer than planned, making informed decisions about their gambling, or knowing how to lodge a gambling-related complaint. To date, no such evaluations of responsible gambling programs have been conducted in Australia.

Outcome Evaluation: Effectiveness in Reducing Problem Gambling

Outcome evaluation focuses on measuring the longer-term effects of a health program and usually corresponds with evaluating its success in bringing about the desired change in the health problem (Hawe et al., 1990). For responsible gambling programs, such an evaluation would involve assessing whether and to what extent the program has reduced problem gambling. Again, no such evaluations have been conducted in Australia. Instead, all existing responsible gambling programs have been developed using a top-down approach, developing practices and processes that are assumed to reduce problem gambling and promote responsible gambling. What is needed is a bottom-up approach that evaluates which practices are actually effective in addressing problem gambling. However, inherent challenges would be encountered in such an evaluation. These challenges include the need for a prevalence study of problem gambling in a community before and after program implementation, isolating the effects of the program from other intervening effects, and ensuring that any measure of problem gambling is valid, reliable, and robust.

CONCLUSION

Many advances have been made in Australia in addressing the most apparent social impact of gambling—problem gambling. Reconceptualizing it as a public health issue has been central to this advancement. Korn and Shaffer (1999) pointed out that such a perspective focuses attention on all levels of prevention, as well as treatment and rehabilitation issues, and on the influence of organizational and political behavior on problem gambling, not just individual behavior. They also noted that viewing problem gambling through a public health lens can encourage multiple strategies and points of intervention because it recognizes a continuum of risk, resiliency, and protective factors that can influence the development and maintenance of gambling-related problems. Some of these multiple strategies have been implemented in Australia, with this chapter detailing those pursued by governments and gambling providers. However, further progress is required to ensure the widespread and consistent implementation of these measures, their efficacy in changing risky gambling behaviors, and their effectiveness in reducing problem gambling.

REFERENCES

Anglicare. (1996). *More than just bob each way: Tasmania takes the gamble out of service delivery*. Hobart: Department of Premier and Cabinet.

Australian Institute for Gambling Research. (1997). *Definition and incidence of problem gambling, including the socio-economic distribution of gamblers*. Melbourne: Victorian Casino and Gaming Authority.

Caldwell, G. T., Young, S., Dickerson, M. G., & McMillen, J. (1988). *Social impact study, Civic section 19 development and casino: Casino development for Canberra: Social impact report*. Canberra: Australian Government Publishing Service.

Hawe, P., Degeling, D., & Hall, J. (1990). *Evaluating health promotion: A health worker's guide*. Sydney: MacLennan and Petty.

Hing, N., Dickerson, M. G., & Mackellar, J. (2001). *Australian Gaming Council summary responsible gambling document*. Melbourne: Australian Gaming Council.

Independent Pricing and Regulatory Tribunal of NSW. (1998). *Report to government: Inquiry into gaming in NSW*. Sydney: Author.

Korn, D., & Shaffer, H. (1999). Gambling and the health of the public: Adopting a public health perspective. *Journal of Gambling Studies, 15*(4), 289-365.

Lesieur, H. (1996). Measuring the costs of pathological gambling. In B. Tolchard (Ed.), *Toward 2000: The future of gambling, proceedings of seventh national conference of the National Association for Gambling Studies* (pp. 11-22). Adelaide: National Association for Gambling Studies.

McMillen, J. (1996). *Perspectives on Australian gambling policy: Changes and challenges*. Paper presented at the National Conference on Gambling, Darling Harbour, Sydney.

Productivity Commission. (1999). *Australia's gambling industries* (Report No. 10). Canberra: AusInfo.

Queensland Treasury. (2005). *Responsible Gambling Community Awareness Campaign*. Available online at: http://www.responsiblegambling.qld.gov.au/gamble =resp/awareness=camp/index.shtml.

Sylvan, R., & Sylvan, L. (1985). The ethics of gambling. In G. Caldwell, B. Haig, M. G. Dickerson, & L. Sylvan (Eds.), *Gambling in Australia* (pp. 217-231). Sydney: Croomhelm Australia.

Tasmanian Gaming Commission. (2002). *Australian gambling statistics 1975-76 to 2000-01*. Hobart: Author.

Wootton, R. (1996). Problem gambling: A successful community education program in Victoria. In B. Tolchard (Ed.), *Toward 2000: The future of gambling, proceedings of the seventh national conference of the National Association for Gambling Studies* (pp. 189-209). Adelaide: National Association for Gambling Studies.

Chapter 11

Economics of Australian Casinos

Jeremy Buultjens

The rapid expansion of casinos into the Australian gambling environment has been a relatively recent phenomenon. Their introduction marked the beginning of a shift in government gambling policy away from community benefit to a more pragmatic, economic focus. Casinos were seen as a solution to declining economies, a shrinking tax base, and an intractable unemployment problem. Despite the perceived benefits, there was, and continues to be, vigorous public opposition to the introduction and expansion of casinos in some jurisdictions. Much of this opposition has been based on the economic and social costs associated with the expansion of gambling and casinos in particular.

The purpose of this chapter is to examine the economic impacts of casino gambling in Australia. This chapter begins by providing a brief description of the development of the industry and the economic imperatives influencing government policy. The next section discusses the industry and its market structure. This is followed by an examination of the economic benefits and costs associated with the development of the sector. The constraints on the industry and future prospects are outlined after the benefits and costs have been reviewed.

A BRIEF HISTORY OF THE CASINO INDUSTRY

Since the introduction of the first casino in 1973, the expansion of casino gambling in Australia has been striking. For example, since the establishment of Wrest Point Casino in Tasmania in 1973, Australian casinos have expanded their market share from nil to 20 percent of total gaming expenditure in 2000-2001 (Tasmanian Gaming Commission, 2002). In 2001, gambling expenditure in Australian casinos was $2,543.3 million, with the largest share, $945.7 million, being spent in the state of Victoria (Tasmanian Gaming Commission, 2002).[1] The average profit margin for a casino is 3.4 percent or $93 million (Australian Bureau of Statistics, 2000). In addition, casinos contributed about $500.8 million in state and territory taxes in 2001-2002 (ACIL Consulting, 2002). This expansion of the sector is even more impressive considering that all forms of commercial gaming in Australia expanded rapidly during this period.

The casino industry in Australia developed through three distinct stages or waves (McMillen, 1995). This development was covered in Chapter 1. Despite the development taking place over three distinct stages, the establishment of all casinos in Australia (see Figure 11.1) was "linked fundamentally to changes in the global economy" (Australian Institute of Gambling Research [AIGR], 1999, p. 119).

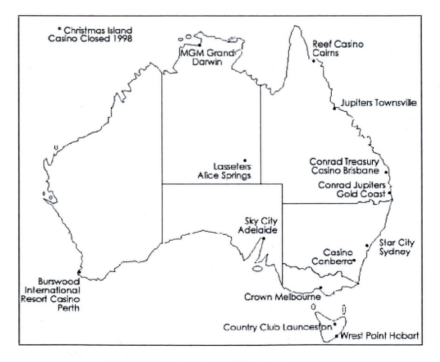

FIGURE 11.1. Location of Australian casinos.

The first of the thirteen legal casinos were established in Tasmania and the Northern Territory in the early 1970s. The economies of these two regions were underdeveloped at the time and their governments were hoping the establishment of casinos would help revitalize them (AIGR, 1999; McMillen, 1995). The casinos in Tasmania and the Northern Territory were low-key developments in relatively remote destinations designed to attract tourists and boost local economic activity.

The continued recession in Australia and the success of the casino in Tasmania and to a lesser extent in the Northern Territory encouraged other states to consider casinos as a means of stimulating economic growth. The next stage of casino development occurred in Perth, the Gold Coast, Adelaide, Canberra, Townsville, and Christmas Island in the mid to late 1980s. These casinos were based in states that were trying to diversify their economies away from primary production and manufacturing toward services, including tourism, as a way of boosting economic growth. In addition, at this time, these states were under increasing pressure to self-fund a larger share of their revenue due to reduced funding from the commonwealth government. The second-wave casinos were much larger American-style establishments aimed at the mass tourism market (AIGR, 1999). They were located in large urban centers and attracted patronage from local residents as well as tourists (McMillen, 1995).

The final stage of casino development occurred in the 1990s. The states in Australia without casinos were increasingly under pressure to establish them to prevent a leakage of their share of the gambling market into other states and territories. This final stage of development was also characterized by state needs to overcome fiscal problems and depressed economic growth arising from the recession of the late 1980s and early 1990s (AIGR, 1999). Megacasinos in the major urban centers of Melbourne, Sydney, Brisbane, and the tourist destination of Cairns were the outcome of this final development stage.

MARKET STRUCTURES AND OWNERSHIP REGIMES

A number of casinos attract some of the highest per capita gaming expenditures because of their geographic proximity to the high-roller markets in Asia. In 2000-2001, net gambling takings in Australia from international tourists were $611 million, an increase of 13 percent from the previous year. Of this, premium players (high rollers) contributed $500 million, an increase of 8 percent on the previous year (Australian Bureau of Statistics [ABS], 2001). In 1998-1999, the casino industry earned $2.2 billion in takings from gaming tables, $867 million from electronic gaming machines, and $24 million from keno. This represented a 24 percent increase in electronic gaming income from the previous year and a 7 percent reduction in table income for the same period (ABS, 2000).

In contrast to a number of countries, for example Holland, Austria, and the Philippines, where governments own casino operations outright, Australia has allowed private ownership of the majority of its casinos (Eadington, 1999). Private ownership also contrasts with the majority of earlier forms of Australian gaming, which had been directly administered by state governments, although this is no longer the situation.

The license for the Wrest Point Casino in Hobart was awarded to Federal Hotels Ltd. with no attempt by the government to call for tenders. The casino license was renewable annually, and for the first twenty-five years, no other license was to be issued for the southern division of Tasmania. This presented the license holder with a virtual monopoly. Also, a 38 percent limit was placed on foreign ownership of the venture.

The establishment of the casinos in the Northern Territory was based on Tasmania's statutes. However, in this state, submissions were called for from prospective developers. Initially, the Darwin casino did not accommodate any machine gambling; however, this situation changed after eighteen months. Since the early 1970s, there have been several changes to casino operations and regulations in the Northern Territory.

The two casinos that were established in Tasmania and the Northern Territory set the pattern of regional monopolies, which was to become a characteristic of Australian casino policy (AIGR, 1999). Therefore, the Australian industry is based on monopoly provision in major cities, as well as in a few destination resort locations (Mossenson, 1991). However, the monopoly status of casinos has been undermined in all states except Western Australia through the provision of electronic gaming machines in other types of establishments, such as hotels and clubs. The existence of other gaming venues has limited, to a certain extent, the profitability of the casinos.

THE IMPACTS OF CASINOS

Identifying and assessing the impacts of gaming in general, and casinos in particular, is a complex issue. Although gaming can have both positive and negative impacts, and although these might be primarily social or economic in nature, these categories are not always so distinct.

The difficulty of assessing the impacts of gaming is compounded by the following considerations:

- Types of impacts. These can include such diverse areas as tourism, crime, taxation, employment, and problem gambling.
- The level of analysis. The impacts of gambling can be considered at the state, regional, community, and individual/family levels.
- Types of gambling. Impacts of gambling vary significantly for each type of gambling (e.g., gaming machines, casino gaming, bingo, and wagering).
- Time frame. The impacts of gambling might vary between short-term and longer-term impacts.
- People, groups, and organizations affected. Gambling impacts differently on different people, groups, and organizations. Furthermore, these impacts might vary in their nature, extent, and whether they are predominantly positive or negative.
- Nature of impacts. Gambling can have economic, social, cultural, and political impacts.
- Extent of impacts. Some impacts affect only those directly involved in gambling, that is, gamblers, while others have much broader impacts on a range of stakeholders.

Despite these considerations, as shown in Table 11.1, it is possible to identify impacts from the development of casinos. The AIGR

TABLE 11.1. Anticipated direct impacts of the expansion of gaming on tourism, entertainment, and leisure.

Development	Case	Tourism, entertainment, and leisure impact
Expansion of gaming	Establishment of casino complex	Increased patron demand—brings international, interstate, and intrastate tourists as well as local patronage.
		Enhanced destination image—results in extended product range, parity with regional competition.
		Improved promotional opportunities—provides a major role in destination promotion with flow on effects for smaller enterprises.
		Increased convention marketing opportunities—demonstrates suitability and sophistication of destination.
		Increased provision of major events/shows—this demonstrates suitability and sophistication of destination, contributes to sponsorship.
		Increased entertainment and leisure options.
Increased gaming expenditure	Crown Casino	Expanded international tourism expenditure.
		Displaced interstate/intrastate tourism, entertainment, and leisure expenditure.
		Displaced local entertainment and leisure expenditure.
		Increased community sponsorships and donation.

Source: Australian Institute for Gambling Research (2000, p. 16).

(2000) determined that the establishment of a casino complex in Melbourne would, among other things, enhance the image of the destination, provide additional entertainment and leisure options as well as increase tourism expenditure, and displace local entertainment and leisure expenditure. Many of these impacts are examined in the following sections.

THE ECONOMIC BENEFITS FROM CASINOS

Consumer Benefit

The potential gains from the development of casinos fall into three major areas. The first benefit is that casinos provide substantial consumer benefit or enjoyment to people who are able to gamble moderately. If there is strong moral criticism of gambling within a society, then Eadington (1999) suggests that the level of consumer surplus be discounted to account for this criticism.

As Australians have become more affluent and their potential discretionary spending rises, they have increasingly pursued various forms of gaming as recreational and leisure opportunities. Figure 11.2 illustrates the growth in Australian gaming industries in terms of real (adjusted for inflation) expenditure since 1976-1977 and shows where the major growth areas have been. Although over 7,000 busi-

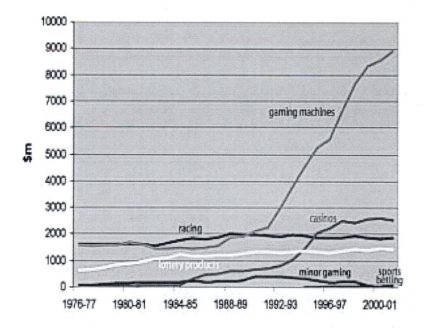

FIGURE 11.2. Real expenditure on different types of gambling in Australia, 1972-1973 to 1998-1999. *Source:* Compiled from Tasmanian Gaming Commission, 2004.

nesses provide gaming services throughout Australia (Productivity Commission, 1999), major growth has occurred in the casino, club, and hotel sectors (and more recently in sports betting), curtailing growth in the lotteries, racing, and minor gaming sectors. Accompanying this overall growth has been increased diversity in legalized gambling options available.

Gaming, especially in casinos, is now seen as a legitimate recreational activity for Australians to pursue. The increasing popularity of gambling in casinos is reflected by the increases in gaming expenditure shown in Table 11.2. The Productivity Commission (1999) contended that the major benefit of gaming derives from consumer gains from access to a service that gives people enjoyment. The commission noted that this enjoyment may flow from the venue, the social interaction, the risk, the thrill of anticipation, or some combination of all or some of these. It also noted that gaming venues can provide an accessible, comfortable, and safe social environment, which many people find appealing. Further, gamblers are buying the hope of a win. For recreational gamblers, that anticipation is part of the enjoyment; but for problem gamblers, it is a big part of their problem.

The establishment of casinos around the country has ensured that communities and individuals benefit through the enhancement of leisure facilities. For example, the Crown Casino in Melbourne not only provides gambling opportunities but also offers other forms of entertainment, a number of restaurants, and retail outlets. In addition, where new gaming opportunities attract high numbers of tourists, expenditure in related industries can also increase. For example, many clubs in close proximity to the Crown Casino in Melbourne reported increased trade due to an overflow from the crowded casino when it first opened, although this situation may have changed over the longer term.

The Productivity Commission (1999) estimated the consumer surplus from gambling in Australia ranged between $2.6 and $4.5 billion, with an estimated $305 to $495 million consumer surplus arising from casino games and $1.4 to $2.3 million resulting from gaming machines, including those in casinos. The commission also cited another study undertaken by Swain in 1992 that estimated the consumer surplus from the establishment of the Star City Casino in

TABLE 11.2. Growth in gaming expenditure in casinos by state ($ million).

Year	New South Wales	Victoria	Queens-land	South Australia	Western Australia	Tasmania	Australian Capital Territory	Northern Territory	Total
1975-76	—	—	—	—	—	6.59	—	—	6.59
1976-77	—	—	—	—	—	7.90	—	—	7.90
1977-78	—	—	—	—	—	8.33	—	—	8.33
1978-79	—	—	—	—	—	10.33	—	—	10.33
1979-80	—	—	—	—	—	11.08	—	4.63	15.72
1980-81	—	—	—	—	—	11.70	—	6.11	17.81
1981-82	—	—	—	—	—	14.22	—	10.62	24.84
1982-83	—	—	—	—	—	17.73	—	10.64	28.37
1983-84	—	—	—	—	—	21.60	—	13.46	35.06
1984-85	—	—	—	—	—	23.49	—	11.60	35.10
1985-86	—	—	47.69	32.49	35.67	25.62	—	16.29	157.75
1986-87	—	—	93.31	54.72	72.89	28.92	—	26.62	276.47
1987-88	—	—	118.30	61.09	76.80	31.85	—	24.57	312.60
1988-89	—	—	143.13	75.21	113.03	39.80	—	33.18	404.34
1989-90	—	—	162.31	82.75	147.59	41.41	—	11.92	445.98
1990-91	—	—	171.20	86.61	188.53	44.39	—	35.01	525.73
1991-92	—	—	186.59	88.59	202.31	48.13	—	32.70	558.32
1992-93	—	—	194.51	100.40	261.73	48.44	21.32	30.39	656.78
1993-94	—	—	230.10	116.20	354.16	57.75	34.63	33.51	826.34
1994-95	—	357.85	253.79	83.56	395.04	58.87	39.58	36.85	1225.53
1995-96	279.40	490.90	371.96	76.54	429.57	62.39	29.28	58.40	1798.44
1996-97	361.45	578.97	432.00	70.71	375.30	74.23	17.80	45.86	1956.32
1997-98	443.20	742.29	468.30	76.01	358.83	75.64	17.28	47.41	2228.96
1998-99	479.70	721.85	476.80	76.65	285.76	82.17	16.29	54.28	2193.49
1999-00	486.40	823.87	531.70	75.83	288.56	77.07	17.70	62.39	2362.52
2000-01	529.00	945.75	543.00	80.74	281.06	76.27	18.39	69.11	2543.32

Source: Compiled from Tasmanian Gaming Commission (2004) figures.

New South Wales to be worth $162 million per annum. This was equal to 29 percent of anticipated casino revenue. Clearly, significant consumer surplus is associated with casinos in Australia.

Economic Growth

The second economic benefit from casino development is that it provides increased economic growth in the state or region providing the service, resulting in increased employment for the area. Economic benefits are captured by exporting casino gaming to customers from regions where the activity does not occur or by encouraging local gamblers to draw on their savings. Encouraging local gamblers to switch consumption expenditure to gambling does not add to overall economic well-being, since this is just a transfer of expenditure within the economy.

In addition, the establishment of casinos is likely to boost tourism generally by portraying the host city as a sophisticated destination, allowing it to be marketed as a convention destination. The establishment of a casino may also deter Australian gamblers from leaving Australia in search of gambling holidays.

A number of studies in Australia and overseas have attempted to quantify the economic gains and growth stimulated from gambling providers, including casinos. The Productivity Commission (1999) noted that this expansion of the industry is unlikely to provide significant economic and employment gains in the long term. One reason for this assessment is that net benefits from tourism are small. For example, in 1996-1997, only 13.6 percent of casino visitors were from outside the local region and only 3.2 percent were international visitors.

Another reason for the limited long-term impact is that any local gambling funded by discretionary savings will result in a short-term economic boost, but in the long term there will be even greater reductions in future consumption expenditure. The limited economic gains from the expansion of the industry are likely to limit the resultant increased employment opportunities.

Australian gaming industries employ large numbers of people, both directly and indirectly. The Productivity Commission (1999) estimated that over 107,000 people, or 1 percent of the Australian workforce, were directly employed in Australian gambling industries in 1997-1998. These comprised:

- over 20,000 people employed in casinos;
- over 13,000 people employed at tabs, sports betting shops, and bookmakers;
- nearly 3,000 people in lottery businesses; and
- about 70,000 people in clubs, pubs, taverns, and bars as a result of gambling (excluding employees in food and beverage, administration, etc.).

Of the 20,342 people employed in the casino sector, 59 percent were permanent full-time employees, 17 percent were part-time employees, and 24 percent were casual employees. Approximately 39 percent of staff were employed as licensed gaming operators, 13 percent as waiters/waitresses, 8 percent as clerical and administrative staff, and nearly 7 percent as managers (ABS, 2000).

Clearly, there has been direct employment generation from new forms of gambling, such as casinos and the introduction of gaming machines, in various states. In fact, creating employment opportunities has been a stated objective when legalizing many new forms of gambling. For example, the introduction of electronic gaming machines into Victorian hotels and clubs and the establishment of Crown Casino in Melbourne have generated about 24,000 jobs to date in Victoria (National Institute of Economic and Industry Research, 2000). Further, as gambling venues respond to increased customer demand, employment is created for bar and restaurant staff, clerical staff, and machine managers. In addition, contracted services will generate employment for entertainers, accountants, auditors, repairers, cleaners, security services, and the like. Construction-related jobs have also been generated by expansions in gambling establishments. However, many of these jobs would probably have been created even if the gambling industry had not been developed because consumption expenditure would have taken place in another sector of the economy. This idea is explored in greater depth in the following section on economic costs.

Revenue to the Public Sector

The third major benefit from the development of casinos is the additional source of revenue that it provides the public sector. Table 11.3 shows the level of government revenue that states and territories receive from gaming, including casinos. The collection of tax revenue has been a major reason underpinning the expansion of gambling in Australia. Indeed, total real (adjusted for inflation) government revenue from gambling in Australia increased from about $1.5 billion in 1975-1976 to $3.7 billion in 2000-2001 (Tasmanian Gaming Commission, 2004), with around 70 percent of this collected in New South Wales and Victoria (Productivity Commission, 1999). Taxation from gambling now represents around 12 percent of all taxation revenue in Australia (Productivity Commission, 1999).

However, while recognizing that gambling taxes contribute to overall government revenue that is spent on community services and infrastructure, such as schools, hospitals, and police, considerable debate has existed for some time regarding the appropriateness of raising taxation revenue through gambling. An interesting assessment of the equity, economic efficiency, administrative costs of gambling revenues, and revenue collected is provided by Johnson (1985) and summarized in the following points. Although his figures are now outdated, the principles by which gambling taxes have been evaluated are worthy of comment:

- Equity refers to the principle that individuals in similar economic positions should bear roughly equal taxes and that individuals in unequal positions should pay different amounts of taxes. However, gambling taxes are regressive in that low-income earners pay proportionately more of their income in gambling taxes than do higher-income earners. This is particularly the case for gaming machines and lotteries (Productivity Commission, 1999).
- Economic efficiency refers to the principle whereby taxes should be neutral and not alter native decisions regarding purchasing of other goods and services. That is, the ratio of tax to retail price should be roughly equal for all goods and services, unless the government needs to protect local industries or where the con-

TABLE 11.3. Real total government revenue from gambling ($ million).

Year	Racing	Gaming	Sports betting	Total
1975-76	701.77	762.84		1464.61
1976-77	683.62	805.45		1489.07
1977-78	673.52	831.04		1504.56
1978-79	662.69	882.08		1544.76
1979-80	663.45	979.04		1642.49
1980-81	653.41	1025.07		1678.48
1981-82	630.84	1094.91		1725.75
1982-83	616.84	1136.73		1753.57
1983-84	656.42	1224.84		1881.26
1984-85	691.07	1331.98		2023.06
1985-86	721.71	1330.09		2051.80
1986-87	710.39	1347.56		2057.95
1987-88	744.17	1411.76		2155.93
1988-89	780.17	1393.71		2173.88
1989-90	798.41	1586.99		2385.40
1990-91	781.97	1641.76		2423.73
1991-92	771.07	1696.61		2467.68
1992-93	791.49	1877.78		2669.27
1993-94	794.00	2214.56		3008.56
1994-95	738.98	2593.99	4.33	3337.30
1995-96	694.10	2905.23	3.69	3603.02
1996-97	672.59	3087.13	3.51	3763.23
1997-98	626.18	3534.05	4.05	4164.28
1998-99	526.44	3900.12	6.15	4432.71
1999-00	483.23	4173.03	8.03	4664.29
2000-01	325.95	3334.30	5.85	3666.10

Source: Compiled from Tasmanian Gaming Commission (2002).

sumption of certain goods or services generates costs for the community. Although gambling is taxed more highly than most activities, these higher taxes have a role to play in redirecting some gambling industry profits to the community, given the remaining government restrictions on gambling (Productivity Commission, 1999). In fact, the commission could not find a strong or unambiguous case for a reduction in gambling taxes, with the exception of the lottery. In fact, it suggested that current taxes appear to be too low in the case of gaming machines in clubs.

• Costs of gambling administration and compliance include some government regulatory activities in addition to tax collection efforts. Johnson (1985) noted that there is no evidence to suggest that these costs are abnormally high—compliance with tax collection is extremely high; taxpayers find the tax convenient to pay; and there are few complaints.

• Revenue raised from gambling amounts to a significant proportion of Australian state taxes and has increased substantially in the last decade. However, gambling expenditure is not very sensitive to increases in income (Johnson, 1985) and so gambling revenue is unlikely to maintain its current proportion of all taxes collected. Indeed, the Productivity Commission (1999) noted that increased gambling revenues in the past ten years are almost entirely due to expanded numbers of gaming machines and casino licenses, rather than higher incomes.

THE ECONOMIC COSTS OF CASINO DEVELOPMENT

Despite the economic benefits that arise from the expansion of gambling in general and casinos specifically, a number of perceived costs are associated with the industry. The nature of the employment generated in the industry, overreliance by governments on gambling taxes, and the diversion of expenditure in the retail sector toward gambling are three common perceived costs associated with gambling. There are also the economic costs associated with problem gamblers, loss of job productivity as a result of problem gambling, increased crime, and political and economic corruption. Some of these costs can be measured in dollars, for example, the cost of social services for compulsive gamblers; however, other costs such as the damage done to persons and families are not easily quantified (Oddo, 1997). In addition, many of these issues are not well researched and therefore linkages with the advent of casino gambling are not well understood (Margolis, 1997). Despite the uncertainty surrounding the economic costs associated with the development of the casino industry, they are considerable and may, as some people would argue, outweigh the benefits generated (see Starr, 1995; Kindt, 1994).

The Nature of Employment

Although the number of jobs generated by the liberalization of gambling in recent years is impressive, the nature of those jobs has raised some concerns. For example, a 1995 impact study of the introduction of gaming machines in Queensland raised three issues concerning the quality of the new employment generated (AIGR, 1995). These were the dominance of part-time jobs, impact on the youth labor market, and career paths and occupational segregation. Concern was expressed that about 65 percent of new positions created by the introduction of the machines were part-time, with most on a casual basis, and that almost 80 percent of part-time employees were women, who were also significantly underrepresented in full-time and managerial positions. Although nothing intrinsic to part-time work reflects on its quality, the report noted that a significant majority of these jobs are relatively mundane activities without a recognized career path. Thus, these positions were seen as unlikely to underpin full-time, skilled work. Nevertheless, it was noted that any new employment is welcome, especially of the type that provides a comparatively high proportion of jobs for young people, as the industry does. In fact, 33.8 percent of all jobs in the industry were performed by those in the fifteen-to-twenty-four-year-old age bracket, although 68.3 percent of these were part-time. The report concluded that this increasing trend toward casualization and greater flexibility in staff utilization would increase the volatility of employment conditions and that lack of career paths and consequent lack of training and skill development, particularly in many smaller establishments, were of concern.

At the national level, the Productivity Commission (1999) also observed that gambling businesses are characterized by a high proportion of part-time, casual, and female employment. It noted that, in 1997-1998, over 50 percent of employment in businesses in which gambling was the primary activity was on a part-time or casual basis and women were employed in 51 percent of these positions. It should be noted that casinos have lower levels of part-time and casual employment.

Reduced Business Opportunities in Other Sectors

Another cost of casinos is that they may actually result in depressing economic development, despite the perceptions of increased development. Macisaac (1995) contended that casinos can actually kill other businesses by sucking money out of an economy. This occurs because increased gambling opportunities can reduce expenditure in other industries, such as retail, tourism, leisure, and recreation. For example, some entertainment and restaurant industries have been vocal opponents of increased gambling opportunities, due to the competitive threats they pose. It appears that some of their fears are well grounded. For example, 18.8 percent of respondents in a Queensland study of the impacts of poker machines said that, if not for poker machines, they would have spent the money on other forms of entertainment (AIGR, 1995). Spending in cafés and restaurants declined immediately following the opening of the casino in Darwin. This means that despite the increase in employment in casinos, jobs in other industries may have been lost if gambling has diverted consumer spending away from them (Productivity Commission, 1999).

Increased Government Reliance on Gambling Revenues

The increasing reliance on gambling tax revenues may also be seen as a cost of gambling. This trend has focused increased public attention on the blatant economic agenda pursued by many state governments in their gambling policies. The dominance of market criteria in gaming development and the widespread perception that some commercial gambling interests hold privileged positions in the policy process have provoked a political backlash by concerned community groups (McMillen, 1996). Although gambling taxes are generally considered to be relatively palatable and invisible (McMillen, 1996) and able to be increased without a political backlash (Blaszczynski, 1987), they are a regressive consumption tax whereby lower-income earners pay proportionately more of their income than higher-income earners (Johnson, 1985). This is exacerbated given that lower-income earners tend to spend more than their wealthier counterparts on certain forms of gambling, notably gaming machines (State Government of Victoria, 1994; DBM Consultants, 1995; Delfabbro & Winefield, 1996). Further, Australian governments have demonstrated increased reliance on gambling taxes, which increased by 69 percent between 1989-1990 and 1994-1995, compared to 18 percent for most other taxes (McCrann, 1996).

Problem Gambling

Major economic and social costs are associated with problem gambling, but it is very difficult to determine the extent to which problem gambling is exacerbated by the establishment of casinos. Additional difficulties are associated with separating personal costs from social costs (Eadington, 1999). In undertaking a benefit-cost analysis of casino gambling, many economists argue that it is important to consider only social costs and not individual or household costs. An economic evaluation should only include costs borne by the society and not by individuals because it is assumed that the costs borne by individuals are a result of informed personal choices. However, the Productivity Commission (1999) suggested that is very unlikely in the case of a problem gambler. The commission also suggested that externality costs will accrue to those people, especially family members, who have a relationship with a problem gambler.

Another consideration when measuring the opportunity costs of legalized gambling is the need to compare the current results with a reasonable alternative situation (Eadington, 1999). For example, if legalized gambling was not allowed and a state of prohibition existed, it is likely that a degree of illegal gambling would be undertaken, with many of the same costs occurring. Therefore, to compare the current situation against an environment where no gambling is occurring would be misleading. Unfortunately, it is very difficult to determine the costs associated with illegal gambling.

Regardless of the difficulties associated with the measurement of problem gambling, the economic costs will be substantial. As discussed in Chapter 10, the Productivity Commission (1999) estimated that approximately 2.1 percent of the adult Australian population (around 290,000 people) are problem gamblers. Although the estimates indicate that the number of problem gamblers represents a very small minority of the Australian population, national survey data suggest that problem gamblers comprise around 15 percent of regular, nonlottery gamblers. The average gambling losses for problem gamblers are around $12,000 per head or 22.1 percent of household income before tax (Productivity Commission, 1999).

The Productivity Commission (1999) noted that there was a range of estimates for the costs of problem gambling, from a low of US$560 to a high of US$52,000 per problem gambler. This discrepancy in the figures can, to a large extent, be explained by whether the researchers viewed problem gamblers' spending and transfer payments as a social cost. Dickerson et al. (1996), in a study of problem gambling in New South Wales, estimated the costs of the effects of excessive gambling on employment, productivity loss, court costs, bankruptcy, divorce, and rehabilitation at $48 million in the state. However, it is difficult to estimate how much of this cost can be attributed to casino gambling. It may be possible to attribute 20 percent of this figure (casinos' share of gambling), or $9.6 million, to casino gambling. In contrast, Walker (1998) suggested that casino gambling may add as much as an extra $16 million to the figure cited by Dickerson et al. Walker noted that the Dickerson et al. (1996) study took place shortly after the establishment of the Star City Casino in Sydney, New South Wales, and that gambling-related problems emerge over an extended period of time. The AIGR (1999) estimated the costs from problem gambling in New South Wales to be in the vicinity of $50 million (see Table 11.4).

In the United States, it is estimated that costs to individuals from such effects as poor physical and mental health and job loss are US$1,000 to US$2,000 per year. It is also estimated that additional lifetime costs from divorce, bankruptcy, or arrests amount to US$5,000 to US$6,000 per affected individual. This represents a crude measure of approximately US$3.5 billion per annum for the United States

TABLE 11.4. Economic and social costs of problem gambling to the NSW community.

Impact on NSW	Estimated annual cost (thousand $)
Employment impacts	28,474
Productivity loss	20,796
Job change	5,258
Unemployment	
Legal costs	17,846
Court costs	5,376
Prison costs	9,978
Police costs	
Financial costs	66
Bankruptcy	
Personal costs	732
Divorce	391
Acute treatment	
Existing services	3,191
Total	50,309

Source: Australian Institute for Gambling Research (1999, p. 86).

(Eadington, 1999). In Australia, the total cost is estimated between $1.8 and $5.6 billion per annum (Productivity Commission, 1999).

Community Perceptions and Impacts

Many people in Australia feel substantial disquiet about the increasing pervasiveness of gambling, including casinos. Economic costs are associated with such strong aversions to gambling, but they are very difficult to quantify. In most situations, these preferences are of minor importance and they are usually ignored when considering policy. However, in some situations, people's preferences may be significant, for example passive smoking (Productivity Commission, 1999). This may also be the case with disquiet about the expansion of gambling.

The expansion of gambling may also have additional costs in terms of adverse community impacts. For example, some people may feel that the character of the local community has been adversely changed. These costs are difficult to quantify, and it may be difficult to attribute the change to the impact from gambling (Productivity Commission, 1999). Nevertheless, policymakers need to be aware that such costs exist and are legitimate.

NET ECONOMIC ASSESSMENT

Clearly, given the difficulties in accurately quantifying many of the benefits and costs associated with gambling, it is problematic determining the overall net economic outcomes from the industry. As stated previously, there are various ways to categorize certain outcomes and the categorizations will significantly influence the economic analysis. Therefore, any net assessment needs to be treated with caution. The other issue related to a net assessment is that there can be variations between states and within regions. For example, in certain jurisdictions, gaming machines are concentrated in lower socioeconomic neighborhoods; therefore, the net economic outcome in these areas will be different than in areas with lower concentrations.

The Productivity Commission (1999) estimated the net economic outcomes from gambling ranged from a community cost of $1.2 billion to a community benefit of $4.3 billion. For casino gaming, the commission estimated a range for community benefit of $431 to $723 million; and for gaming machines, the range was from a community cost of $2.3 billion to a community benefit of $1.1 billion.

CONSTRAINTS ON CASINOS

The casino industry has been subject to considerable constraints and controls throughout the world because the industry has been and continues to be viewed in some jurisdictions as a morally questionable and controversial consumption industry (Eadington, 1998). In Australia, a number of harm minimization measures, such as limits on granting of credit, limits on advertising, maximum limits on bets, and the provision of information, have been introduced. From an economic perspective, these controls can be seen as preventing the market from reaching equilibrium, resulting in inefficiencies and an undersupply of casino gaming products (Eadington, 1999). The restrictions placed on casinos may allow alternative providers a competitive advantage unless they are subject to the same restrictions. For example, cruise ships operating out of some ports in Australia provide gaming facilities similar to those of land-based casinos. These ships are not subject to the same controls as casinos, therefore will have lower costs than land-based casinos. This could result in land-based casinos losing some of their economic rent to cruise ship operators. In addition, governments are likely to lose through reduced tax earnings from land-based casinos.

It may also be questionable whether these restrictions actually result in reducing the social costs associated with gambling. This would mean that the costs associated with gaming controls and restrictions are not matched by benefits from reduced levels of problem gambling. If this is the case, these would be economically inefficient policy measures resulting in reduced net economic benefit for the community. Another outcome of these measures, if they are not applied uniformly to all types of gambling providers, is a loss of competitiveness and profits for the casino industry. A result of such a situation may be that casinos will reduce their investment in the provision of nongaming amenities due to the lower expected return on investment (Eadington, 1999).

THE FUTURE

Industry analysts and operators express disquiet about market expectations and future growth of the casino sector. What makes this argument so notable is that the casino sector has been seen as the golden goose of Australian gaming, a source of unprecedented revenues and a major force in the gaming expansion of the last decade. Despite some casinos in Australia being well positioned geographically to take advantage of the growing global market for casino gaming, the sector was showing signs of saturation and limited opportunities for future growth by the mid-1990s.

Competition for casino gaming in Australia has increased sharply at three levels: between casinos and club/hotel gaming, between each casino (and thus between regions and states), and between Australian casinos and overseas competitors for international tourists and junket players. The increased competition and unusually high abnormal expenses saw the operating profit margin register a low of –10.8 percent (a loss) in 1997-1998. The profit margin was down from 8.9 percent in 1995-1996 and 6.5 percent in 1994-1995 (ABS, 2000). The operating profit before tax per person employed was $4,600 in 1998-1999, $1,200 in 1998-1999, and $10,700 in 1995-1996 (ABS, 2000). The increased terrorism threat and severe acute respiratory syndrome (SARS) epidemic exacerbated the situation for casinos. The stagnation and fall in profitability experienced by Australian casinos may influence state governments to grant tax concessions to maintain viability.

Casino operators, like lottery managers, are responding to the changing gaming environment by searching for new market opportunities and ways to improve their competitiveness. But the general view of the industry is that some existing casinos will not be able to match the resources and marketing capacity of their rivals. The size of the casino is a factor that will determine future success. This will probably result in the sector becoming even more concentrated than it currently is. In June 1999, the casinos operated by the four largest enterprises accounted for 81 percent of employment and 85 percent of income during 1998-1999 (ABS, 2000).

The introduction of new technology is likely to have a considerable impact on the casino sector. The introduction of innovative changes to electronic gaming machines based on new computer-based technologies are likely to encourage higher levels of gambling among consumers (Eadington, 1999). This may increase earnings of the gaming sector, including casinos. However, new technology allowing Internet gambling could have substantial negative economic impacts on casinos. Currently, the Australian government has restricted domestic access to Internet gambling, but this approach may change, with flow-on consequences for casinos.

The continuing disquiet among some members of the community about gambling may also have impacts on casinos in the future. Currently, all governments have some strategies in place to minimize the impacts from gaming. However, if governments are forced to increase these measures, consequences will occur for all gambling providers, in term of reduced earnings.

CONCLUSION

The casino industry in Australia has experienced rapid growth since the early 1970s. It currently accounts for 20 percent of all gaming income in the country. The development of casinos was encouraged because they were seen as a solution to declining economies, a shrinking tax base, and an intractable unemployment problem. Despite the economic benefits that have flowed from their establishment, the sector has continued to attract criticism because many people argue that the benefits are outweighed by the costs associated with the expansion of the industry. Undertaking an economic assessment of the industry is problematic because a number of benefits and costs are difficult to quantify and can be categorized in different ways. In its assessment of casino gaming, the Productivity Commission (1999) estimated the community benefit ranged from $431 million to $723 million. The estimated range for gaming machines (including casino machines) was from a community cost of $2.3 billion to a community benefit of $1.1 billion. The net economic estimates for all forms of gaming ranged from a community cost of $1.2 billion to a community benefit of $4.3 billion.

NOTE

1. All dollar figures quoted are Australian unless otherwise stated.

REFERENCES

ACIL Consulting. (2002). *Casino industry survey 2001-02: Summary of results.* Canberra: Australian Casino Association.

Australian Bureau of Statistics. (2001). *Casinos* (Catalogue No. 8683.0). Canberra: AGPS.

Australian Institute for Gambling Research. (1995). *Report of the first year of the study into the social and economic impact of the introduction of gaming ma-*

chines to Queensland clubs and hotels. Brisbane: Department of Family Services and Aboriginal and Islander Affairs.

Australian Institute for Gambling Research. (1999). *Australian gambling: Comparative history and analysis.* Melbourne: Victorian Casino and Gaming Authority.

Australian Institute for Gambling Research. (2000). *The impact of gaming on the tourism, entertainment and leisure industries.* Melbourne: Victorian Casino Gaming Authority.

Blaszczynski, A. (1987). Does compulsive gambling constitute an illness? Responsibility of the state in rehabilitation. In M. Walker (Ed.), *Faces of gambling: Proceedings of the second national conference of the National Association for Gambling Studies* (pp. 307-315). Sydney: National Association for Gambling Studies.

DBM Consultants. (1995). *Report on the findings of survey of community gambling patterns.* Melbourne: DBM Consultants.

Delfabbro, P. H., & Winefield, A. H. (1996). *Community gambling patterns and the prevalence of gambling-related problems in South Australia, with particular reference to gaming machines.* Adelaide: University of Adelaide, Department of Family and Community Services.

Dickerson, M., Allcock, C., Blaszcynski, A., Nicholls, B., Williams, J., & Maddern, R. (1996). *An examination of the socio-economic effects of gambling on individuals, families and the community including research into the costs of problem gambling in New South Wales.* Sydney: Casino Community Benefit Fund, NSW Government.

Eadington, W. (1998). Contributions of casino style gambling to local economies. *Annals of the American Academy of Political and Social Sciences, 556,* 5-65.

Eadington, W. (1999). The economics of gambling. *Journal of Economic Perspectives, 13*(1), 173-192.

Johnson, J. (1985). Gambling as a source of government revenue in Australia. In G. Caldwell, B. Haig, M. Dickerson, & L. Sylvan (Eds.), *Gambling in Australia* (pp. 78-93). Sydney: Southwood Press.

Kindt, J. (1994). The economic impacts of legalised gambling activities. *Drake Law Review, 43,* 51-95.

Macisaac, M. (1995). Casino gambling: A bad bet. *Readers Digest, 146,* 71-74.

Margolis, J. (1997). Casinos and crime: An analysis of the evidence. Washington, DC: American Gaming Association.

McCrann, T. (1996, March 30-31). Why the wages of sin is a GST. *The Weekend Australian,* p. 28.

McMillen, J. (1995). The globalisation of gambling: Implications for Australia. *National Association for Gambling Studies Journal, 8*(1), 9-19.

McMillen, J. (1996). Perspectives on Australian gambling policy: Changes and challenges. In B. Tolchard (Ed.), *Proceedings of the National Conference on Gambling* (pp. 1-9). Sydney: Darling Harbor. Adelaide: Flunders Press.

Mossenson, D. (1991). The Australian casino model. In W. Eadington & J. Cornelius (Eds.), *Gambling and public policy: International perspectives* (pp. 303-362). Reno, NV: University of Nevada.

National Institute of Economic and Industry Research. (2000). *The economic impact of gambling.* Melbourne: Victorian Casino and Gaming Authority.

Oddo, A. (1997). The economics and ethics of gambling. *Review of Business, 18*(3), 4-8.

Productivity Commission. (1999). *Australia's gambling industries.* Canberra: Commonwealth of Australia.

Starr, O. (1995). Riverboat gambling does not help local economies. In C. Cozic & P. Winters (Eds.), *Gambling: Current controversy series,* (pp. 153-156). San Diego: Greenhaven Press.

State Government of Victoria. (1994). *Review of electronic gaming machines in Victoria (*Vol. 1). Melbourne: Author.

Tasmanian Gaming Commission. (2004). Australian gambling statistics 2004. Tasmanian Gaming Commission: Hobart.

Walker, M. (1998). *Gambling government: The economic and social impacts.* Sydney: UNSW Press.

Chapter 12

Impacts of Casinos in Korea

Ki-Joon Back
Choong-Ki Lee

INTRODUCTION

The first casino opened in Korea in 1962, as a way to attract inbound tourists from overseas. Today, a total of fourteen casinos are in
operation in Korea. Among these casinos, thirteen operate exclusively for foreign customers, and one legally accommodates domestic players. One of the most positive impacts of casinos on the Korean
economy is their ability to generate considerable foreign receipts. In
2001, the Korean casino industry earned almost US$3 million in total
foreign casino receipts from the thirteen casinos. In addition, the
Kangwon Land Casino, the only casino open to the domestic market,
exerted even more positive economic impacts on the Korean economy after its opening in 2000. These impacts included revitalization
of a rundown coal mining community, job creation, increased income
levels, and the development of community tourism infrastructures,
such as roads, transportation systems, and attractions.

However, a number of concerns have been expressed about the
negative social impacts of gaming, and these should not be over-
looked. Numerous people become problem gamblers and their behaviors cause bankruptcies, the destruction of families, and even suicide. The casino industry has been developing rapidly in Korea, as it
has in other countries in today's global market. It is the responsibility
of government policymakers, casino operators, and academics to
clearly understand the pros and cons of casino development. Specifically, methods for minimizing the potential negative impacts of ca-

sinos need to be developed and implemented, including developing awareness and treatment programs for problem gamblers.

The main focus of this chapter is the positive economic and negative social impacts of casino development. In addition, this chapter deals with current practices and recommendations relating to responsible gaming issues.

ECONOMIC IMPACTS
OF FOREIGN CASINO RECEIPTS

One way of estimating the economic impacts of the casino industry is an input-output (I-O) analysis, which has been widely used in practical tourism research (Archer, 1977; Fletcher, 1989; Blaine, 1993; Heng & Low, 1990; Khan, Chou, & Wong, 1990; United Nations, 1990; Lee, 1992; Lee & Kwon, 1995, 1997). The essence of the I-O framework developed by Leontief (1936) is an input-output transactions table, which consists of three major sectors: intermediate input (processing), primary input, and final demand sectors. The intermediate input sector is defined as the processing sector, which purchases inputs from the primary and its own sector and, at the same time, sells its output to intermediate and final demand sectors. Primary input, such as wages, salaries, and value-added components, is defined as inputs purchased by the intermediate sector. The final demand sector is defined as final users that purchase output from the processing sector.

In this chapter, casino multipliers are derived from the Korean I-O transactions tables (Bank of Korea, 2001). Economic impacts of the Korean casino industry are estimated by multiplying total casino receipts by the corresponding casino multipliers (Lee, 2003) in terms of total output, income, employment, value-added components, indirect tax, and imports. In 2001, total foreign casino receipts in the thirteen Korean casinos were US$296 million (Korean Casino Association, 2003). As shown in Table 12.1, these casino receipts generated US$750 million of output as a result of their direct, indirect, and induced impacts. The total casino receipts also generated US$143 million in personal income to residents, US$397 million in value added,

TABLE 12.1. Total economic impact of the casino industry.*

Output impact	Income impact	Employment impact	Value-added impact	Indirect tax impact	Import impact
$750,283,000	$143,347,000	37,451 persons	$397,116,000	$55,122,000	$42,557,000

Source: Lee, 2003.

*Currency in U.S. dollars.

and US$55 million in government revenue. The casino receipts also produced US$43 million of import goods.

Another positive economic impact of the casino industry may be the creation of employment opportunities. Foreign casino receipts created 37,451 full-time equivalent jobs through direct, indirect, and induced impacts. The casino employment multiplier appears to be much higher than those of other major export industries, such as automobiles and semiconductors. In comparison, ninety-eight employees are created for every 1 million Korean won (US$1 = 1,200 won) of casino receipts. For the same amount of money, forty-two employees in the semiconductor industry, forty-four employees in the automobile industry, eighty employees in the lodging industry, and fifty-five employees in the transportation industry are generated.

The Korean casino industry contributed to the country's balance of payments by generating foreign exchange earnings of approximately US$278 million in 2001 with a foreign exchange earnings rate of 94 percent. The rate of foreign exchange earnings shown in Table 12.2 was computed by multiplying the exports of each sector by that sector's import multiplier, subtracting the product from its exports, and finally dividing the result by its exports, or [{exports – (exports × import multiplier)}/exports]. The rate of foreign exchange earnings for the casino sector was found to be 94 percent, meaning that for every dollar in export (foreign casino receipts), 94 cents were generated as net foreign exchange earnings. However, for every dollar in export of semiconductor products, only about 40 cents were produced as net foreign exchange earnings. Thus, the casino sector appears to have

TABLE 12.2. Rate of foreign exchange earnings.[a]

		Foreign exchange earnings	
Number	Sector	Rate (%)	Rank[b]
Export			
1	Textiles/apparel/leather	64.3	8
2	TVs	60.0	9
3	Semiconductors	39.3	10
4	Passenger cars	79.5	6
Tourism			
5	Shopping (retail trade)	93.9	1
6	Restaurants	90.5	5
7	Hotels	92.2	3
8	Transportation and communication	78.2	7
9	Culture and recreation services	91.7	4
10	Casinos	93.7	2

[a][{exports – (exports × import multiplier)}/exports]

[b]The sector ranked 1 is the sector having the strongest effect on foreign exchange earnings whereas the sector ranked 10 has the weakest effect.

the largest effect on foreign exchange earnings among all export sectors and all other tourism sectors, except for the retail trade.

Specifically, the casino industry earned US$473 per foreign customer in 2001. Receiving one foreign casino customer is equivalent to exporting twenty-four semiconductors or two television sets. The casino industry, in accommodating twenty-two casino customers, would be making as much money as would result from selling one passenger car to a foreign country (Lee, 2003). Using this formula, gross revenues for the casino industry in 2001 were equivalent to exporting 28,354 passenger cars.

ECONOMIC IMPACTS
OF KANGWON LAND CASINO

Kangwon Land Casino was legalized to revitalize the economy of former coal mining areas. This is the only Korean casino that allows domestic players. After opening the Kangwon Land Casino to domestic customers, numerous positive economic impacts were reported. Kangwon Land Casino (2003) reported that it received about 2,500 customers daily in 2002. Due to the visitor volume, revenues for local lodging operations and restaurants also increased up to 50 percent (Lee & Back, 2003). The number of train passengers increased two to three times, while the number of taxi passengers doubled since the casino opening.

By the end of fiscal year 2002, Kangwon Land Casino earned approximately US$220 million in revenues and paid over US$100 million in taxes to the central government and taxes and donations to the local government (Kangwon Land Casino, 2003). As the main casino opened in March 2003, casino revenues were doubled.

Those taxes and donations to the local government were used to revitalize the local economy and enhance the welfare of the local people. Also, Kangwon Land Casino (2003) created more than 12,000 jobs in the community. Among those positions, 3,200 employees are working full time in the hotel and casino and the rest are involved in the construction of the casino and the resort properties, including a hotel, golf course, theme park, ski slopes, and condominiums. According to a Kangwon Land Casino (2003) report, 61 percent of all employees were from the local community, which is positive evidence of economic revitalization. In addition, thirty local companies in Kangwon Province handled 32 percent of the total construction of the casino. Furthermore, Kangwon Land Casino purchased 80 percent of its food and beverage inventories from local vendors.

SOCIAL IMPACTS

As Oh (1999) mentioned, assessing the social impacts of gaming poses many conceptual difficulties because it is not easy to separate social impacts from economic impacts. There are many definitional overlaps between economic and social impacts. Also, social impacts should be assessed at both the societal and individual levels. Numerous secondary data sources can be used to measure the impact at the societal level, such as community, city, state, or country. However, the social impacts on an individual level are not often reported, although they are more important because the casino industry has a major impact on the quality of life among residents in the community.

Societal Level

Although the casino industry provides numerous positive economic impacts, it is associated with some negative social impacts, such as gambling addiction, bankruptcy, and crime. In Korea, gaming has been traditionally perceived as an immoral activity. Numerous traditional gambling activities have jeopardized the quality of life of individuals and families in the past. Pathological gamblers could lose all their assets and even their lives. A typical gambling problem starts with an increasing amount of debt, and may escalate to the committing of crimes by gambling-addicted individuals. Many studies have indicated that pathological gamblers sometimes abuse their children and spouses, resulting in divorce. In extreme cases, some commit suicide when they discover that they cannot control themselves (Burke, 1996; Littlejohn, 1999; Lorenz & Shuttlesworth, 1983).

Several researchers have studied symptoms of pathological and compulsive gambling problems. Burke (1996) stated that problem gamblers often suffer from profound marital difficulties. As a matter of fact, Nevada has the highest divorce rate in the United States, which is more than double the national average (Littlejohn, 1999). A study by Lorenz and Shuttlesworth (1983) showed that 50 percent of spouses experienced physical abuse from problem gamblers. In addition, Bland, Newman, Orn, and Stelesky (1993) found that about 17 percent of children of pathological gamblers were physically and verbally abused.

Littlejohn (1999) concluded that problem gamblers assessed to be at the highest risk for suicide were more likely to be separated or divorced. Many studies also found that 20 percent of problem gamblers attempted suicide (McCormick, 1993; Lesieur, 1998; Thompson, Gazel, & Rockman, 1996). Furthermore, Littlejohn (1999) stated that Nevada has the highest suicide rate in the United States.

Since the Korean government deregulated the overseas travel policy in 1989, Korean outbound travel to casinos in foreign countries has led to numerous unfortunate instances of financial difficulties, involving money laundering, paying extremely high interest rates on debts, and suicide. This problem has become more serious since the government legalized a casino in the domestic market in 2000. Many customers perceived casinos as a way to change their social status if they could hit a jackpot. According to a survey, typical visitors to the Kangwon Land Casino appeared to lose an average of US$4,000 per visit and more than 80 percent were found to be repeat customers (Choe, 2000).

Lee, Lee, and Ahn (2002) conducted a study to identify problem gamblers. The person-to-person survey was conducted with 620 casino visitors at Kangwon Land Casino between July 15 and 19, 2002. Twenty questions used by Gamblers Anonymous were presented to the respondents. Results of the study showed that 29.5 percent of the respondents were found to be problem gamblers, while the rest appeared to be responsible players. Problem gamblers had visited Kangwon Land Casino an average of ninety-six times since it opened. Furthermore, the length of their stay was found to be an average of eight days. The two groups, problem gamblers and responsible players, were statistically significantly different with regard to demographic characteristics, illusion of control, enduring involvement, benefit sought, and casino facilities and programs desired.

Individual Level: An Exploratory Study

Several researchers have mentioned that measuring social impacts on individuals is difficult (Oh, 1999; Rudd, 1999). Specifically, it is difficult to assess an individual's perception of social impacts in a city where the local gaming industry has impacted individuals' daily lifestyle.

Despite these difficulties, Lee and Back (2003) conducted a study to explore the changing attitudes of residents toward Kangwon Land Casino before and after its opening. Specifically, this study was conducted to explore the underlying factors of casino impacts, namely, social, economic, and environmental impacts, on residents' perception of benefits received and their support level. The presurvey was conducted at the end of June 2000, before the casino opened. The number of subjects was proportionately allocated based on occupation, using the official statistics of Chongsun County and Taeback City, Kangwon Province. A self-administered questionnaire was given to those who preferred to complete the questionnaire by themselves. Otherwise, the field researchers completed the questionnaire via personal interview. Informing respondents that the researchers would return to conduct a postsurvey, the surveyors asked for respondents' names and phone numbers so that the same respondents could be identified in the postsurvey. A total of 517 usable questionnaires were collected during the presurvey. In December 2000, the postsurvey was administered to those who had responded to the presurvey after the Kangwon Land Casino opened. During the postsurvey, a total of 404 usable questionnaires were collected, fewer than those collected in the presurvey.

A theoretical model was developed based on social exchange theory. Many researchers have used social exchange theory to integrate factors influencing residents' reactions to casino development. Social exchange theory assumes that residents' opinions are affected by their perceptions of the exchange they are making (Gursoy, Jurowski, & Uysal, 2002). Jurowski, Uysal, and Williams (1997) stated that residents' support for tourism development should be considered based on the social exchange theory to indicate their willingness to make an exchange with tourists.

The model postulates that causal factors (i.e., impacts of a casino) have both direct and indirect effects on residents' perceived benefits received and support for a casino. The theoretical model tested involved eight constructs: negative social, negative environmental, negative economic, positive social, positive environmental, and positive economic factors, as well as benefit and support. Residents' perceptions were measured on a five-point Likert-type scale: 1 = strongly disagree, 3 = neutral, and 5 = strongly agree. Respondents were asked to rate how much they agreed with each item on the scale.

Results of paired t-tests indicated that residents' perceptions were significantly different before and after the casino opening, as shown in Table 12.3. Mean values of most variables were found to be lower in the postsurvey than in the presurvey. Results indicated that residents perceived all negative and positive impact factors less strongly after the casino opened than they did prior to the opening. However, residents held stronger perceptions of some negative social impacts, such as gambling addiction, encouraging speculative gambling, increasing bankruptcy rates, and destructive effects on the family, after the casino opening. On the other hand, some negative impact factors scored significantly lower in the postsurvey than in the presurvey. For negative environmental impact factors, residents perceived that envi-

TABLE 12.3. Results of paired *t*-tests between pre- and postsurvey.

Variable	Mean score[a]		Mean difference[b]	*t*-value
	Presurvey	*Postsurvey*		
Negative social				
Occurrence of gambling addicts	3.55	3.94	0.39	4.57**
Speculative gambling	3.54	3.86	0.32	3.74**
Bankruptcy	3.51	3.79	0.28	3.41**
Destruction of family	3.47	3.52	0.04	0.52
Prostitution	3.62	3.21	−0.41	5.22**
Divorce	3.45	3.09	−0.36	4.79**
Alcoholism	3.51	3.11	−0.40	4.81**
Crime	3.59	3.36	−0.23	2.79*
Political corruption	3.47	3.27	−0.20	2.55*
Negative environmental				
Crowding due to visitors	3.89	3.13	−0.76	11.63**
Traffic congestion	4.02	3.56	−0.46	6.76**
Quantity of litter	4.16	3.51	−0.64	9.05**
Noise level	4.02	3.36	−0.66	9.39**
Water pollution	4.01	3.22	−0.79	10.88**
Destruction of natural environment	4.06	3.39	−0.67	8.91**
Negative economic				
Cost of living	3.24	2.93	−0.32	4.67**
Increased tax burden	3.35	3.09	−0.26	3.97**
Leakage of casino revenues	3.78	3.54	−0.24	3.08**
Positive social				
Quality of life	3.11	2.34	−0.77	11.94**
Consolidation of community spirit	2.76	2.50	−0.26	3.63**
Improvement of educational environment	2.38	1.99	−0.39	6.02**
Pride of local residents	3.19	2.55	−0.64	9.34**
Positive environmental				
Preservation of historic sites	2.88	2.47	−0.41	7.10**
Natural beauty	3.72	3.09	−0.63	8.94**

TABLE 12.3 *(continued)*

Variable	Mean score[a]		Mean difference[b]	t-value
	Presurvey	Postsurvey		
Positive economic				
Investment and business	3.96	2.89	−1.07	15.73**
Employment opportunities	3.63	3.01	−0.62	9.58**
Tourist spending	3.94	3.17	−0.78	11.96**
Tax revenues	3.73	3.01	−0.72	11.29**
Public utilities and infra-structure	4.00	3.21	−0.79	11.95**
Standard of living	3.42	2.32	−1.10	19.26**
Benefit				
Benefit to myself	3.18	2.43	−0.75	10.41**
Benefit to local residents	3.27	2.91	−0.36	4.87**
Support				
Future is bright due to casino	3.48	3.15	−0.33	4.42**
I am proud that I live in this city	2.85	2.63	−0.22	3.23**
Casino makes this city a better place to live	3.15	2.66	−0.49	6.51**
I support casino development	3.22	3.02	−0.20	1.93
Casino is the right choice for this city	3.33	3.00	−0.33	4.26**

Source: Lee and Back, 2003.

[a]Mean value based on a five-point Likert-type scale, where 1 = strongly disagree, 3 = neutral, and 5 = strongly agree.

[b]Mean difference (pre–postsurvey).

*p $\leq$ .01; ** p $\leq$ .001

ronmental concerns, such as crowding, traffic problems, and noise levels, were not really as bad as they had thought before the casino opening. Respondents' scores were also lower in the postsurvey regarding negative economic impact factors, indicating that they did not experience those economic problems to the extent that they had expected.

In contrast, residents perceived fewer positive impacts in the post-survey than in the presurvey. First, respondents scored somewhat higher than neutral about quality of life (mean = 3.11) and pride of local residents (mean = 3.19) during the presurvey. During the post-survey, respondents revealed more disagreement (mean = 2.34 and 2.55, respectively). Second, respondents scored lower for positive environmental factors. Respondents perceived that casino development did not help preserve historic sites and natural beauty of the community. Third, respondents expressed agreement with positive economic impact factors during the presurvey (mean ranged from 3.63 to 4.00). After the casino opening, respondents' scores were much lower on positive economic impact factors. Standard of living scored especially low (mean = 2.32).

Benefit factors scored slightly lower, indicating greater disagreement, in the postsurvey. Respondents also scored support factors slightly lower in the postsurvey than in the presurvey. Respondents had neutral perceptions of benefit and support factors before the casino opening; these perceptions changed to be more negative as they experienced the existence of a casino.

Furthermore, Lee and Back (2003) conducted a structural equation modeling analysis to examine the direct and indirect effects of those impacts of the casino opening on residents' perception of benefits received from the casino opening and on their support for casino development. Results showed that positive economic impact was the most significant in determining the benefit level; the magnitude of the impact was further enhanced after the casino opened. Also, respondents' perceived positive social impacts were the most significant in affecting the support level both before and after the casino opening. This study had several implications: (1) the social exchange model fits very well in explaining residents' attitudes toward casino operation with both pre- and postsurvey data; (2) policymakers should identify how to provide benefits to local residents so that they can support casino development further; and (3) casino operators and policymakers should make efforts to minimize the negative social impacts, because increase in the level of quality of life or standard of living was not only due to the positive economic impact but also significantly affected by negative social factors, such as gambling addiction problems (Back & Lee, 2003).

By conducting a series of longitudinal studies, researchers should be able to evaluate changes in residents' attitudes and identify new positive or negative impacts of the casino. Consequently, policymakers can take appropriate actions to make the community a pleasant place to live and to improve the quality of life for residents.

MINIMIZING NEGATIVE IMPACTS OF CASINOS

Gambling can be considered as either a leisure activity or a pathological problem, depending on how an individual perceives it. If a person has the ability to control his or her time and money, spending some time in the casino would not be dangerous, compared to someone who has pathological or compulsive gambling problems. Pathological gambling can be defined as gambling that causes serious damage to a person's social, vocational, or financial life. Often referred to as compulsive gambling and less frequently as disordered gambling, it is considered by most to be an impulse control disorder (Bland et al., 1993).

By learning from data associated with problem gambling in other countries, Korea can minimize many negative impacts to its society. Those problems can be prevented through proactive educational programs and treatment in a clinical environment. Proper regulation of gambling can make the industry healthy and ensure that the economic impact of recreational gaming activities remains beneficial. For instance, local residents of the community where Kangwon Land Casino is located may be restricted to enter the casino only once a month by showing an identification card at the entrance. This policy is specifically designed to minimize potential gambling problems in the community.

Furthermore, the government and businesses should support an effective compulsive gambling treatment program. A portion of the casino operation's profits could be used for this purpose. Currently, the Kangwon Land Casino spends a great deal on the Korea Gambling Problem Center (KGPC, 2003). The objectives of this problem gambling center are to (1) develop and provide prevention and treatment programs, (2) link with a clinical help line, (3) offer education pro-

grams for youth and local residents, and (4) increase public awareness of potential problem behaviors.

Specifically, the KGPC provides a telephone hotline for immediate
contact for pathological gamblers, potential gamblers, family members of problem gamblers, and other interested persons. The hotline
telephone number is posted in the casino, on its Web site, and in brochures. Once a person contacts the KGPC, a trained professional
helps screen the severity of the caller's problem and refers the caller
to visit the KGPC. After discussion with a professional at KGPC, the
person will join the treatment program and may be contacted by a
clinic. The hotline also provides additional information and resources
for help, such as Gamblers Anonymous (GA, or "Dandobak" in Korean), or the Korean Institute of Brief Family Therapy (BFT). The
KGPC works closely with GA and provides callers with information
regarding GA group meetings, locations, and times. The BFT provides consulting services for families who have problems associated
with marriage, parenthood, and addictions to gambling, drugs, or
alcohol.

When an individual's gambling problem seems to be serious, the
gambler may likely be referred to the KGPC's intensive outpatient
program. In the outpatient program, individuals meet with a professional counselor. Since KGPC is still in the initial stage, group activities are not developed yet. Individual interactions between pathological gamblers and the counselor may require additional support from
government, clinical, and religious groups. Individuals may also seek
help from KGPC in solving financial, legal, marital, or employment
issues caused by their gambling problems.

REFERENCES

Archer, B. H. (1977). Tourism multiplier: The state of the art. In J. Revell (Ed.),
    Bangor occasional papers in economics: No. II. Cardiff: University of Wales
    Press.
Back, K. J., & Lee, C. K. (2003). Structural equation modeling of residents percep-
    tions toward casinos: Pre- and post-casino development. *Proceedings of Interna-
    tional CHRIE 2003 Conference* (CD-ROM). Palm Springs, CA: CHRIE.
Bank of Korea. (2001). *1998 Input-output tables.* Seoul: Government Printer.
Blaine, T. W. (1993). Input-output analysis: Application to the assessment of the
    economic impact of tourism. In M. Khan, M. Olsen, & T. Var (Eds.), *VNR's en-*

cyclopedia of hospitality and tourism (pp. 663-670). New York: Van Nostrand
    Reinhold.
Bland, R. C., Newman, S. C., Orn, H., & Stelesky, G. (1993). Epidemiology of
    pathological gambling in Edmonton. Canadian Journal of Psychiatry, 38, 108-
    112.
Burke, J. D. (1996). Problem gambling hits home. Wisconsin Medical Journal, 95,
    611-614.
Choe, Y. (2000, November 22). Casino development. Korea Herald, p. A1.
Fletcher, J. E. (1989). Input-output analysis and tourism impact studies. Annals of
    Tourism Research, 16(4), 514-529.
Gursoy, D., Jurowski, C., & Uysal, M. (2002). Resident attitude: A structural mod-
    eling approach. Annals of Tourism Research, 29(1), 79-105.
Heng, T. M., & Low, L. (1990). Economic impact of tourism in Singapore. Annals
    of Tourism Research, 17(2), 246-269.
Jurowski, C., Uysal, M., & Williams, D. R. (1997). A theoretical analysis of host com-
    munity resident reactions to tourism. Journal of Travel Research, 36(2), 3-11.
Kangwon Land Casino. (2003). Casino visitors and revenues. Kangwon-do: Author.
Khan, H., Chou, F. S., & Wong, K. C. (1990). Tourism multiplier effects on Singa-
    pore. Annals of Tourism Research, 17(3), 408-409.
Korea Gambling Problem Center. (2003). Understanding gambling addictions.
    Available: http://www.gamblerclinic.or.kr.
Korean Casino Association. (2003). Casino visitors and receipts. Seoul: Author.
Lee, C. K. (1992). The economic impact of international inbound tourism on the
    South Korean economy and its distributional effects on income classes. Unpub-
    lished doctoral dissertation, Texas A&M University, College Station.
Lee, C. K. (2003). A long-term strategy for the Korean casino industry. Seoul: Para-
    dise Walker-Hill Casino.
Lee, C. K., & Back, K. J. (2003). Pre and post casino impact of residents' percep-
    tion. Annals of Tourism Research, 30(4), 868-885.
Lee, C. K., & Kwon, K. S. (1995). Importance of secondary impact of foreign tour-
    ism receipts on the South Korean economy. Journal of Travel Research, 34(2),
    50-54.
Lee, C. K., & Kwon, K. S. (1997). The economic impact of the casino industry in
    South Korea. Journal of Travel Research, 36(1), 52-58.
Lee, C. K., Lee, B. K., & Ahn, B.Y. (2002). Comparison of characteristics between
    problem gamblers and leisure-oriented seekers in Kangwon Land Casino.
    Kangwon-do: Author.
Leontief, W. (1936). Quantitative input and output relations in the economic system
    of the United States. Review of Economic Statistics, 18(3), 105-125.
Lesieur, H. R. (1998). Costs and treatment of pathological gambling. Annals of the
    American Academy of Political and Social Science, 556(1), 153-171.
Littlejohn, D. (1999). The real Las Vegas: Life beyond the strip. New York: Oxford
    University Press.
Lorenz, V. C., & Shuttlesworth, D. E. (1983). The impact of pathological gambling
    on the spouse of the gambler. Journal of Community Psychology, 11(1), 67-76.

McCormick, R. A. (1993). Disinhibition and negative affectivity in substance abusers with and without a gambling problem. *Addictive Behaviors, 18,* 331-336.

Oh, H. M. (1999). Social impacts of casino gaming: The case of Las Vegas. In C. Hsu (Ed.), *Legalized casino gaming in the United States* (pp. 177-199). Binghamton, NY: The Haworth Press.

Rudd, D. (1999). Social impacts of Atlantic City casino gaming. In C. Hsu (Ed.), *Legalized casino gaming in the United States* (pp. 201-220). Binghamton, NY: The Haworth Press.

Thompson, W. N., Gazel, R., & Rockman, D. (1996). The social costs of gambling in Wisconsin. *Wisconsin Policy Research Institute Report, 9*(6), 1-44.

United Nations. (1990). *Guidelines on input-output analysis of tourism.* New York: Author.

Chapter 13

Gambling and Chinese Culture

Grace C. L. Chien
Cathy H. C. Hsu

Chinese records of betting on dice and Chinese chess matches date back to around 300 BC; some studies indicate that in China and Hong Kong, in the late 1800s, everyone would gamble for everything (Galletti, 2002). "Basically all Chinese have the gambling gene," says a source in the casino industry in Macao (Casino City, 2002). Even the act of buying meat from a street vendor became a gambling game, in which instead of simply paying for the meat, the client would gamble with the vendor, willing to risk getting nothing for the chance of possibly winning three times as much (Nepstad, 2000).

The Chinese are a nation of gamblers (Abel, 1997; Nepstad, 2000), who are naturally higher risk takers, quicker to adopt new technologies, and more money focused (Cullen, 2000). Modern games of chance, such as roulette, dice, lottery, and baccarat, and competitive games of skill, such as chess, checkers, and billiards, are so addictive that some Chinese become the pawns of destiny, and others, fully aware of the inevitable outcome, still persist in pursuing their course.

Gambling is a form of Chinese culture. This chapter examines the phenomenon of gambling as a cultural expression among the Chinese. Many different forms of gambling activities beginning with ancient China are introduced. Gambling policies and cultural factors in the modern gambling practice of different Chinese societies are discussed as well.

CHINESE GAMING HISTORY

Games of chance and of skill have been found in China's aesthetic and social traditions since ancient times. Divine associations in games of chance are evident in archaeological finds in China, Israel (formerly Palestine), Sumeria, Assyria, Babylonia, Greece, Rome, India, and Japan, and in ancient Egyptian tomb paintings (Brenner & Brenner, 1990). The ancient Chinese divination manual and book of mystical speculations *I Ching* (The Chinese Book of Changes) consists of eight basic trigrams and "sixty-four hexagrams formed by their combinations," symbolizing "all the possible situations or mutations of creation" (Bary, 1960, p. 192). The book may be the oldest text in Chinese. It was first written by the legendary Chinese Emperor Fu Hsi (2953-2838 BC) and further commentaries were added by the Duke of the Chou Dynasty in the eleventh century BC and Emperor Wen of the Sui Dynasty (AD 581-618) (*The I Ching,* 1963). *I Ching* could be used for fortune telling, commonly using coins or sticks. Fifty yarrow stalks, the original instruments of calculation, were used to predict and interpret future events (Bary, 1960).

The ancient Chinese also applied to inspired and divinely authoritative communications for help, advice, or information based on tortoise-shell readings. Because tortoise shells "concealed the secrets of heaven and of earth" (Eberhard, 1986/1983, p. 294), their cracks and patterns were considered to contain such communications. Placed over a flame, the tortoise shell would crack, forming ordered and disordered squares that were interpreted accordingly by seers, shamans, and oracles (von Franz, 1980) who then set down their predictions in some form of writing. Divination writing itself originated from an intelligent Chinese who needed to read into future events, and thus to gamble on things to come. Other forms of divination were and are still popular for similar reasons (Eberhard, 1986/1983). Early predictive writings have also been found on long strips of bamboo, silk, and wood.

Also popular during the Han dynasty (206 BC-AD 220) was the game of liubo, involving dice and played on a board reminiscent of a Chinese sundial. The playing of liubo was accompanied by ritualized gestures performed with each throw of the dice. Several types of chess, card games, and dominoes were also favored (Eberhard, 1986/1983).

Confucius, however, condemned such pastimes, referring to Lao-tzu, the founder of Taoism, as an "ignorant good man" who foolishly encouraged the use of lucky charms and gambling. Since no social good derived from gambling, most Han Dynasty philosophers also frowned on this form of moneymaking (Aero, 1980). Centuries later, women and men of all classes took to betting on nearly everything: butchers on cuts of meat, bakers on cakes, and fruit dealers on the number of pits in orange sections. Interestingly, the winners of orange games received three times the original stake. In another popular game, the one who guessed the winning animal out of a possible thirty-six animals was awarded thirty times what he or she had pledged (Aero, 1980).

The most common gambling games in Chinese culture are animal fighting, dice, dominoes, chess, cards and mah-jongg (Aero, 1980). Fighting crickets and quail matches were popular in the Chin Dynasty (221-206 BC) and Han Dynasty, and dice throwing was popular in the Tang Dynasty (AD 618-907). Dominoes originated from a pot-throwing game in the Tang Dynasty; chess and cards were becoming popular in the Ming Dynasty (AD 1368-1644). Bettors during the Qing Dynasty (AD 1659-1911) preferred to wager on foot-shuttlecock, kite flying, quail fighting, cricket fighting, chess, cards, dice, and seed-catching birds (Werner, 1994). In addition, the game mah-jongg has been popular since the Qing Dynasty (Hsieh, 2002).

The gambling culture can also be demonstrated by the presence of gambling in great masterpieces of ancient literature. In *The Story of Miss Li* (AD 79), a Tang Dynasty tale by Po Hsing-chien, the young male protagonist was willing to gamble considerable sums to win his lady love. *The Pearl-Sewn Shirt* (AD 1466), by the Ming dynasty tale-teller Feng Meng-lung, revolved around the more than strange fate of a wife named Fortune. Certain sequences in China's great classical novel *The Dream of the Red Chamber* (AD 1791) by Tsao Hsueh-chin are replete with gambling games (Beal, 1975).

CHINESE GAMES

Chinese Cards

The exact origin of playing cards is unknown. However, if cards were not invented in Europe, they must have come from the East

(Parlett, 1990). The old idea that cards reached Europe from China in or following the thirteenth-century voyages of Marco Polo is no longer credible. However, it is true that playing cards were then known to the Chinese, and probably invented by them (Parlett, 1990). Playing cards of some sort are known to have existed in China from early times, at least as early as the Tang Dynasty, although none has survived from a period earlier than the eighteenth century. There appears to be no word in the Chinese language for "playing cards," which are lumped together with other gaming devices, such as dice, dominoes, and chess pieces under a generic title meaning "objects for gambling." This sums up the Chinese attitude toward playing cards as just another form of gambling (Beal, 1975).

One of the legends about the origins of playing cards is that the custom was born in the inner chambers of the Chinese imperial palace. The inner chambers were where the royal "sleeping staff" lived. The "veiled ladies" secluded therein were numerous, since the emperor's recognized establishment for some 2,000 years included one empress, three consorts, nine spouses, twenty-seven beauties or concubines, and eighty-one attendant nymphs or assistant concubines. The numbers three and nine were held in particular regard by Chinese astrologers (Tilley, 1973).

The "mistresses of the bed" kept regular night watches, the eighty-one attendant nymphs sharing the imperial couch for nine nights in groups of nine, the twenty-seven beauties for three nights in groups of nine, the nine spouses and three consorts for one night each as a group, and the empress for one night alone. These arrangements lasted from, roughly, the early years of the Chou Dynasty (1122-256 BC) to the beginning of the Sung Dynasty (AD 950-1279) when the order broke down and had to be abandoned according to a contemporary policy, because of the absolutely uncontrolled and ungoverned competition of no less than 3,000 ladies of the palace. By the time of the Sung Dynasty, the occupants of the inner chambers had even less to do than ever before, and their days must have been wearisome to the point of inducing mental breakdown. As a result, says the legend, in 1120, playing cards were conceived by a member of the Chinese imperial harem as a pastime for relieving perpetual boredom (Tilley, 1973).

The Chinese legend may indeed hold more than a grain of truth because the ladies of the harem not only had urgent need for such an invention but also had the necessary time to give to the matter, and more important, the talent. Two further points appear to be relevant and supportive of the legend. The first is that the Emperor Hui Tsung, who reigned from 1100 to 1125, was a painter of the first rank and a noted calligrapher. Could he not have sympathized with his women and lent his brush to them? The second point is that the period was one of the finest in the history of printing from woodblocks in China (Tilley, 1973).

The legend matches a Chinese encyclopedia published in 1678, which gave the year 1120 as the date of the invention of playing cards (Beal, 1975). Ashton (1898) also confidently attributed the origin of cards to China, where they were known, he claimed, in the twelfth century. However, the statement is still open to some debate (Beal, 1975). Another work dated to Chinese New Year's Eve in AD 969 reported that the Emperor Mu-Tsung of the Sung Dynasty played cards with his wives (Dummett, 1980), and these cards were evidently domino cards (Parlett, 1990).

Chinese cards varied considerably and were usually black and white, as straight and narrow as a moral principle (Tilley, 1973). The cards were always long and narrow, varying in size from about 65 × 20 mm to something like 120 × 30 mm (Beal, 1975). According to Beal (1975), they can be classified into six main groups: mah-jongg cards, word or phrase cards, number cards, money cards, domino or dice cards, and chess cards. Each type of card has different designs and rules for playing.

Mah-jongg

Mah-jongg has for centuries been the favorite game of the Chinese, and tradition has it that its name comes from the sound made by the tiles clicking together during the game. Some mah-jongg aficionados claim that the word is a composite of *mah* (meaning flax or hemp and associated with the sound made by the leaves of plants "clicking in the wind") and *jong,* identified with the chattering of the sparrow. Thus the derivation of the name mah-jongg, popular in China, and indeed throughout the world in both past and contemporary times, is uncertain. According to Parlett (1990), mah-jongg, a nineteenth-century invention in China, is clearly a version of the three-suited money-card pack. A mah-jongg set has 144 tiles, which may be classified into four suits: the bamboo, circle, character, and wind. Each suit has thirty-six tiles (Photo 13.1). When playing mah-jongg, the unseen tiles make the game interesting. The players understand the subtleties and extreme complexities of the game by its many terms, the speed with which they make their moves, and the varieties of ways in which the game may be played (Whitney, 1975).

Most people in China have participated in the game using some playing chips or a few dollars just for the pleasure of playing. Since mah-jongg is associated with gambling, unlike Chinese chess or wei qi (both are very popular official games), no official mah-jongg competition is held anywhere in China. Mah-jongg was forbidden during the Chinese Cultural Revolution (1966-1976); however, it is now popular again. One might even hear the sound of playing when passing by the home of Chinese neighbors at night. Mah-jongg is also now available online. Players can log in to a Web site and play the game with other online players.

PHOTO 13.1. The Chinese game of mah-jongg.

CHINESE PLAYERS IN THE MODERN GAMING MARKET

Gaming has been a pastime for Chinese people in all parts of the world. Abel (1997) revealed the popularity of gambling among Chinese immigrants to North America and the prevalence of Chinese at all-night gambling operations. The Chinese were among the pioneer settlers of the American West. They established enclaves of Chinese culture in Chinatowns in various cities and gambling was one of the three types of economic activity, besides prostitution and opium, that the Chinese engaged in during the nineteenth century (Chen, 1992).

Chinese players have been and will continue to be an integral part of the gaming industry. Nowadays, an entire gaming industry has sprung up to cater to Chinese players (Casino City, 2002) because the gaming industry is aware of the importance of Chinese customers. Considering the potential difference that Chinese customers can make in the casino bottom line, casino managers should be extremely interested in appreciating such customers (Galletti, 2002). Understanding elements of Chinese culture can help generate repeat visits to casinos. For example, games of chance and skill are popular year round in Chinese communities, but gambling activities are particularly prevalent during the Chinese New Year festivities (Aero, 1980; Toledano, 1997). Casinos consider the Chinese New Year the best gambling weekend in the year, when thousands of Chinese go to Las Vegas to celebrate and gamble (Galletti, 2002). Understanding their culture, needs, and expectations can lead to improvements in customer service and therefore increase customer satisfaction.

Las Vegas and Australia are the top picks for many Chinese gamblers. Las Vegas is a favorite destination for the Chinese and 85 percent of the high rollers that play in Las Vegas come from China, Taiwan, and Japan (ABC News, 2002). Even though the volume of Japanese visiting Las Vegas is greater than the volume of Chinese visitors, the amount of money Chinese are willing to gamble is exorbitant (Galletti, 2002). Statistics show that in Las Vegas, losses by Chinese have been extraordinary (Pomfret, 2002). Casino operators in Las Vegas have reported that in recent years the number of Chinese gamblers has increased dramatically, probably because it has become easier for Chinese citizens to travel to the United States for business or conferences. According to tour operators, most Chinese visitors go to Las Vegas as part of their itinerary in the United States (Biers, 2001).

In Australia, the report *The Impact of Gaming on Specific Cultural Groups* by the Victorian Casino and Gambling Authority (2000) indicated that problem gamblers were more prevalent in the Chinese community than in the general population. Specifically, among Chinese gamblers, 10.7 percent were problem gamblers; the figure for the Vietnamese community was 10.5 percent, for the Greek community 9.0 percent, and for the Arabic community 7.2 percent (Victorian Casino and Gambling Authority, 2000). The median outlay of individual Chinese gamblers each week was A$10, compared to A$3 by individuals in the general population. Another study has also found that problem gambling is more than six times more prevalent in Australia's Asian community than in the community at large (Marshall, 2000).

Similarly, in some Canadian cities, such as Toronto or Montreal, Chinese problem gambling treatment services have been developed for the growing number of Chinese-speaking individuals in these cities (Harvard Medical School, 1997). Sin (1996) conducted an exploratory study examining gambling and problem gambling behaviors and attitudes among Chinese residents in Quebec. Sin concluded that Chinese Canadians may develop higher rates of problem gambling; however, this finding could be a function of different cultural perspectives. For example, although playing mah-jongg may have been considered a social activity for many Chinese in their country of origin (Au & Yu, 1997), playing mah-jongg for money is considered gambling within the Canadian context (Harvard Medical School, 1997).

CHINESE CULTURAL TRAITS

Many people understand culture in terms of geography; however, culture is not confined to nations or countries. Rather, culture is the unique combination of characteristics of a social group, the values and norms shared by its members that set them apart from other social groups (Lytle, Brett, & Shapiro, 1999). "[T]o the extent that members of a social system share particular symbols, meanings, images, rule structures, habits, values, and information processing and transformational patterns they can be said to share a common culture" (Ruben, 1983, p. 139).

People of Chinese origin love to gamble. Gambling has also been associated with Chinese culture (Toledano, 1997). Throughout Chinese history, a large percentage of the Chinese population has been poor. Therefore, people have always hoped for a miracle, a streak of good luck, a big win. Another theory relates the gambling tradition to the Confucian worldview that stresses that favors from the gods can be secured through prayers, so Chinese people hoped to secure favors for their endeavors, in other words, to have good luck. Therefore, luck and the quest for good luck became important components of Chinese culture (Nepstad, 2000), even though Confucius condemned gambling and the quest for luck.

Chinese Superstitions

The Chinese in general have a strong belief in the existence of good luck or bad luck compared to Westerners, and the Chinese associate many things with good or bad luck. In this section, Chinese superstitions about colors, numbers, plants, dining, and gift giving related to gaming management are discussed. An understanding of Chinese superstitions can provide gaming operators with clues on how to improve customer satisfaction, or at least to avoid dissatisfaction, and increase repeat visits among Chinese gamblers.

Color

Color is not only an aesthetic issue but also a cultural one. The Chinese like red because it represents happiness (Ding & Bone, 1995; Galletti, 2002). However, writing in red is not appropriate for Chinese because it is thought to shorten a person's life. Gaming operators should pay special attention when printing invitations or special materials to be sent to Chinese customers. Because the colors white and black are used in Chinese funerals, not too much black or white should be used in a gaming room (Galletti, 2002).

Numbers

It is believed that numbers can determine a person's fate in Chinese culture. The number four is very unlucky as in Chinese it sounds like the word for death (Chinatown Online, 2003; Simmons & Schindler, 2003). In contrast, the number eight is associated with prosperity and good luck, whereas six is believed to make things run smoothly (Galletti, 2002; Simmons & Schindler, 2003). Many casinos have already removed seat number four from table games and room number four from guest or gaming rooms to adjust to this Chinese belief (Galletti, 2002). The role of superstitions about numbers provides guidance for gaming operators in managing casinos and setting prices for the increasingly important Chinese market.

Plants

Lucky bamboo is a must-have plant that symbolizes health, love, and good luck. Bamboo is said to bring good fortune to those who own it and is one of the plants recommended by feng shui masters to create a space where people supposedly will feel safe and more energized (Galletti, 2002). Many Chinese like plum blooms too because plum blooms are associated with perseverance and integrity. However, chrysanthemums in white or yellow are associated with death because they are the flowers used in funerals. When decorating hotel guest rooms or casino gaming floors that cater to Chinese players, gaming operators should carefully study the most appropriate type and color of plants to use so that a comfortable environment can be created for Chinese customers.

Dining

When conducting business with the Chinese, it is useful to understand Chinese dining etiquette. When gaming operators host a meal for Chinese customers, the serving staff should pay special attention to Chinese dining traditions and table manners (Galletti, 2002; Reiman, 2003). At Chinese banquets, seating arrangements should be made based on the seniority and social rank of the diners present. Dining is a social event and the Chinese like to speak loudly around the dining table. Toasting is an important part of the meal. Before food is delivered, an elaborate process of toast-giving begins the event. The Chinese like to empty their glasses each time, usually in one go, then seek an immediate refill to be ready for the next toast (Reiman, 2003).

Banquets usually consist of ten to fifteen courses (Seligman, 1983) and can run for hours. Placing chopsticks upright in a bowl of rice is believed to attract death (Galletti, 2002); thus, servers should be instructed not to do so and to remove the chopsticks immediately if they observe such situations. When serving fruits, pears are not supposed to be shared because sharing a pear, *fen li,* has the same pronunciation as the word for separation in Chinese.

Gift Giving

Gift giving is a delicate issue among the Chinese; they have precise rules governing it (Reardon, 1982; Galletti, 2002). Gift-giving actions not only reveal concern and offer friendship but also communicate clues about certain relationships called *guan xi,* which can be translated as social relations, personal connections, or particularistic ties (Kipnis, 1996). The determination of the proper gift recipient is as important as choosing the proper gift (Reardon, 1982) and it is acceptable to give gifts either in private or to a group as a whole to avoid embarrassment because of the Chinese collectivist orientation (Galletti, 2002). Because gift giving can be confused with bribery, gifts should be limited to small items (Seligman, 1983). The most acceptable gift is a banquet, such as a welcoming or departure party (Seligman, 1983; Galletti, 2002); quality writing pens are also considered favored gifts (Galletti, 2002). Some gifts and colors are associated with bad luck, death, or separation, and thus should not be given to the Chinese under any circumstances.

Examples of unwelcome gifts are clocks and umbrellas ("No umbrellas," 1992). Giving a clock *(song zhang)* has the same pronunciation as "sending off at the end," which is also a term used for funerals; therefore, giving a clock as a gift is a major no-no. One should also never give umbrellas *(san)* as gifts to family, friends, or customers, unless one wishes to dissolve *(san)* the bond between. Gaming operators should carefully review information about gifts and their meanings so that proper gifts can be offered to Chinese customers (Galletti, 2002).

In addition to these beliefs, Chinese do not have the same sense of privacy as Westerners do. To build *guan xi,* many Chinese expect others to ask about their age, family, and career, among other things, as this shows that they are becoming friends. Even though it may sound very uncomfortable for a person from the West to ask or be asked such questions, gaming staff should be aware of the types of conversation that will make a Chinese customer perceive himself or herself as a friend rather than just a customer (Galletti, 2002).

Feng Shui

A very important component of Chinese culture is feng shui, which is a Chinese discipline indicating that the placement of objects influences peace, prosperity, and health (Galletti, 2002). Feng shui is translated as "wind water" and traditionally symbolizes the space between heaven and earth, the environment where people live. The underlying philosophy recognizes that people and their environment are sustained by an invisible, yet tangible, energy that moves like the wind and is called chi (Wong, 2001). Chi is called yin as a negative energy, or yang as a positive energy. Feng shui principles teach one how to attract and enhance positive life energy (chi) based on how the home or the environment is arranged (Wong, 2001). Understanding these disciplines is important for gaming operations seeking to offer an environment that will make Chinese customers feel comfortable, because the combination of materials, shapes, and locations where objects are placed can strongly impact a Chinese person's perception of a good and comfortable environment. Therefore, feng shui should be carefully reviewed by gaming operators in terms of gaming floor plans and decorations.

Many casinos have hired feng shui experts to ensure that the environment is properly presented (Central News Agency, 1997; Galletti, 2002) from the perspectives of gaming operators themselves and of Chinese customers. Often the Chinese make a corner shop, hotel, or bank entrance slanted so that access to the business is widened and chi can go in, which means people and money are drawn in. For years, these slanted doors have been used by gambling operations in markets such as Macao (Rossbach, 1983).

The first thing that a feng shui expert does is to conduct an external inspection of the building to detect anything that might cause "problems." Problems could come from surrounding buildings, freeways, an overpass, or other objects. The feng shui expert uses a Chinese compass *(lo pan)* to make a feng shui chart that involves several calculations. From the results, one can tell which direction could bring good or bad influences. Each direction is associated with a particular star and number, and each star has its own particular energy (chi). For example, if the number eight star shows, it corresponds to money. Other stars may represent illness, celebration, success, relationship, luck (good or bad), popularity, birth, and death (Wong, 2001).

Bagua is another common map used in feng shui to find out which part of the building or environment correlates with a particular situation in a person's life. This map enables the feng shui expert to evaluate and adjust the environment. Using this *bagua* map, one can select and arrange objects in a room to create harmony and encourage the proper flow of energy. Each of the directions on the *bagua* is believed to govern a different aspect of life, such as health, wealth, fame, marriage, children, helpful people, career, knowledge, and family. Each of these aspects is influenced by the five elements of earth, fire, wood, metal, and water. Every object around and in the building is characterized by a certain element. The way objects and their elements interact is believed to influence the environment (Wong, 2001).

In feng shui, sunlight is believed to bring or encourage positive energy. Main doors and windows of gaming buildings can be arranged to face south to get more sunshine and be free of obstructions. In addition, water flowing means prosperity, so fountains are often placed in various areas of a building. Usually, the feng shui expert uses *lo pan* and *bagua* to determine the exact place where the fountain would be most effective in bringing in cash (Galletti, 2002).

Money and the Chinese

The Chinese view money differently than people of other cultures do. "Chinese feel there is one pocket for saving, the other for playing money," says Larry Yu, the founder of Schwab's Asia Pacific Services in the United States (Cullen, 2000). The Chinese are willing to take more risks with their playing money (Cullen, 2000). Although North American gamblers tend to adjust their bets slowly at the gaming tables, Chinese gamblers, in contrast, tend to make huge bet variations as their sense of luck changes. Casino operators report that it is not unusual to see a Chinese player increase a $100 bet to $10,000. This willingness to risk large amounts of money on a single bet and the propensity to gamble for long periods of time make the Chinese one of the favorite groups of customers for Las Vegas casinos (Galletti, 2002).

The Chinese propensity to gamble can be reflected in a study of American and Chinese proverbs in regard to economic values by Weber, Hsee, and Sokolowska (1998). The study found that Chinese proverbs generally advocated greater risk-taking than did American proverbs. The result helps explain earlier research that found Chinese citizens were indeed more willing to take financial risks than Americans. In addition, due to the collectivist nature of the Chinese culture, their willingness to take financial risks can be linked to traditional norms, such as group harmony and collaborative spirit, that ensured the safety of family members. A traditional familial safety net in Chinese culture means that gamblers would not land in the poorhouse, as would be likely to happen in individualistic cultures where the sense of community and family protection is not as strong (Taylor, 1999).

Chinese gamblers have particular characteristics, such as the size of their bets and the ability to play for several days with no sleep (Biers, 2001). The Chinese gambling style tends to be more intense and erratic compared to that of average North American gamblers (Galletti, 2002). All these factors have caught the attention of gaming companies for this emerging market. The Asian regional marketing director for Harrah's Las Vegas, Bill Chu, stated that "Asians are the only growing segment of the casino market, and the Chinese are the only people in Asia with cash" (Pomfret, 2002, p. A1).

Analysis of Hofstede's Cultural Dimensions

To study cultural influences on a society, one needs typologies (Schein, 1985) or dimensions (Hofstede, 1980) for analyzing the behaviors, actions, and values of its members (Low & Shi, 2002). According to Ogbor (1990), the frameworks used to describe the assumptions that a particular society may have about reality may be grouped into three categories as cultural dimensions (Hofstede, 1980, 1984, 1985, 1991), cultural paradigms (Schein, 1985), and cultural patterns (Geertz, 1973) or pattern variables (Parsons & Shils, 1952). This section discusses one of the most widely quoted frameworks, cultural dimensions as espoused by Hofstede (1980), which was adopted as the conceptual framework by Galletti (2002) for the analysis of Chinese gamblers. Hofstede's model is commonly referred to as the four-dimension culture model (Holt, 1998). The four dimensions are power distance, uncertainty avoidance, individualism-collectivism, and masculinity. Redpath and Nielsen (1997) added one more dimension, Confucian dynamism, to Hofstede's model. This particular dimension differentiates Chinese from Western cultural values.

Power Distance

Power most often symbolizes higher status, respect, and more rights and wealth (Hofstede, 1980). The high power distance between ranks among the Chinese indicates that inequalities of power and wealth have been allowed to grow within the society and that opportunities and equality for everyone are not embraced (Galletti, 2002). The Chinese highly respect elders, who should not be called by their first names. In the West, calling someone by his or her first name may represent friendliness; for the Chinese, this would be considered a disrespectful way to communicate with an elder. According to Galletti (2002), power distance means gaming operators should be aware that Chinese customers value seniority, rank, and title; therefore, they would feel more valued when high executives of the gaming institution show attention to players' needs and respect to them by using their last names with titles.

Uncertainty Avoidance

The uncertainty avoidance dimension refers to the extent to which members of a culture feel threatened by ambiguity and uncertainty and the extent to which they try to avoid these situations (Hofstede, 1980). As Redpath and Nielsen (1997) noted, because of insecurity, people try to control their environment by creating laws and rules, and forming groups or institutions. Cultures high in uncertainty avoidance, such as the Chinese, have policies, procedures, and rules to stipulate what actions to take under certain conditions, thereby attempting to limit risk and uncertainty (Volkema & Fleury, 2002). The Chinese attempt to limit risk and uncertainty when gambling by knowing the exact rules and mastering the skills of playing the game. Very often, Chinese players at table games look very serious, partly because some players have a large amount of money at stake; however, for the most part, Chinese players are serious about the games because they want to be in control of the situation. Brochures specifying the rules of various games and beginners' tables could be offered to orient new players so that they are equipped to minimize uncertainty.

Individualism-Collectivism

The individualism-collectivism dimension focuses on the degree to which a society reinforces individual or collective achievement and interpersonal relationships (Hofstede, 1980). The Chinese culture is high in collectivism rather than individualism and the Chinese emphasize group harmony, social order, relationships between people, loyalty, and group reputation (Chang, 2003). In practical terms, gaming operators should know that the Chinese tend to emphasize group identity and group relations; the Chinese see themselves as a group and not as individuals. For example, it is more appropriate to offer a gift to the group as a whole rather than to an individual group member. Gifts to individuals should be given in private and not in front of group members to avoid embarrassment (Galletti, 2002).

Masculinity

The masculinity dimension focuses on the degree to which a society reinforces the traditional masculine role models of male achievement, control, and power (Hofstede, 1980). The Chinese high masculinity rating indicates that people experience a high degree of gender differentiation, and males dominate a significant portion of the society and power structure. In Chinese communities, females are not treated as equal to males in all aspects of society and are limited in their participation in managerial and professional ranks (Galletti, 2002; Chang, 2003). Also, females would feel more comfortable dealing with men than with women in a negotiation process (Chang, 2003) and opposite-gender attraction might be the reason. Galletti (2002) suggested that gaming operators should be aware of the norms and rules of complementary gender-role behaviors among the Chinese.

Confucian Dynamism

People who adhere to Confucianism may have certain qualities, such as loyalty, a sense of reciprocal obligation, and honesty in dealing with others (Hill, 1994). Chinese are ranked extremely high in long-term orientation based on Confucian dynamism; this indicates the value of long-term commitments and respect for tradition by the Chinese (Galletti, 2002). When doing business with the Chinese, respecting their values and being polite and honest will help build a long-term business relationship (Chang, 2003). Therefore, Galletti (2002) suggested that gaming operators should invest time in establishing long-term relationships with such customers as a way to keep their business.

GAMING LEGALIZATION IN CHINESE SOCIETIES

Gambling has become legal and almost ubiquitous throughout the world. The freedom to lose money has become established in most ideological environments. However, gambling has been regarded as a sin, a vice, and a crime in Chinese communities. This attitude persists among many Chinese even to this day (Hsieh, 2002). Gambling is officially illegal in China, where the government has regarded it with some disfavor (Beal, 1975; "China's uncertain odds," 1995), even though China inaugurated a state lottery on July 31, 1933 (Brenner & Brenner, 1990). Lotteries are not unfamiliar to the Chinese; *hwo-wei,* a form of illegal lottery in the 1930s, was very popular among the lower classes in Shanghai (Brenner & Brenner, 1990).

Over the past several decades, China has made remarkable strides in developing a mature mix of lotteries. After the formation of the People's Republic of China in 1949, all forms of gambling were forbidden. The policy changed in 1987 with the approval of the first instant lottery, which initially only offered the relatively primitive break-open tickets (Compulot, 2000). There are two authorized lottery organizations in China: the Welfare Lottery, designed to support social charities, and the Sports Lottery, which channels its proceeds to sports development projects (Asia-Pacific News Service, 2001), both of which now have computerized lottery systems (Compulot, 2000). The China Welfare Lottery Issuing Center was established in Beijing in 1987 (World Lottery Association, 2003). Later, the Sports Lottery started in 1994, and its center was established in Beijing as well (World Lottery Association, 2003).

National lotteries are now a promising industry in China as they create job opportunities, increase tax revenues, and generate funds for the government ("China to tighten," 2002). The lottery industry in China is expected to create 50,000 job opportunities ("Lawmaker says," 2001). For example, in Beijing, the Sports Lottery has already created more than 3,000 jobs. Players have splurged 44 million yuan (US$5.5 million) on the lottery, more than three times the original projection, with an average of 5 million yuan awarded twice weekly. The fifteen new millionaires and other jackpot winners have paid a total of approximately 1.8 million yuan in income taxes (Asia-Pacific News Service, 2001).

Thirty percent of funds collected from the issuance of the computerized Sports Lottery tickets are invested in facilities related to the 2008 Olympic Games. From 1994 to 2001, more than 2.3 billion yuan (US$280 million) from the Sports Lottery were collected to finance part of the Olympic construction program ("China approves," 2001). Lotteries netted only 18 million yuan in 1987, the first year they were reintroduced ("China's finance chiefs," 2000); however, the Welfare Lottery and Sports Lottery raised a combined 28 billion yuan (US$3.5 billion) in 2001. The Welfare Lottery has reached more than 95 percent of the counties and cities in China. Over 60 percent of residents in major cities, including Beijing, Shanghai, Guangzhou, and Wuhan, have purchased lottery tickets (World Tibet Network News, 2002).

Lottery proponents pointed out that China has a very big potential given that only some 6 percent of its 1.26 billion people have bought lottery tickets (Asia-Pacific News Service, 2001). Chinese on average spend barely six yuan each year on the lottery, placing it in a lowly ninety-seventh place worldwide, well behind countries such as France, Japan, and the United States (Agence France-Presse, 2001). Per capita sales only have to increase marginally to record a further significant increase in revenue. The national target in the next several years is to generate some 10 billion yuan in annual sales, or an average lottery spending of seven yuan per person (Asia-Pacific News Service, 2001).

National lotteries face stiff competition from illegal rivals. However, the illegal lotteries have not stopped the growth of the national lotteries. According to the government's lottery research center, China's legitimate lottery market should reach 84 billion yuan by 2010, a massive fivefold increase over sales in 1999 (Agence France-Presse, 2001). On the other hand, it is believed that China is in need of national laws to guide the rapid new development of its lottery industry. Since 2002, the Ministry of Finance of the Chinese government has managed to tighten supervision over the country's lottery industry to maintain a fair market in order to avoid unfair competition between gaming institutions ("China to tighten," 2002). Previously, the two lottery operations were administered by the People's Bank of China. The administration of the lotteries is now consolidated under the Ministry of Finance, and the lottery proceeds are apportioned to various ministries and functions rather than being earmarked solely for sports and social welfare projects (Compulot, 2000).

As for casino development in China, an American-style casino resort was approved in 1994 for Hainan as part of China's economic diversification into global tourism (McMillen, 1996). Hainan is an island in the southern part of China and has been given the status of an economic trade zone by the central Beijing government, which gives it, among other things, free trade status. The Beijing government is keen to develop tourism and sees Hainan as a natural tropical destination for the Asian market. MGM Grand Inc. signed a letter of intent with the provincial government of Hainan to explore the development of two resorts that would offer gambling as well as other entertainment. MGM Grand, in late 1994, was then granted a six-month exclusive period to undertake the necessary due diligence and complete definite agreements with the province (Kasselis & Landos, 1995). However, the project continued to be pending. MGM Grand had hoped to use the special status of Hainan to obtain Beijing's approval for table game operation for foreigners only and slot machines for both foreigners and locals (Kasselis & Landos, 1995), but it turned out unsuccessfully.

Gambling in Hong Kong is dominated by a thriving horse racing and lottery industry. The Hong Kong Jockey Club was established in 1846 (Cheung, 2002) and the Hong Kong Lotteries Board was established in 1975 (World Lottery Association, 2003). All gambling is controlled by the Hong Kong Jockey Club, which is a nonprofit organization, regarded as one of the most prestigious racing establishments in the world. The Hong Kong Jockey Club operates both horseracing and lottery facilities; the club, with two racetracks in Happy Valley and Sha Tin, has the highest turnover in the world ("Gambling laws," 2003).

As well as authorized legal gambling, there is extensive illegal gambling in Hong Kong. Local illegal bookmakers and unauthorized offshore operators offer betting on Hong Kong and overseas races, the Mark Six lottery, and take bets on a wide range of overseas sporting events, especially European football matches. Soccer is a popular spectator sport among Hong Kong residents as part of the British heritage remaining after more than a century of colonialism. The legalization of soccer betting was debated in recent years due to its popularity and the numerous illegal operations. The Hong Kong government first floated the need to legalize soccer betting in 2000 amid growing concern over illegal gambling and soaring budget deficits (Cheung, 2002). The Hong Kong government executive committee announced the legalization of soccer betting on November 26, 2002, granting an exclusive five-year license to the Hong Kong Jockey Club commencing in the summer of 2003 (Hsu, 2003).

Macao, another predominantly Chinese society, has had a thriving gaming industry. Details of the development and state of Macao's gaming are discussed in Chapter 3.

Casinos continue to be banned by the market-oriented government of Taiwan (McMillen, 1996). In Taiwan, charity raffles have been popular for many decades. The establishment of casinos, particularly in the Penghu archipelago, has been an unsolved issue since 1987 (Hsieh, 2002). Despite the pending legalization of casinos, the first modern state lottery, issued in 1999, has grown in popularity at an accelerating pace; gambling has undergone a marked change in image for people on the island (Yu, 2001).

Many countries and regions in Asia, with the notable exception of China and Taiwan, have conceded to the realization that casinos can generate economic development. The attitudes of Chinese policy-makers toward gambling are dominated by stereotypes of organized crime and political corruption, as well as concern over the social damage that could occur from widespread gambling. All these factors have reflected the tendency for policymakers to concentrate on social impacts of commercial gaming. Even though gambling has been pop-ular among the Chinese for thousands of years, in comparison to Western countries, gambling policy in Chinese society is considered to be more conservative and has been more focused on social rather than economic concerns.

REFERENCES

ABC News. (2002, April 24). Downtown Las Vegas. *ABC News,* p. A12.

Abel, A. (1997, June 16). A night at the races. *Sports Illustrated, 86*(24), 22-24.

Aero, R. (1980). *Things Chinese.* Garden City, NY: Doubleday.

Agence France-Presse. (2001, August 30). *China banks on lottery fever for Olympic funding.* Available: http://www.lotteryinsider.com/lottery/chinaspo.htm.

Ashton, J. (1898). *A history of gambling in England.* London: Duckworth.

Asia-Pacific News Service. (2001, January 19). China's lottery industry targets $10 billion in annual sales. Available: http://www.lotteryinsider.com/lottery/chinaspo.htm.

Au, P., & Yu, R. (1997, June). *Working with problem gambling in the Chinese community: A Toronto experience.* Paper presented at the Second Biannual Ontario Conference on Problem and Compulsive Gambling, Toronto, Ontario.

Bary, W. T. (1960). (Ed.). *Sources of Chinese tradition.* New York: Columbia University Press.

Beal, G. (1975). *Playing cards and their story.* New York: Arco.

Biers, D. (2001, March 22). Bright lights, high rollers. *Far Eastern Economic Review, 164*(11), 60-63.

Brenner, R., & Brenner, G. A. (1990). *Gambling and speculation.* New York: Cambridge University Press.

Casino City. (2002). Macau bets future on China: Asian high rollers. *Casino City Newsletter, 3*(86), 2. Available: http://newsletter.casinocity.com/issue86/Page2.htm.

Central News Agency (Producer). (1997, December 24). Casino boss consults feng shui experts to attract Asian high-rollers, p. 1. Taipei: Asia Intelligence Wire from FT Information.

Chang, L. C. (2003). An examination of cross-cultural negotiation: Using Hofstede framework. *Journal of American Academy of Business, 2*(2), 567-570.

Chen, C. Y. (1992). San Francisco's Chinatown: A socio-economic and cultural history, 1850-1882. *UMI ProQuest Digital Dissertations: Full Citation and Abstract,* AAT9234773.

Cheung, J. (2002, November 27). Jockey Club wins soccer betting rights. *South China Morning Post,* p. 1.

China approves ticket increase in Olympic sports lottery. (2001, July 21). *China Daily.* Available: http://www.lotteryinsider.com/lottery/chinaspo.htm.

China to tighten supervision of lottery. (2002, June 18). *People's Daily.* Available: http://english.peopledaily.com.cn.

China's finance chiefs eye lotteries in fight against budget gap. (2000, July 31). *South China Morning Post.* Available: http://www.lotteryinsider.com/lottery/chinaspo.htm.

China's uncertain odds. (1995, September 2). *Economist, 336*(7930), 84.

Chinatown Online. (2003). Chinese customs and superstitions: Miscellaneous customs and beliefs. Available: http://www.chinatown-online.co.uk/pages/culture/customs/miscellaneous.html.

Compulot. (2000, February 7). The People's Republic of China's lottery industry is computerised. Available: http://www.lotteryinsider.com/lottery/chinaspo.htm.

Cullen, L. (2000, December). Fortune hunters. *Money, 29*(13), 114-121.

Ding, N., & Bone, C. (1995). Concerning the use of colour in China. *British Journal of Aesthetics, 35*(2), 160.

Dummett, M. (1980). *The game of tarot.* London: Oxford University Press.

Eberhard, W. (1986). *A dictionary of Chinese symbols: Hidden symbols in Chinese life and thought* (G. L. Campbell, Trans.). London: Routledge and Kegan Paul. (Original work published 1983).

Galletti, S. (2002, November 1). Chinese cultures and casino customers services. *Business Times.* Available: http://www.jackpots.com.sg/article/publish/printer_72.shtml.

Gambling laws for Asia. (2003, September 18). *Asia Casino News.* Available: http://www.asiacasinonews.com/gamblelaw/index.php.

Geertz, C. (1973). *The interpretation of cultures.* New York: Wiley.

Harvard Medical School. (1997, June 10). *The Wager: The Weekly Addiction Gambling Educational Report, 2*(1). Available: http://www.thewager.org/Backindex/Vol2pdf/w223.pdf.

Hill, C. W. L. (1994). *International business: Competing in the global marketplace.* Burr Ridge, IL: Irwin.

Hofstede, G. (1980). *Culture's consequences: International differences in work-related values.* Beverly Hills, CA: Sage.

Hofstede, G. (1984). Cultural dimensions in management and planning. *Asia Pacific Journal of Management, 1*(2), 81-99.

Hofstede, G. (1985). The interaction between national and organizational value system. *Journal of Management Studies, 22*(4), 347-357.

Hofstede, G. (1991). *Cultures and organizations: Software of the mind.* London: McGraw-Hill.

Holt, D. D. (1998). *International management: Text and cases.* Fort Worth, TX: Dryden Press.

Hsieh, C. M. (2002). The policy-making analysis of casino gambling in Penghu County, Taiwan. *National Dissertations Database of Taiwan,* 90NTU02227017.

Hsu, C. H. C. (2003). Residents' opinions on gaming activities and the legalization of soccer betting. *Asia Pacific Journal of Tourism Research, 9*(1).

The I Ching: Book of changes (2nd ed.). (1963). (J. Legge, Trans.). New York: Dover.

Kasselis, P. A., & Landos, P. D. (1995). *Gaming in the Asia/Pacific—Joining the international bandwagon.* Sydney: Arthur Andersen.

Kipnis, A. B. (1996). The language of gifts: Managing quanxi in a north China village. *Modern China, 22,* 285.

Lawmaker says China needs national laws to guide the development of its fledgling lottery industry. (2001, March 8). *China Daily.* Available: http://www.lottery insider.com/lottery/chinaspo.htm.

Low, S. P., & Shi, Y. (2002). An exploratory study of Hofstede's cross-cultural dimensions in construction projects. *Management Decision, 40*(1), 7-16.

Lytle, A. L., Brett, J. M., & Shapiro, D. L. (1999). The strategic use of interests, rights and power to resolve disputes. *Negotiation Journal, 15*(1), 31-49.

Marshall, D. (2000). No chance: Electronic gaming machines and the disadvantaged in Melbourne. *Geodate, 13*(4), 5-8.

McMillen, J. (1996). From glamour to grind: The globalisation of casinos. In J. McMillen (Ed.), *Gambling cultures: Studies in history and interpretation* (pp. 263-287). London: Routledge.

Nepstad, P. (2000, April 1). Gambling history and tradition in China. *Illuminated Lantern,* No. 2. Available: http://www.illuminatedlantern.com/gamblers/.

No umbrellas, please. (1992, January 16). *Washington Post,* p. A26.

Ogbor, J. (1990). Organizational change within a cultural context: The interpretation of cross-culturally transferred organizational practices. In A. T. Malm (Ed.), *Lund studies in economics and management* (Vol. 8, pp. 1-402). Lund, Sweden: Lund University.

Parlett, D. S. (1990). *The Oxford guide to card games.* New York: Oxford University Press.

Parsons, T., & Shils, E. A. (Eds.). (1952). *Toward a general theory of action.* Cambridge, MA: Cambridge University Press.

Pomfret, J. (2002, March 26). China's high rollers find a set at table. *Washington Post,* p. A1.

Reardon, K. K. (1982). International gift giving: Why and how it is done. *Public Relations Journal, 38*(6), 16-20.

Redpath, L., & Nielsen, M. O. (1997). A comparison of native culture, non-native culture and new management ideology. *Canadian Journal of Administrative Sciences, 14*(3), 327-339.

Reiman, C. A. (2003). China and the business of doing lunch. *Consulting to Management, 14*(2), 17.

Rossbach, S. (1983). *Feng shui: The Chinese art of placement.* New York: Dutton.

THE HAWORTH HOSPITALITY PRESS®
Hospitality, Travel, and Tourism
K. S. Chon, PhD, Editor in Chief

CULTURAL TOURISM: GLOBAL AND LOCAL PERSPECTIVES edited by Greg Richards. (2007).

GAY TOURISM: CULTURE AND CONTEXT by Gordon Waitt and Kevin Markwell. (2006).

CASES IN SUSTAINABLE TOURISM: AN EXPERIENTIAL APPROACH TO MAKING DECISIONS edited by Irene M. Herremans. (2006). "As a tourism instructor and researcher, I recommend this textbook for both undergraduate and graduate students who wish to pursue their careers in parks, recreation, or tourism. The text is appropriate both for junior and senior tourism management classes and graduate classes. It is an excellent primer for understanding the fundamental concepts, issues, and real-world examples of sustainable tourism." *HwanSuk Chrus Choi, PhD, Assistant Professor, School of Hospitality and Tourism Management, University of Gueph*

COMMUNITY DESTINATION MANAGEMENT IN DEVELOPING ECONO-MIES edited by Walter Jamieson. (2006). "This book is a welcome and valuable addition to the destination management literature, focusing as it does on developing economies in the Asian context. It provides an unusually comprehensive and informative overview of critical issues in the field, effectively combining well-crafted discussions of key conceptual and methodological issues with carefully selected and well-presented case studies drawn from a number of contrasting Asian destinations." *Peter Hills, PhD, Professor and Director, The Centre of Urban Planning and Environmental Management, The University of Hong Kong*

MANAGING SUSTAINABLE TOURISM: A LEGACY FOR THE FUTURE by David L. Edgell Sr. (2006). "This comprehensive book on sustainable tourism should be required reading for everyone interested in tourism. The author is masterful in defining strategies and using case studies to explain best practices in generating long-term economic return on your tourism investment." *Kurtis M. Ruf, Partner, Ruf Strategic Solutions; Author,* Contemporary Database Marketing

CASINO INDUSTRY IN ASIA PACIFIC: DEVELOPMENT, OPERATION, AND IMPACT edited by Cathy H.C. Hsu. (2006). "This book is a must-read for anyone interested in the opportunities and challenges that the proliferation of casino gaming will bring to Asia in the early twenty-first century. The economic and social consequences of casino gaming in Asia may ultimately prove to be far more significant than those encountered in the West, and this book opens the door as to what those consequences might be." *William R. Eadington, PhD, Professor of Economics and Director, Institute for the Study of Gambling and Commercial Gaming, University of Nevada, Reno*

THE GROWTH STRATEGIES OF HOTEL CHAINS: BEST BUSINESS PRAC-TICES BY LEADING COMPANIES by Onofre Martorell Cunill. (2006). "Informative, well-written, and up-to-date. This is one title that I shall certainly be adding to my 'must-read' list for students this year." *Tom Baum, PhD, Professor of International Tour-*

ism and Hospitality Management, The Scottish Hotel School, The University of Strathclyde, Glasgow

HANDBOOK FOR DISTANCE LEARNING IN TOURISM by Gary Williams. (2005). "This is an important book for a variety of audiences. As a resource for educational designers (and their managers) in particular, it is invaluable. The book is easy to read, and is full of practical information that can be logically applied in the design and development of flexible learning resources." *Louise Berg, MA, DipED, Lecturer in Education, Charles Sturt University, Australia*

VIETNAM TOURISM by Arthur Asa Berger. (2005). "Fresh and innovative.... Drawing upon Professor Berger's background and experience in cultural studies, this book offers an imaginative and personal portrayal of Vietnam as a tourism destination.... A very welcome addition to the field of destination studies." *Professor Brian King, PhD, Head, School of Hospitality, Tourism & Marketing, Victoria University, Australia*

TOURISM AND HOTEL DEVELOPMENT IN CHINA: FROM POLITICAL TO ECONOMIC SUCCESS by Hanqin Qiu Zhang, Ray Pine, and Terry Lam. (2005). "This is one of the most comprehensive books on China tourism and hotel development. It is one of the best textbooks for educators, students, practitioners, and investors who are interested in china tourism and hotel industry. Readers will experience vast, diversified, and past and current issues that affect every educator, student, practitioner, and investor in China tourism and hotel globally in an instant." *Hailin Qu, PhD, Full Professor and William E. Davis Distinguished Chair, School of Hotel & Restaurant Administration, Oklahoma State University*

THE TOURISM AND LEISURE INDUSTRY: SHAPING THE FUTURE edited by Klaus Weiermair and Christine Mathies. (2004). "If you need or want to know about the impact of globalization, the impact of technology, societal forces of change, the experience economy, adaptive technologies, environmental changes, or the new trend of slow tourism, you need this book. *The Tourism and Leisure Industry* contains a great mix of research and practical information." *Charles R. Goeldner, PhD, Professor Emeritus of Marketing and Tourism, Leeds School of Business, University of Colorado*

OCEAN TRAVEL AND CRUISING: A CULTURAL ANALYSIS by Arthur Asa Berger. (2004). "Dr. Berger presents an interdisciplinary discussion of the cruise industry for the thinking person. This is an enjoyable social psychology travel guide with a little business management thrown in. A great book for the curious to read a week before embarking on a first cruise or for the frequent cruiser to gain a broader insight into exactly what a cruise experience represents." *Carl Braunlich, DBA, Associate Professor, Department of Hospitality and Tourism Management, Purdue University, West Lafayette, Indiana*

STANDING THE HEAT: ENSURING CURRICULUM QUALITY IN CULINARY ARTS AND GASTRONOMY by Joseph A. Hegarty. (2003). "This text provides the genesis of a well-researched, thoughtful, rigorous, and sound theoretical framework for the enlargement and expansion of higher education programs in culinary arts and gastronomy." *John M. Antun, PhD, Founding Director, National Restaurant Institute, School of Hotel, Restaurant, and Tourism Management, University of South Carolina*

SEX AND TOURISM: JOURNEYS OF ROMANCE, LOVE, AND LUST edited by Thomas G. Bauer and Bob McKercher. (2003). "Anyone interested in or concerned about the impact of tourism on society and particularly in the developing world, should read this book. It explores a subject that has long remained ignored, almost a taboo area for many governments, institutions, and organizations. It demonstrates that the stereotyping of 'sex tourism' is too simple and travel and sex have many manifestations. The book follows its theme in an innovative and original way." *Carson L. Jenkins, PhD, Professor of International Tourism, University of Strathclyde, Glasgow, Scotland*

CONVENTION TOURISM: INTERNATIONAL RESEARCH AND INDUSTRY PERSPECTIVES edited by Karin Weber and Kye-Sung Chon. (2002). "This comprehensive book is truly global in its perspective. The text points out areas of needed research—a great starting point for graduate students, university faculty, and industry professionals alike. While the focus is mainly academic, there is a lot of meat for this burgeoning industry to chew on as well." *Patti J. Shock, CPCE, Professor and Department Chair, Tourism and Convention Administration, Harrah College of Hotel Administration, University of Nevada–Las Vegas*

CULTURAL TOURISM: THE PARTNERSHIP BETWEEN TOURISM AND CULTURAL HERITAGE MANAGEMENT by Bob McKercher and Hilary du Cros. (2002). "The book brings together concepts, perspectives, and practicalities that must be understood by both cultural heritage and tourism managers, and as such is a must-read for both." *Hisashi B. Sugaya, AICP, Former Chair, International Council of Monuments and Sites, International Scientific Committee on Cultural Tourism; Former Executive Director, Pacific Asia Travel Association Foundation, San Francisco, CA*

TOURISM IN THE ANTARCTIC: OPPORTUNITIES, CONSTRAINTS, AND FUTURE PROSPECTS by Thomas G. Bauer. (2001). "Thomas Bauer presents a wealth of detailed information on the challenges and opportunities facing tourism operators in this last great tourism frontier." *David Mercer, PhD, Associate Professor, School of Geography & Environmental Science, Monash University, Melbourne, Australia*

SERVICE QUALITY MANAGEMENT IN HOSPITALITY, TOURISM, AND LEISURE edited by Jay Kandampully, Connie Mok, and Beverley Sparks. (2001). "A must-read. . . . a treasure. . . . pulls together the work of scholars across the globe, giving you access to new ideas, international research, and industry examples from around the world." *John Bowen, Professor and Director of Graduate Studies, William F. Harrah College of Hotel Administration, University of Nevada, Las Vegas*

TOURISM IN SOUTHEAST ASIA: A NEW DIRECTION edited by K. S. (Kaye) Chon. (2000). "Presents a wide array of very topical discussions on the specific challenges facing the tourism industry in Southeast Asia. A great resource for both scholars and practitioners." *Dr. Hubert B. Van Hoof, Assistant Dean/Associate Professor, School of Hotel and Restaurant Management, Northern Arizona University*

THE PRACTICE OF GRADUATE RESEARCH IN HOSPITALITY AND TOURISM edited by K. S. Chon. (1999). "An excellent reference source for students pursuing graduate degrees in hospitality and tourism." *Connie Mok, PhD, CHE, Associate Professor, Conrad N. Hilton College of Hotel and Restaurant Management, University of Houston, Texas*

THE INTERNATIONAL HOSPITALITY MANAGEMENT BUSINESS: MANAGEMENT AND OPERATIONS by Larry Yu. (1999). "The abundant real-world examples and cases provided in the text enable readers to understand the most up-to-date developments in international hospitality business." *Zheng Gu, PhD, Associate Professor, College of Hotel Administration, University of Nevada, Las Vegas*

CONSUMER BEHAVIOR IN TRAVEL AND TOURISM by Abraham Pizam and Yoel Mansfeld. (1999). "A must for anyone who wants to take advantage of new global opportunities in this growing industry." *Bonnie J. Knutson, PhD, School of Hospitality Business, Michigan State University*

LEGALIZED CASINO GAMING IN THE UNITED STATES: THE ECONOMIC AND SOCIAL IMPACT edited by Cathy H. C. Hsu. (1999). "Brings a fresh new look at one of the areas in tourism that has not yet received careful and serious consideration in the past." *Muzaffer Uysal, PhD, Professor of Tourism Research, Virginia Polytechnic Institute and State University, Blacksburg*

HOSPITALITY MANAGEMENT EDUCATION edited by Clayton W. Barrows and Robert H. Bosselman. (1999). "Takes the mystery out of how hospitality management education programs function and serves as an excellent resource for individuals interested in pursuing the field." *Joe Perdue, CCM, CHE, Director, Executive Masters Program, College of Hotel Administration, University of Nevada, Las Vegas*

MARKETING YOUR CITY, U.S.A.: A GUIDE TO DEVELOPING A STRATEGIC TOURISM MARKETING PLAN by Ronald A. Nykiel and Elizabeth Jascolt. (1998). "An excellent guide for anyone involved in the planning and marketing of cities and regions. . . . A terrific job of synthesizing an otherwise complex procedure." *James C. Maken, PhD, Associate Professor, Babcock Graduate School of Management, Wake Forest University, Winston-Salem, North Carolina*

Order a copy of this book with this form or online at:
http://www.haworthpress.com/store/product.asp?sku=5541

CASINO INDUSTRY IN ASIA PACIFIC
Development, Operation, Impact

_____ in hardbound at $39.95 (ISBN-13: 978-0-7890-2345-2; ISBN-10: 0-7890-2345-8)

_____ in softbound at $24.95 (ISBN-13: 978-0-7890-2346-9; ISBN-10: 0-7890-2346-6)

Or order online and use special offer code HEC25 in the shopping cart.

COST OF BOOKS_____

POSTAGE & HANDLING_____
(US: $4.00 for first book & $1.50
for each additional book)
(Outside US: $5.00 for first book
& $2.00 for each additional book)

SUBTOTAL_____

IN CANADA: ADD 7% GST_____

STATE TAX_____
(NJ, NY, OH, MN, CA, IL, IN, PA, & SD
residents, add appropriate local sales tax)

FINAL TOTAL_____
(If paying in Canadian funds,
convert using the current
exchange rate, UNESCO
coupons welcome)

☐ **BILL ME LATER:** (Bill-me option is good on
US/Canada/Mexico orders only; not good to
jobbers, wholesalers, or subscription agencies.)
☐ Check here if billing address is different from
shipping address and attach purchase order and
billing address information.

Signature_____

☐ **PAYMENT ENCLOSED: $_____**

☐ **PLEASE CHARGE TO MY CREDIT CARD.**

☐ Visa ☐ MasterCard ☐ AmEx ☐ Discover
☐ Diner's Club ☐ Eurocard ☐ JCB

Account # _____

Exp. Date_____

Signature_____

Prices in US dollars and subject to change without notice.

NAME_____

INSTITUTION_____

ADDRESS_____

CITY_____

STATE/ZIP_____

COUNTRY_____ COUNTY (NY residents only)_____

TEL_____ FAX_____

E-MAIL_____

May we use your e-mail address for confirmations and other types of information? ☐ Yes ☐ No
We appreciate receiving your e-mail address and fax number. Haworth would like to e-mail or fax special
discount offers to you, as a preferred customer. **We will never share, rent, or exchange your e-mail address
or fax number.** We regard such actions as an invasion of your privacy.

Order From Your Local Bookstore or Directly From
The Haworth Press, Inc.
10 Alice Street, Binghamton, New York 13904-1580 • USA
TELEPHONE: 1-800-HAWORTH (1-800-429-6784) / Outside US/Canada: (607) 722-5857
FAX: 1-800-895-0582 / Outside US/Canada: (607) 771-0012
E-mail to: orders@haworthpress.com

For orders outside US and Canada, you may wish to order through your local
sales representative, distributor, or bookseller.
For information, see http://haworthpress.com/distributors

(Discounts are available for individual orders in US and Canada only, not booksellers/distributors.)

PLEASE PHOTOCOPY THIS FORM FOR YOUR PERSONAL USE.
http://www.HaworthPress.com   BOF06